HOME REPAIR AND IMPROVEMENT

ADVANCED WOODWORKING

TIME®
LIFE
BOOKS

HOME REPAIR AND IMPROVEMENT

ADVANCED WOODWORKING

BY THE EDITORS OF TIME-LIFE BOOKS, ALEXANDRIA, VIRGINIA

The Consultants

Jon Arno, a wood technologist residing in Michigan where he works for a family lumber business, is known for his skills in furniture design and cabinetmaking. Mr. Arno has written extensively on the properties and use of wood and is the author of *The Woodworkers Visual Handbook* and a frequent contributor to *Fine Woodworking* magazine. He also conducts seminars on wood identification and early American furniture design.

Mike Dunbar, a woodworker for the past 26 years, fathered the modern revival of North American Windsor chairmaking. He lives in Hampton, NH, where he and his wife run a woodworking school, teaching Windsor chairmaking and related toolmaking and woodworking skills. He is a contributing editor for *American Woodworker* magazine and has written seven woodworking books.

Paul McGoldrick owns and operates Pianoforte, a piano restoration business established in Montreal, Quebec, in 1978. Mr. McGoldrick, who trained as a cabinetmaker, specializes in fine wood finishes and the maintenance and preparation of concert pianos.

CONTENTS

1 Rough Wood to Smooth Boards

Straight boards with flat surfaces and square edges are required for most woodworking projects. To produce such boards from rough-hewn lumber, you first need a basic understanding of the nature of wood. This chapter explains how trees grow and are prepared for use, as well as how to select the best wood for your projects and shape it with both hand and power tools.

Planing the edge of a board →

Understanding Wood

Transforming raw wood into boards is the first step in the process of acquiring workable stock. By understanding how wood grows and how it is milled, you will be able to make well-informed decisions when selecting material for your projects.

Hardwoods and Softwoods: Although technically the terms hardwood and softwood describe the strength of wood, in practice the lumber industry uses them simply to distinguish between wood mostly from deciduous trees and that from conifers, which are predominantly evergreens. Hardwoods come mainly from deciduous trees and are indeed generally hard, but the wood of some—such as basswood—is quite soft. Likewise, the wood of most softwoods is soft, but that of some conifers—such as southern yellow pine—is hard. The hardwoods typically used for fine woodworking have distinctive grain patterns *(page 10)*; and each species has properties that make it suitable for different uses *(page 11)*.

Characteristics of Boards: The part of the tree from which a board is cut *(below)*, and the conditions to which it is exposed before milling *(opposite, top)* affect the quality of the boards derived from it. The method of cutting *(opposite, bottom)* also has an influence on the properties of the individual boards.

Grading Lumber: Boards are graded according to their appearance. Lumber in the top grades, First and Second (FAS), is 80 to 90 percent free of knots and other blemishes on both faces, and at least 6 inches wide and 8 feet long. In the next grade, Select, boards are 80 percent clear on one face, and at least 4 inches wide and 6 feet long. No. 1 Common boards, the next category, classifies boards that are about 65 percent clear on one face. Hardwood grades are based on the poorer of the two faces; softwood grades on the better of the two faces. In general, use the higher-grade lumber for the visible parts of your projects.

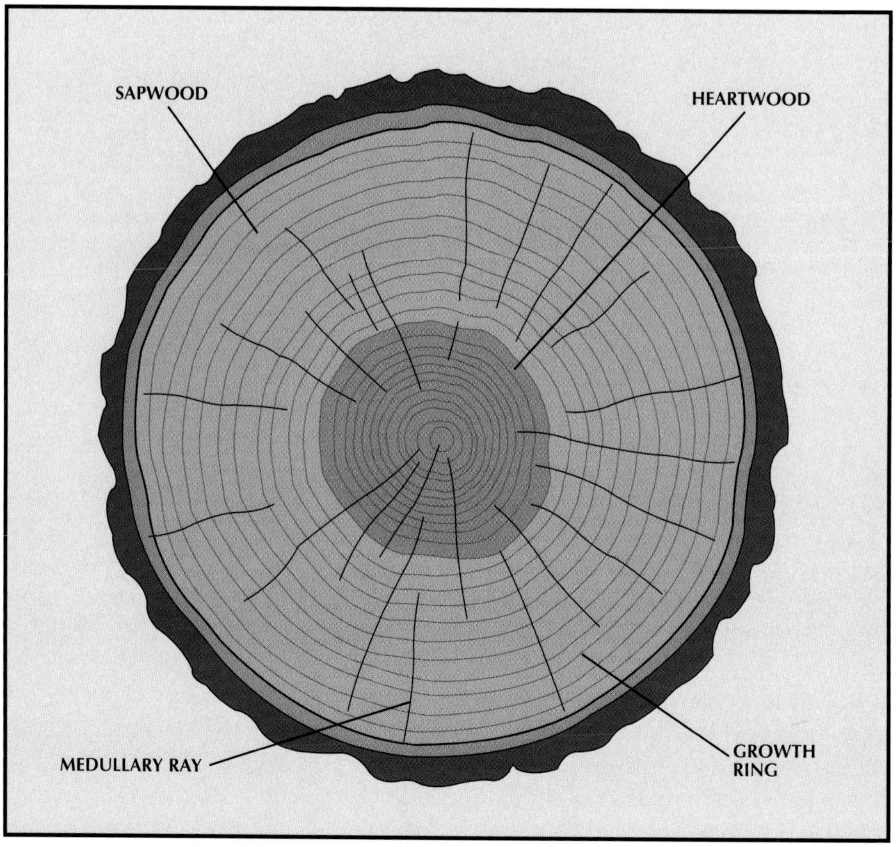

Anatomy of a tree. The first layer of usable wood in a tree is the sapwood, which carries moisture and minerals up from the roots—a function that accounts for the sapwood's receptiveness to moisture. The heartwood is denser, darker, and generally more durable; it contains resins that make it more resistant to rot. Each of the growth rings represents one year of life divided into two growing seasons: the lighter-colored "springwood" and the darker "summerwood"; a high proportion of summerwood to springwood results in a richer, darker color. Radiating outward are the medullary rays, which carry food laterally and in some woods produce a pronounced pattern in the milled lumber.

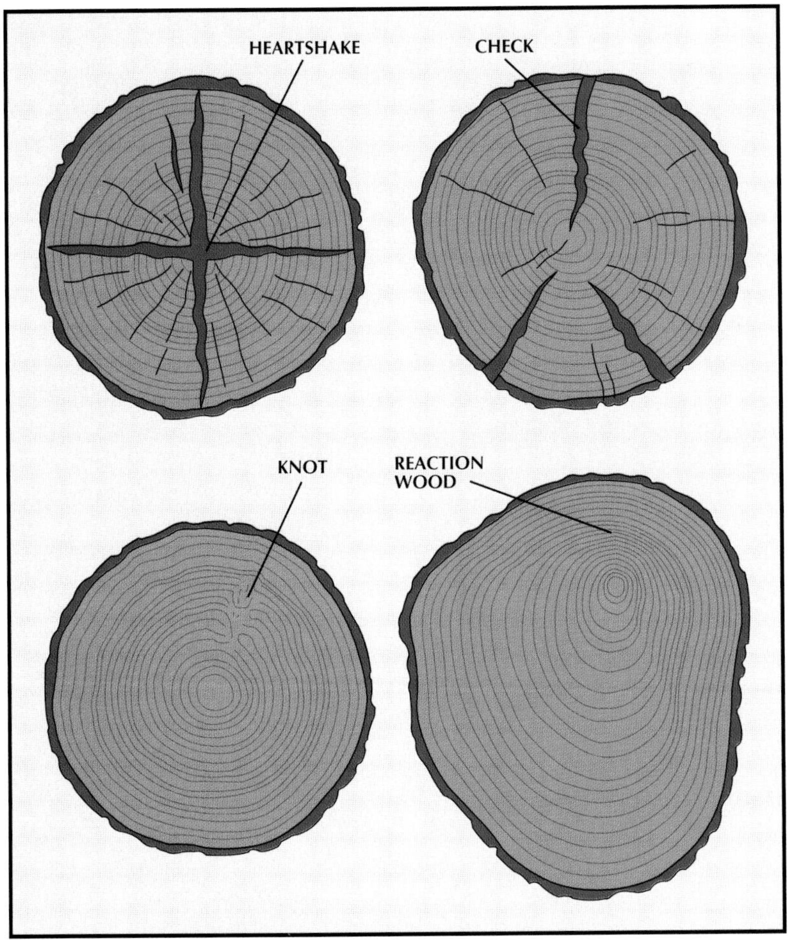

A record of assaults.
Adverse conditions during growth of a tree or poor handling after harvesting can cause defects in a log *(left)*. Heartshake—a result of decay or stress—produces cracks at the center of a tree and splits along the medullary rays. Checks are splits or cracks between the wood fibers along the grain and across the annual growth rings; they occur when a log is dried too rapidly after it is felled. Knots are the ends of broken limbs that have become encased by new growth. Reaction wood, characterized by an off-center pattern in growth rings, occurs in trees that lean to one side due to high winds or a unidirectional light source.

CHARACTERISTICS OF BOARDS

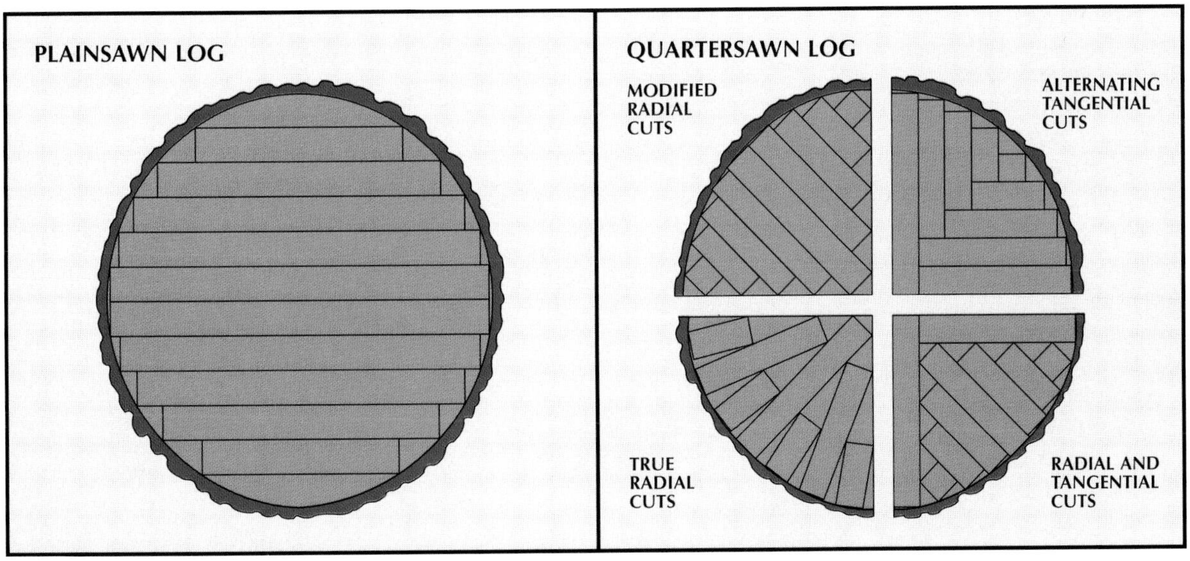

Variations in milling techniques.
In plainsawing *(above, left),* the simplest and most common method of milling boards from a tree, the log is sliced lengthwise into parallel slabs of uniform thickness. This method leaves very little waste, but some of the boards tend to warp as they dry because the growth rings run across the width of the lumber. In quartersawing *(above, right),* the log is cut into quarters, then into slabs. Four cutting patterns may be used to obtain boards from the quarter logs: true radial, modified radial, alternating tangential cuts, and a combination of radial and tangential cuts. In general, boards with grain running along the length, such as those produced by true radial cuts, are more attractive and more stable than those cut by the other methods.

Identifying grain types.

The pattern of the grain on a milled board is largely a reflection of the annual growth rings *(page 8)*, but it can be emphasized or softened by the manner in which the log is cut *(page 9)*. The grain pattern is also a function of the wood species. Straight grain, common in ash and oak, is a sign of strong lumber, but may appear rather plain. When straight grain is deflected by a defect such as a knot, it is called irregular grain. Wood with wavy grain is not as strong as straight-grained lumber, but it does produce attractive patterns; wavy grain is found in many species, including maple, birch, and walnut. Spiral grain follows a corkscrew course up the trunk, producing a diagonal pattern. Interlocked grain, shown here in several slices taken from one wood block, follows one course and then another. It is commonly found in elm and many tropical woods.

In addition to forming distinctive patterns, grain has direction *(inset)*. To determine the grain direction of a board, run your hand over its surface. When you are following the grain, the board feels smooth; against the grain, it feels rough. Or examine the edge of a board. The direction of the grain is the one in which it rises to the face.

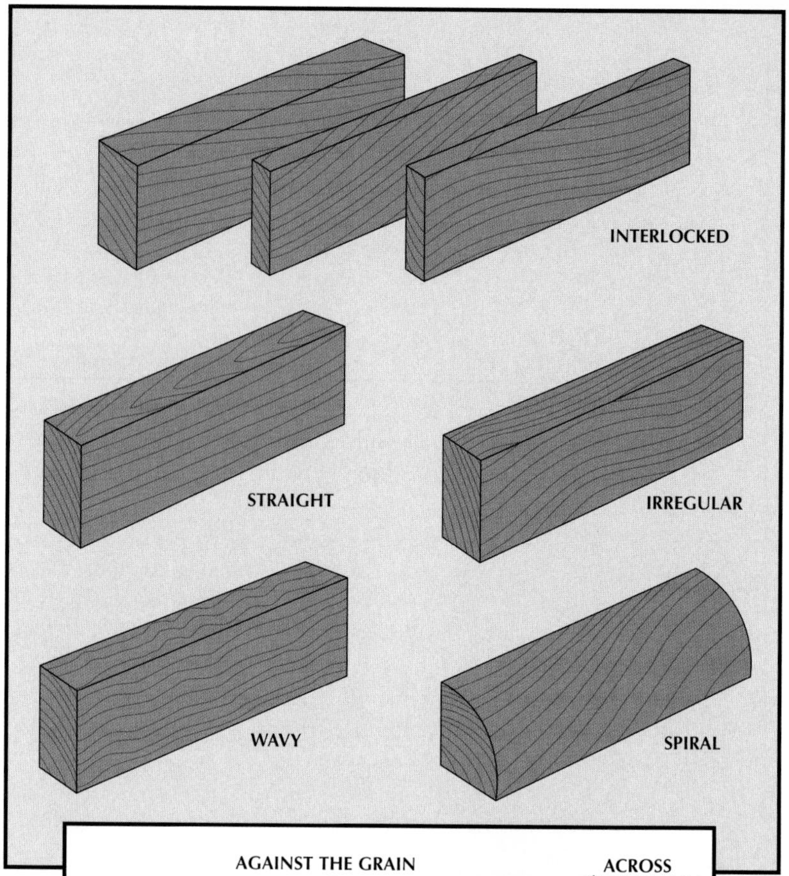

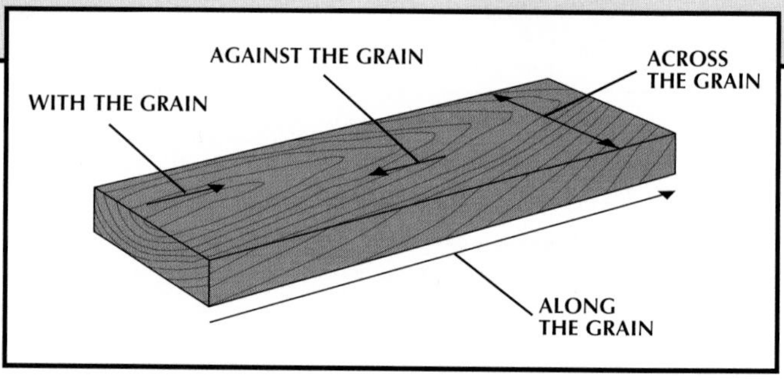

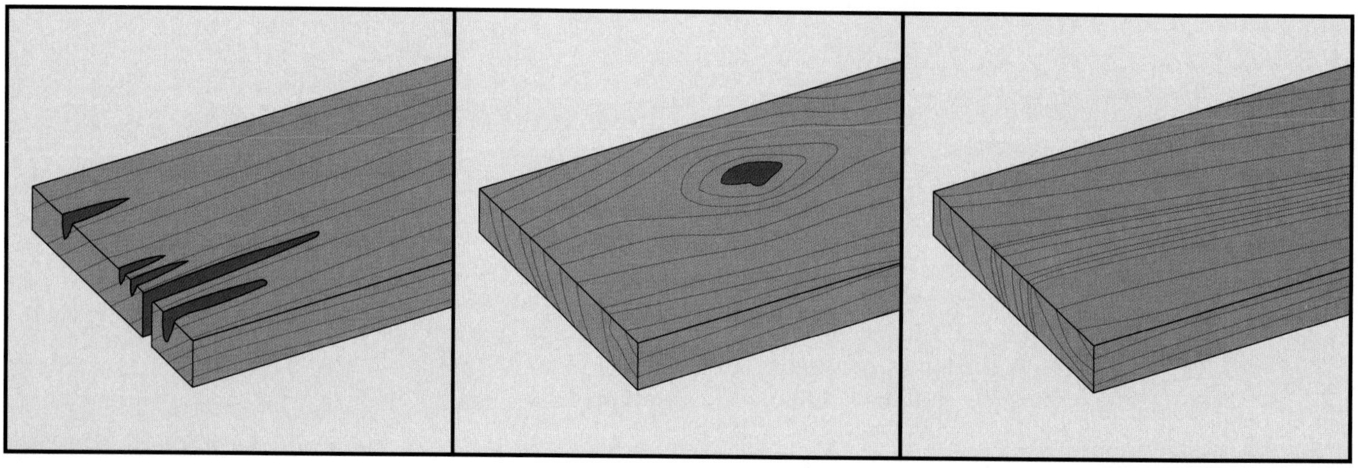

Recognizing defects.

In the milling process, abnormal growth appears as defects that may weaken the wood. Checks *(above, left)* show up as deep cracks in the end of the board or as surface splits; they tend to worsen as the board shrinks and swells. Knots *(above, center)* appear as dark whorls, varying in size from pin knots, less than $\frac{1}{2}$ inch across, to knots more than $1\frac{1}{2}$ inches in diameter. If a knot is encased in dead bark, it may eventually loosen and fall out. Reaction wood *(above, right)* shows up as a dark streak in the grain pattern of a board; the tension of the rings may cause the board to be brittle and shrink unevenly.

A GUIDE TO THE CLASSIC HARDWOODS

Species	Characteristics
Ash	Coarse to medium texture; good strength, excellent bending qualities; fair workability; fair with nails, screws, glue; excellent finishing qualities; commonly used for furniture, interior joinery, turning, tool handles, baseball bats.
Basswood	Very fine texture; excellent workability; good with nails, screws, glue; excellent finishing properties; commonly used for carving and framed panels in furniture.
Beech	Fine, even texture; excellent strength and bending qualities; fair workability; fair with nails, screws; good with glue; good finishing qualities; commonly used for furniture, interior joinery, turning.
Birch	Fine to medium texture; good strength and bending qualities; good workability; good with nails, screws, glue; excellent finishing qualities; commonly used for furniture, veneer, interior joinery, turning.
Cherry	Fine, even texture; good strength and bending qualities; very good workability; good with nails, screws, glue; excellent finishing qualities; commonly used for furniture, veneer, cabinetry, interior joinery, turning.
Hickory	Coarse to medium texture; very good strength, good bending qualities; fair workability (tends to dull blades); difficult with nails, screws; good with glue; fair finishing qualities; commonly used for tool handles, sports equipment.
Maple	Fine texture; very good strength, excellent resistance to wear; good workability; good with nails and screws, fair with glue; good finishing qualities; commonly used for furniture, veneer, turning.
Oak	Coarse texture; excellent strength, good bending qualities; good workability; good with nails, screws, glue; good finishing qualities; commonly used for furniture, veneer, interior joinery.
Sycamore	Smooth texture; very good strength, good bending qualities; fair workability; fair with nails and screws; good with glue; excellent finishing qualities; commonly used for furniture, interior joinery, veneer, turning.
Walnut	Fine texture; excellent strength, good bending qualities; very good workability; good with nails, screws, glue; excellent finishing qualities; commonly used for furniture, veneer, interior joinery, carving, turning.

Comparing woods.
The chart above describes the properties and uses of a variety of hardwoods commonly used in woodworking. The term "texture" applies to the appearance of the grain, rather than its tactile qualities. "Strength" and "bending qualities" refer to the ability of the wood to withstand impact and bend without splitting. "Workability" describes how the wood responds to tools. Each wood is also rated for its ability to hold fasteners and glue, and to take finishes, such as stain or paint.

The Significance of Seasoning

When a living tree is felled, water contained in its cells makes up more than half its weight. This moisture exists as free water and bound water. Once the free water evaporates, the wood is said to be at the fiber-saturation point. Most woods reach this point when their moisture content is about 27 percent.

Moisture Content: As a board dries out and the amount of moisture falls below the fiber-saturation point, it begins to shrink. The process continues until the wood's moisture content is in balance with that of the surrounding atmosphere. The wood is then said to have reached an equilibrium moisture content, and is considered seasoned and ready to be worked.

The fastest way to season lumber is by kiln-drying. In this method, wood is exposed to steam in an oven where the temperature is raised gradually and the humidity lowered until the moisture content reaches the desired level, which, for furniture-making, is about 6 to 8 percent.

Air-Drying Lumber: Since kiln-dried lumber is more expensive than unseasoned wood, you can save money by buying green wood and drying it yourself. Begin by numbering each board and noting the starting date of the drying process. Then stack the wood outdoors, out of direct sunlight, on blocks off the ground. Separate the layers with sticker strips—1-by-2s spaced 18 inches apart across the width of the pile. Place boards of uniform length in each stack; overhanging boards will dry too rapidly and warp. Coat the ends of the boards generously with paraffin or polyurethane varnish to prevent them from drying too fast and splitting. Protect the stack from direct rainfall with plastic sheeting.

Check the moisture content of the wood periodically with a moisture meter *(opposite)*. Or, weigh a board taken from the middle the stack, and mark the weight and date on it. Weigh the wood periodically—the wood will stop losing weight when it reaches its equilibrium moisture content. If the wood is to be used indoors, bring it inside and continue drying it until it reaches its equilibrium moisture content in the environment in which the finished project will be used.

HOW WOOD RESPONDS TO THE DRYING PROCESS

A predictable pattern of shrinkage.
Cuts of lumber, superimposed in their original positions on a log *(right)*, show how wood tends to shrink along the annual rings as it dries, causing variations in shape. A radial cut, which is perpendicular to the rings, shrinks almost half as much as a tangential cut—one roughly parallel to the rings. Shrinkage is uneven in cuts that are both across and along the grain—a square board would distort into a diamond shape, while a circular cutout would become oblong.

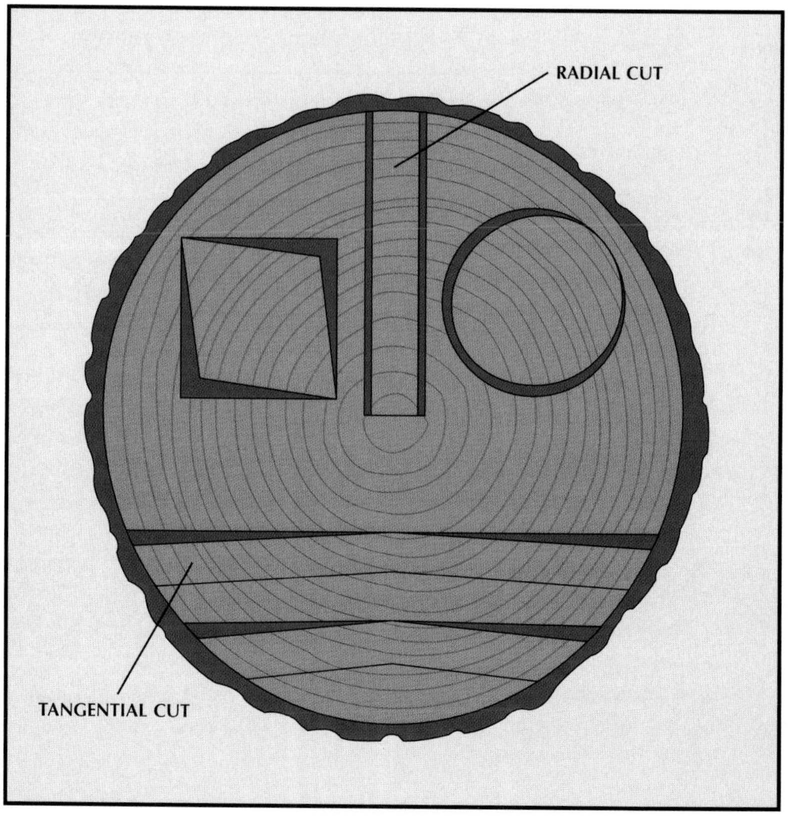

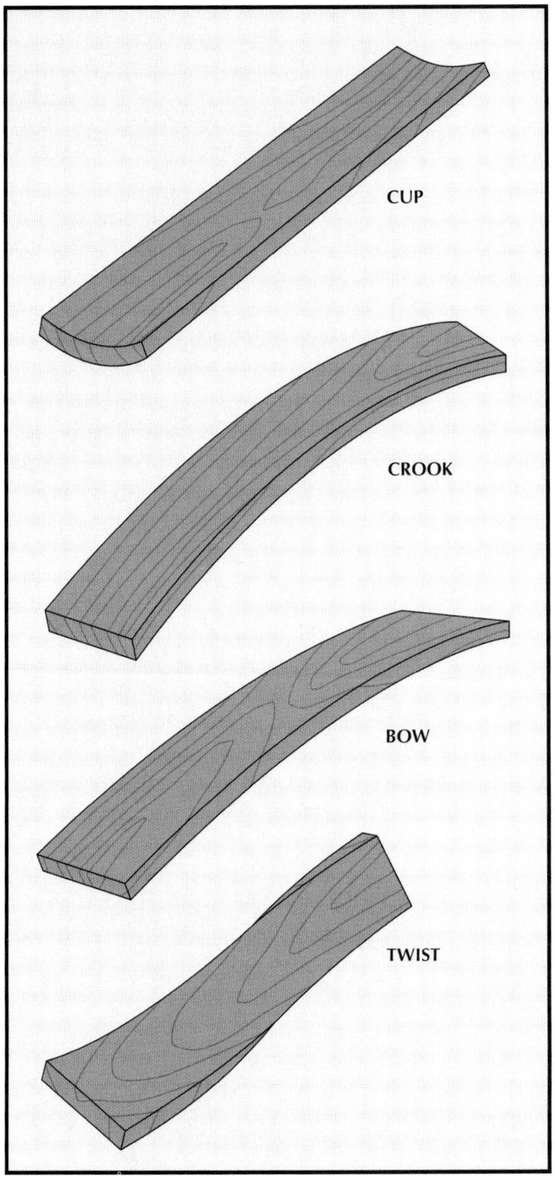

Changes in shape.
Boards can warp in different ways as they dry *(left)*. A cupped board curves into a hollow across the grain; in crooking, the board lies flat but bends along the edges. When a board bows, it arches along the face from one end to the other. In twisting (also called winding), the board lies flat at one end but cups or springs at the other. Although it's best to avoid warped boards, they can sometimes be salvaged by planing.

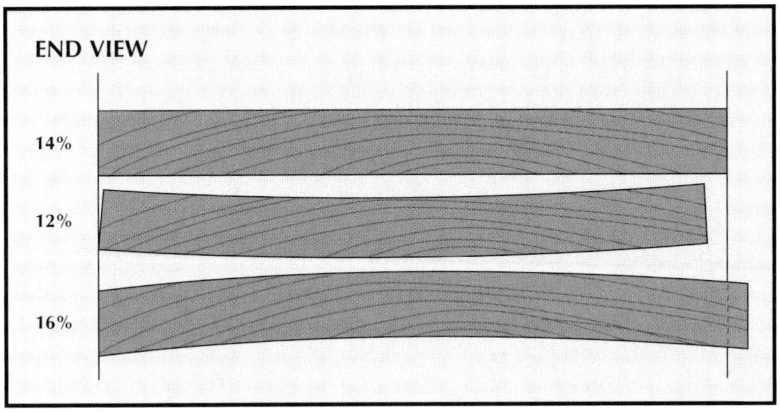

Changes in dimension.
Wood responds to changes in humidity in a predictable way. A board milled straight and square at a given moisture content—14 percent, for example *(top)*—will shrink in width and begin to cup slightly if the humidity drops and the moisture content falls to 12 percent. Conversely, if the humidity rises and the moisture content climbs to 16 percent, the board will swell and cup in the opposite direction. Varnishes and sealers can slow but not stop this process. Kiln-dried wood, which undergoes a change at the cellular level in the kiln, exhibits less pronounced reactions to humidity changes.

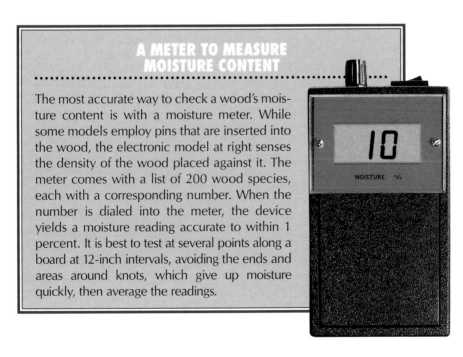

A METER TO MEASURE MOISTURE CONTENT

The most accurate way to check a wood's moisture content is with a moisture meter. While some models employ pins that are inserted into the wood, the electronic model at right senses the density of the wood placed against it. The meter comes with a list of 200 wood species, each with a corresponding number. When the number is dialed into the meter, the device yields a moisture reading accurate to within 1 percent. It is best to test at several points along a board at 12-inch intervals, avoiding the ends and areas around knots, which give up moisture quickly, then average the readings.

Cutting Stock to Length and Width

The first step in any woodworking project is to cut the wood to the approximate size required, producing boards with straight edges and eliminating defects.

Table Saw: For best results, use a table saw equipped with a rip fence, a miter gauge, and a carbide-tipped combination blade to cut boards to width (ripping) and length (crosscutting). You can build a simple jig to cut straight edges on rough stock *(page 16)*. Once the edges are straight, cut the board to length with a miter gauge—or, for more accuracy, make a crosscutting jig *(page 17)*.

A table saw performs best with periodic fine-tuning. Check the alignment of the saw table and the blade: Unplug the saw, raise the blade, and mark one tooth with a crayon. Then, rotate the blade by hand so the marked tooth is even with the table surface at the front of the blade slot, and measure from the tooth to each miter slot. Repeat the procedure with the marked tooth rotated to the back of the blade slot. The two measurements should be equal; if not, adjust the table top according to the manufacturer's instructions—usually by loosening the bolts connecting the table to the base, tapping the table top into alignment with a rubber mallet, then tightening the bolts. Also, check the tilt of the blade and the angle of the miter gauge before each project *(opposite)*.

Milling Tips: Plan your cuts carefully to economize on wood. Also plan cuts to eliminate knots, cracks, and other defects in the wood. When sawing around problem areas, use caution: Knock out loose knots before sawing, to prevent them from being thrown by the blade. Avoid sawing through cracks; doing so can cause a wedge of wood to pop out with great force.

TOOLS

Table saw	Screwdriver
Try square	Push stick
Electric drill	C-clamps
Countersink bit	

MATERIALS

Plywood ($\frac{3}{4}$")	Stop block
Hardwood for runner	Wood screws ($1\frac{1}{4}$", $1\frac{1}{2}$" No. 6)
1 x 6s	Toggle clamps

SAFETY TIPS

Protect your eyes with goggles when operating a power tool.

Safety Rules for Power Tools

Observe the following precautions whenever you are working with a power tool:

- ✔ Always be sure to unplug the tool before making any adjustments.
- ✔ Keep the tool clean and lubricated, and the blade sharp; check the power cord and plug frequently for fraying, nicks, or other damage. Make sure the outlet and plug are properly grounded.
- ✔ Keep the work area and tool surface uncluttered and well lit.
- ✔ Keep children and pets away from the workshop.
- ✔ Do all your planning and marking before turning on the motor; concentrate completely on the cut at hand, and turn the motor off as soon as the cut is done.
- ✔ Never operate a power tool when you are tired or ill, or have been drinking alcoholic beverages or taking medicine. Do not let your mind wander; concentrate on what you are doing.
- ✔ Do not wear clothing or jewelry that could catch in moving parts. Keep shirtsleeves buttoned or rolled up, and long hair tied back.
- ✔ Whenever possible, use the safety aids such as blade guards provided with the tool.
- ✔ Never force a workpiece through a machine at a faster rate than the tool is designed for.

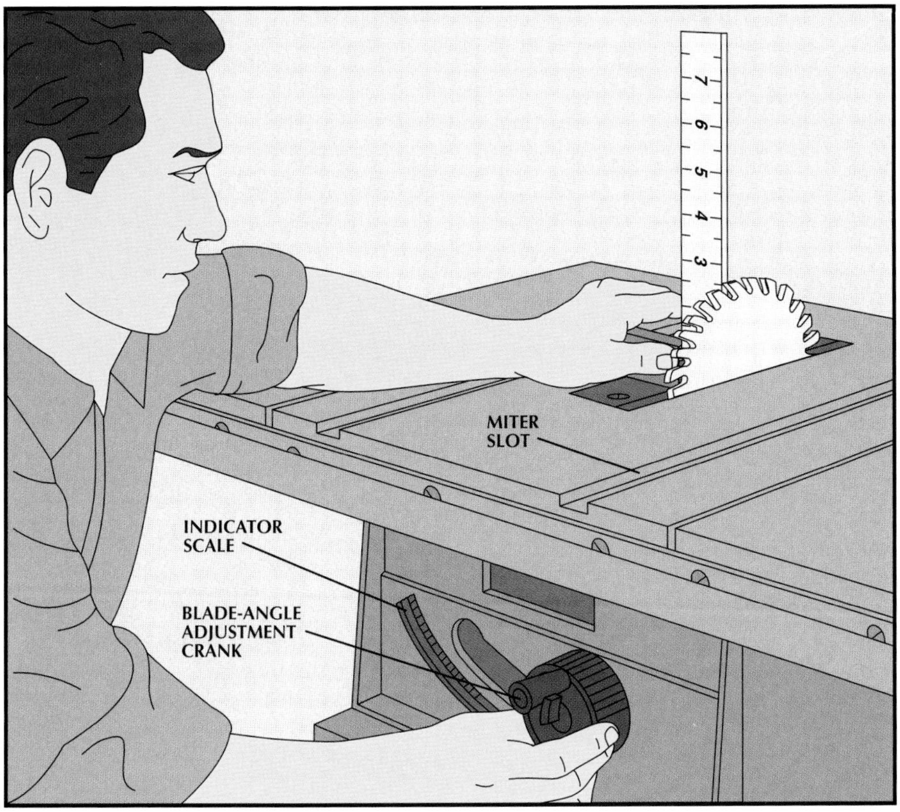

Adjusting blade angle.

◆ To check the vertical alignment of the blade, first unplug the saw and extend the blade to its full height.

◆ Set a try square on the table with its tongue vertical and resting against the blade.

◆ Turn the saw's blade-angle adjustment crank to bring the blade flush against the square, and adjust the pointer on the tilt mechanism's indicator scale to 0 degrees. If the blade does not move easily, check the tilt mechanism track for obstructions.

Table-Saw Safety

In addition to the safety rules for power tools listed opposite, observe these precautions:

✓ Keep the surface of the saw clean and free of wood scraps and tools.

✓ Provide support for large workpieces at the sides or end of the table.

✓ Never saw boards freehand; use the rip fence as a guide for rip cuts, and the miter gauge or a jig when crosscutting.

✓ Use a push stick when ripping narrow stock.

✓ Hold the wood firmly against the fence or the miter gauge while cutting. Avoid awkward hand positions that will be hard to maintain during the cut.

✓ Never reach over the blade.

✓ If the blade stalls, turn off the saw, retract the workpiece, and start the cut again.

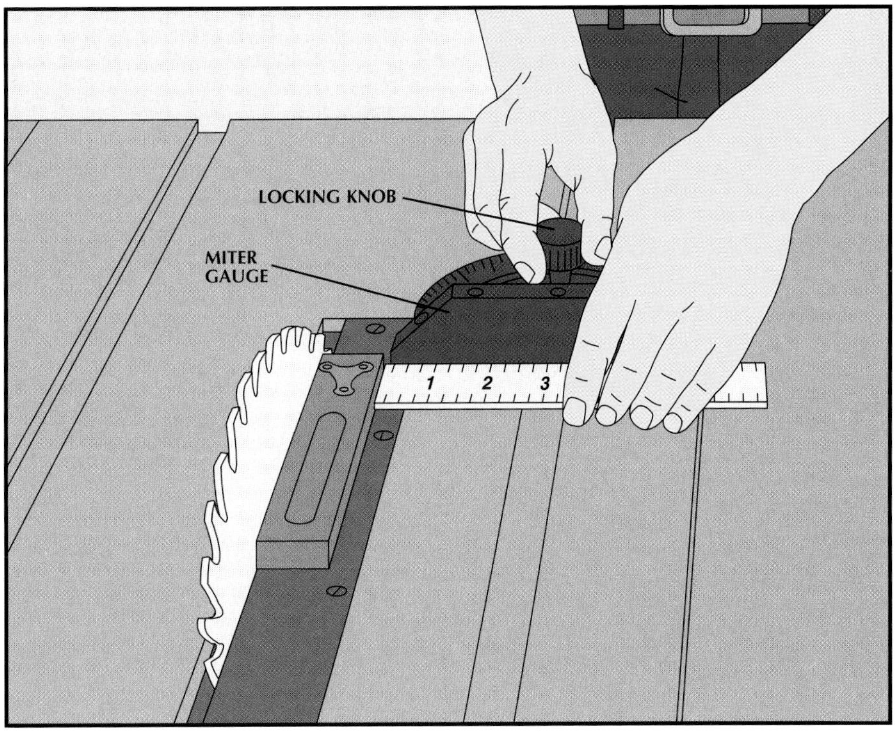

Adjusting the miter gauge to 90 degrees.

◆ Loosen the miter-gauge locking knob, then hold a try square on the saw table so the tongue rests against the gauge and the handle sits against the blade without touching any teeth.

◆ Pivot the miter gauge to bring the square's handle flush against the blade, then tighten the locking knob *(above)*.

RIPPING ROUGH BOARDS

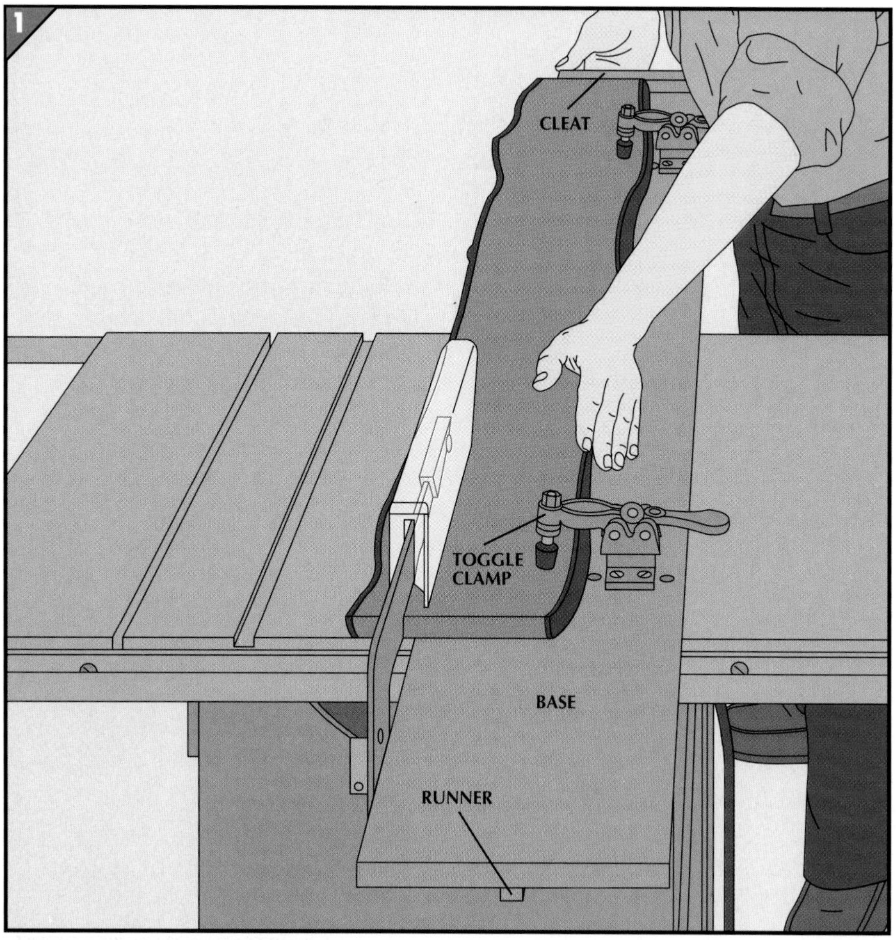

1. Squaring the first edge.
To create straight edges on a rough-cut board, use a table-saw jig like the one shown here. The jig consists of a 6-foot-long base cut from $\frac{3}{4}$-inch plywood, guided by a hardwood runner cut to fit the saw table's miter slot. With countersunk No. 6 wood screws, secure the runner to the base so the edge of the base is 1 inch from the blade with the runner in the slot. Fasten a cleat of $\frac{3}{4}$-inch plywood to one end with $1\frac{1}{4}$-inch screws. Drill rows of screw holes through the base for mounting two toggle clamps, one row near each end. Attach the clamps using the holes that accommodate the width of the board to be trimmed.

◆ With the jig on the saw table with the runner in the miter slot, set the board on the base with one end flush against the cleat and the other end just in front of the blade. Tighten the toggle clamps with an edge of the board to the right of the blade.

◆ Turn on the saw and push the jig across the table, holding the board down against the jig base with one hand *(left)*.

2. Cutting the opposite edge.

◆ Unclamp the board from the jig and remove the jig from the saw table.

◆ Position the rip fence so the blade will saw the uncut edge with the straight one sliding along the fence.

◆ Place the board on the saw table with the straight edge against the fence and one end just in front of the blade. Turn on the saw and slowly push the board into the blade with your right hand, pressing the board against the fence with your left hand *(right)*.

◆ When your hands approach the blade guard, finish the cut with a push stick or a piece of scrap wood held between the saw blade and the fence.

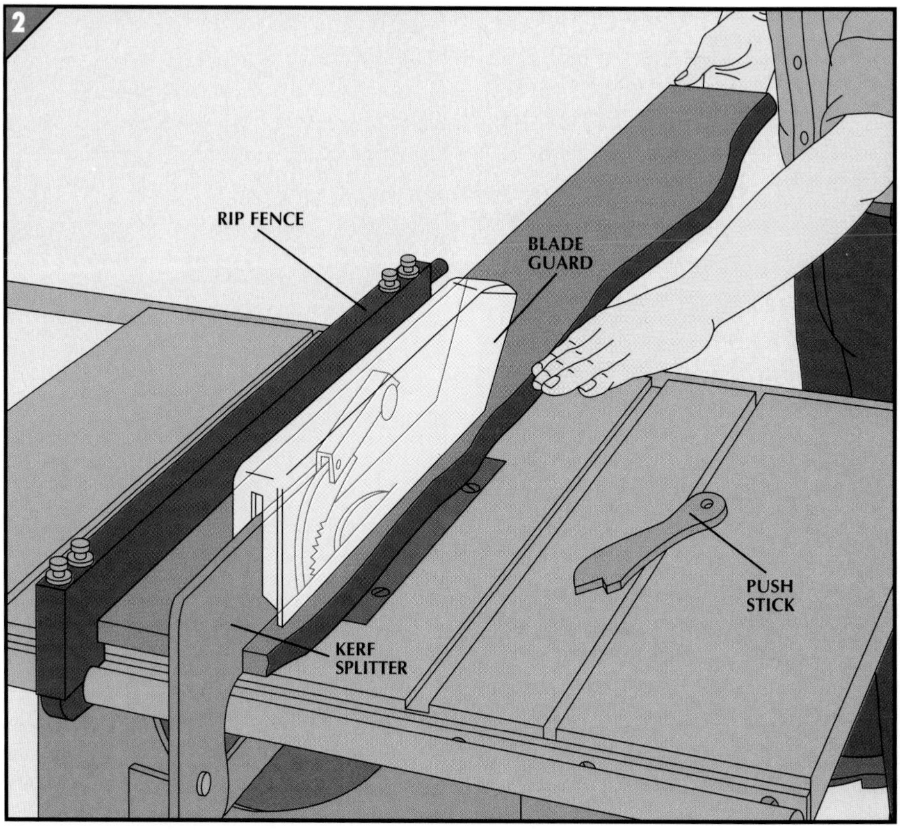

A JIG FOR CROSSCUTTING

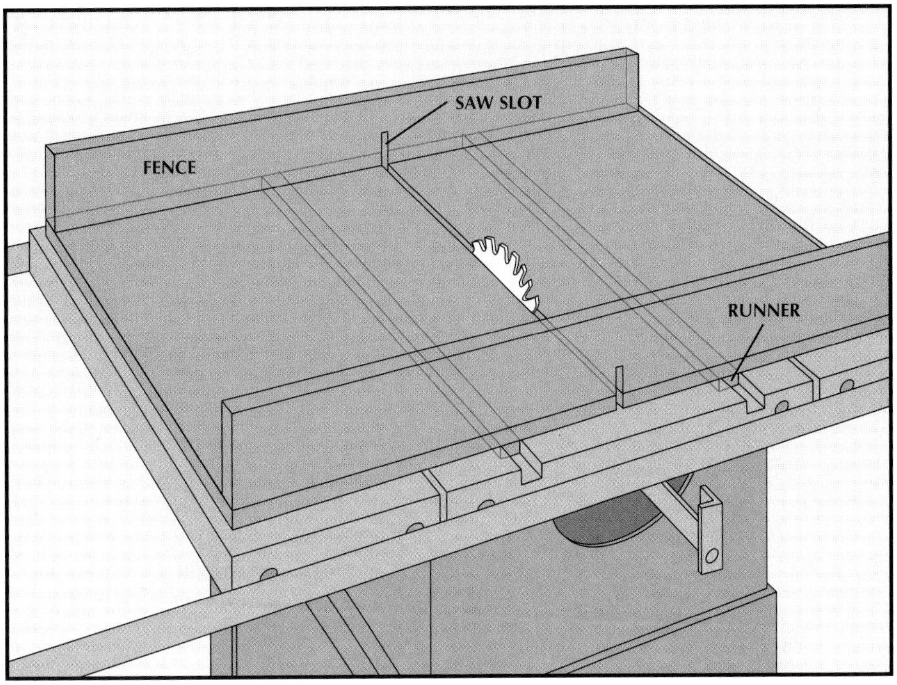

Building the jig.

To crosscut boards safely and precisely, use the jig illustrated at right. From $\frac{3}{4}$-inch plywood, cut the base no larger than the saw table. Make two hardwood runners to fit the saw table's miter slots and attach them with No. 6 countersunk wood screws to the underside of the base. Saw two 1-by-6 fences to the same length as the base and attach them to the base with $1\frac{1}{2}$-inch screws, making sure not to align any screws with the saw blade.

To ready the jig for use, place it on the saw table with the runners in the miter slots and the front-edge fence in front of the blade; set the blade half as high as the fences. Turn on the saw and slide the jig across the table, slotting the fences and base.

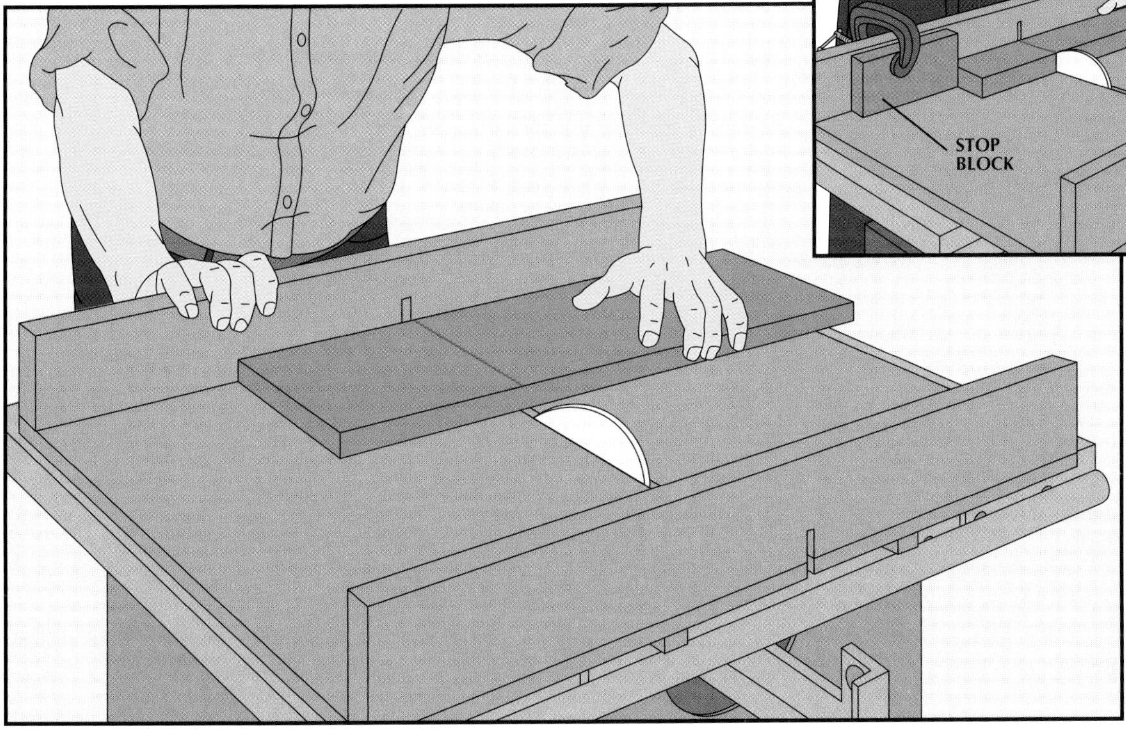

Making crosscuts.

◆ Adjust the blade height $\frac{1}{4}$ inch higher than the thickness of the board to be cut.
◆ Position the crosscut jig on the saw table and place the board on the base with one edge against the back fence and the cutting line over the saw slot.
◆ Turn on the saw and push the jig across the table, using one hand to hold the board against the base and fence *(above)*. Keep both hands well away from the blade.

To crosscut several pieces to the same length, place the first board in the jig, set a wood block against its end as a stop, and clamp the block to the fence. Cut each board as for a standard crosscut, holding it against the fence and stop block *(inset)*.

Resawing Thick Lumber

When rough stock is thicker than you need, you can resaw it into thinner boards. You can also use this method to produce veneer or inlay, since successive slices from the same board yield pieces with mirror-image grain patterns. The best tool for this job is a band saw; because the blade is thin, waste is minimal.

The Band Saw: Models for home use can resaw boards up to 6 inches wide. For a clean cut requiring little effort, use a skip-tooth blade made for resawing; use the widest blade the saw can hold, and adjust it before sawing *(opposite, top).*

Guiding the Cut: The flexible blade of a band saw tends to track along the grain of the wood being cut. You can compensate for this and ensure a straight cut by using a pivot jig *(opposite, bottom).*

To prepare a board for resawing, make one face and one edge square and straight *(pages 26-27)*, and feed these surfaces along the saw table and the jig. After the cut, set the resawn boards aside for two or three days—they may warp slightly as they dry—then plane the pieces to their final dimensions. Planing will also smooth out any rough surfaces left by the saw blade.

TOOLS

- Band saw
- Try square
- Hex wrench
- Hand-screw clamp

MATERIALS

Lumber for pivot jig and push stick

SAFETY TIPS

Goggles will protect your eyes when you are operating a power tool.

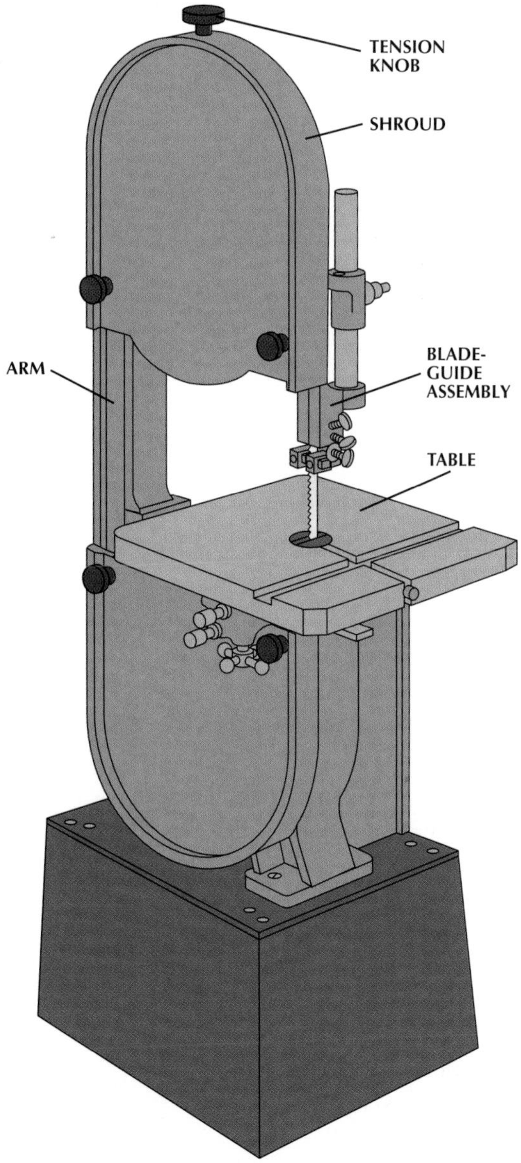

The versatile band saw.
The blade of a band saw loops around two large, shrouded wheels, the lower wheel connected to an electric motor, and the upper wheel turning freely. Blade tension is adjusted by raising or lowering the upper wheel by means of the tension knob. On a typical home-shop band saw, the maximum amount of blade that can be exposed between the blade-guide assembly and the table—which limits the width of boards that can be resawn—is usually just over 6 inches.

Band-Saw Safety

In addition to the safety rules for power tools listed on page 14, observe these precautions:

- ✔ Mount the blade so the teeth are pointing down in the direction the blade moves.
- ✔ Set the blade-guide blocks no more than $\frac{1}{8}$ inch above the wood you are cutting, to protect your fingers and provide maximum support for the blade.
- ✔ Position your hands so your fingers would not hit the blade if the workpiece were to split or move forward suddenly.
- ✔ Hold the stock firmly against the table and against any fence or jig you are using.
- ✔ Avoid backing up in a cut with the saw running—this could pull the blade off the wheels.

ADJUSTING A BAND SAW

Setting the blade clearance.

◆ Check that the blade is properly aligned with the table by holding the handle of a try square against the side of the blade so its tongue is flush against the table. If it is not square, loosen the table-tilt handles and adjust the table so it forms a right angle with the square *(right)*. Tighten the handles.

◆ Turn the lateral-guide adjustment knob so the front edges of the guide blocks rest just behind the gullets of the teeth *(inset)*. With a hex wrench, adjust the blocks so they will hold a piece of paper against the blade, but not so tight as to pinch the blade.

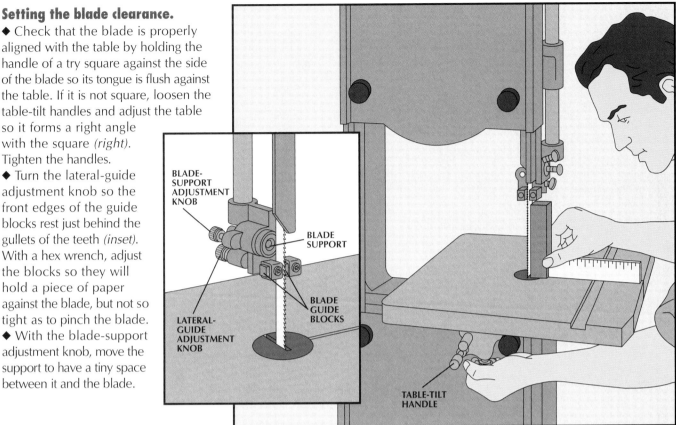

◆ With the blade-support adjustment knob, move the support to have a tiny space between it and the blade.

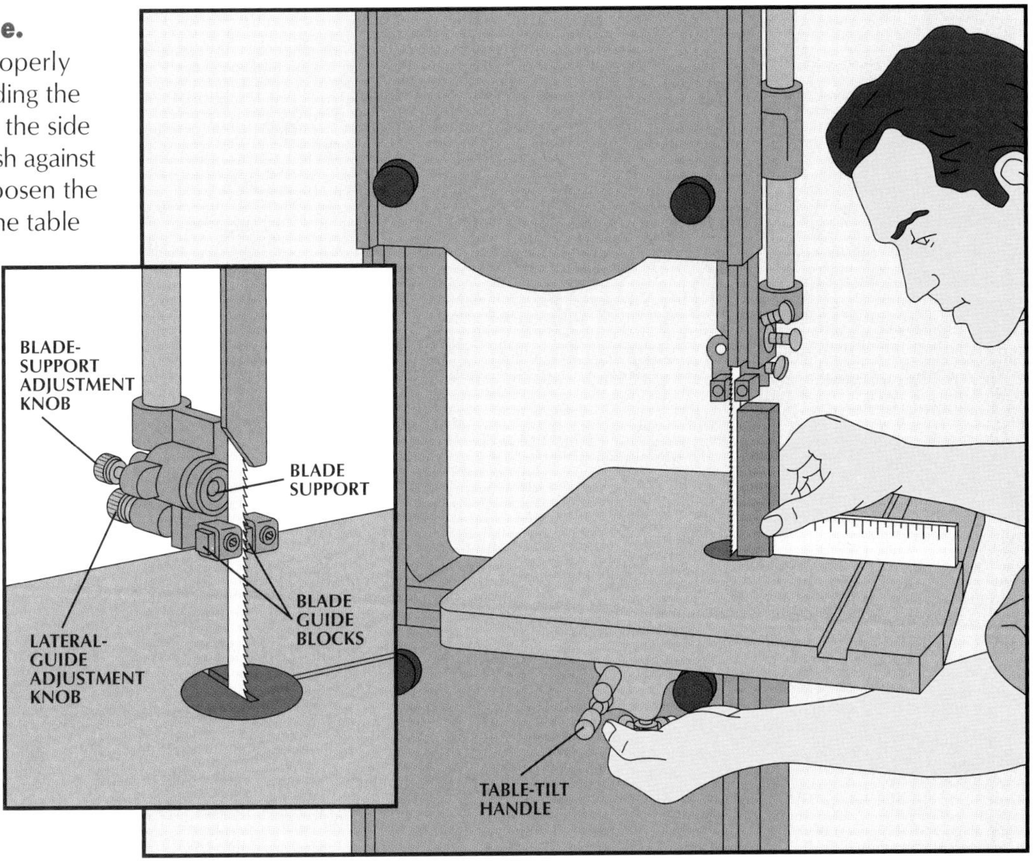

CUTTING THIN SLICES OF WOOD

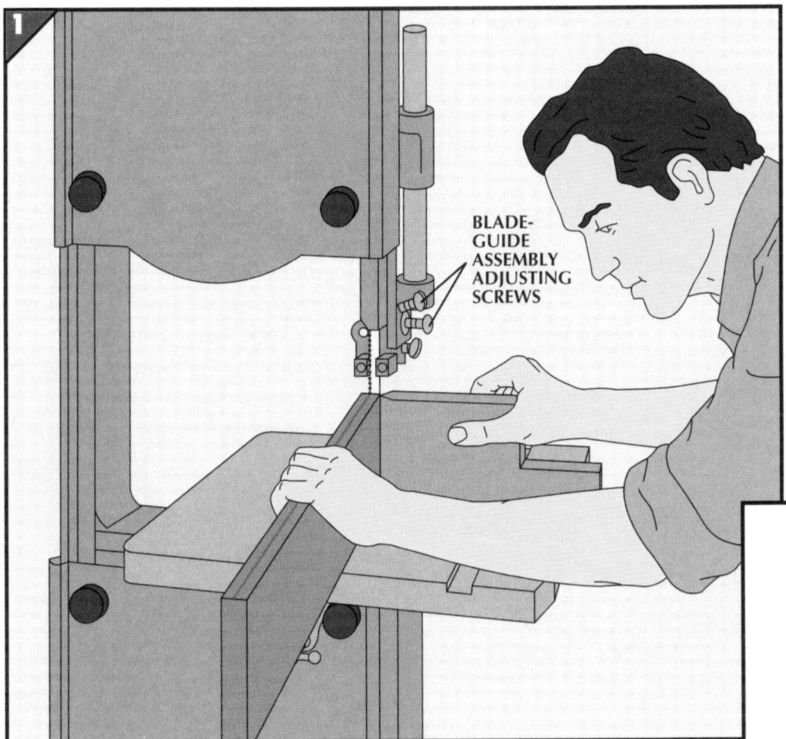

1. Setting the pivot jig.

◆ To make the jig, cut a wood block into an L shape so the tall end is as high as the wood being cut, then bevel the tall end and round it slightly with sandpaper *(inset)*.

◆ Mark a line on the top edge of the stock to indicate the desired thickness.

◆ Set the stock on the saw table so the mark aligns with the blade teeth; position the jig at a right angle to the stock with its nose even with the teeth and the board edge *(left)*. Clamp the jig to the table.

◆ Loosen the blade-guide assembly screws, set the guides $\frac{1}{8}$ inch above the board, then tighten the screws.

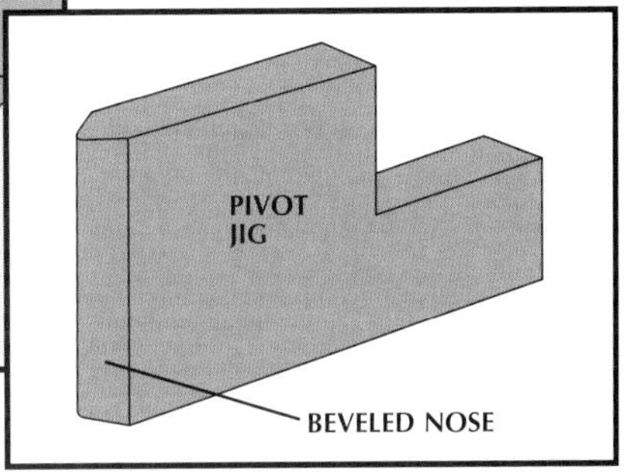

2. Starting the cut.

◆ With the stock clear of the blade, switch on the saw.

◆ Begin pushing the stock forward with your right hand so the blade splits the cutting line. With your left hand, press on the side of the board opposite the beveled nose of the jig *(right)*.

◆ If the blade wanders from the cutting line, pivot the stock against the nose of the jig to realign the blade with the line.

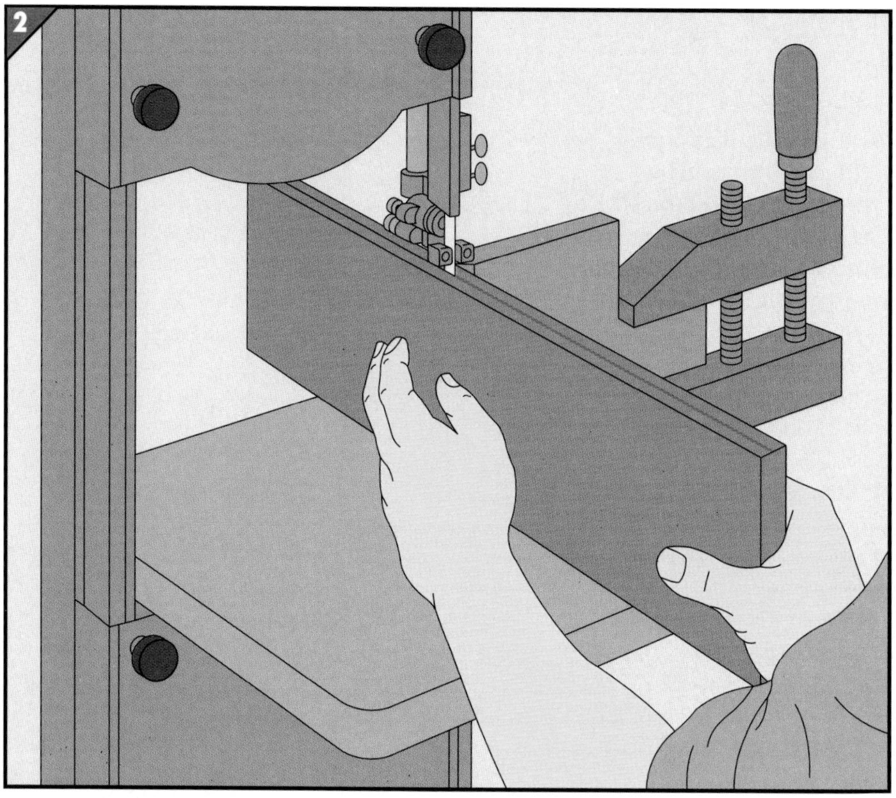

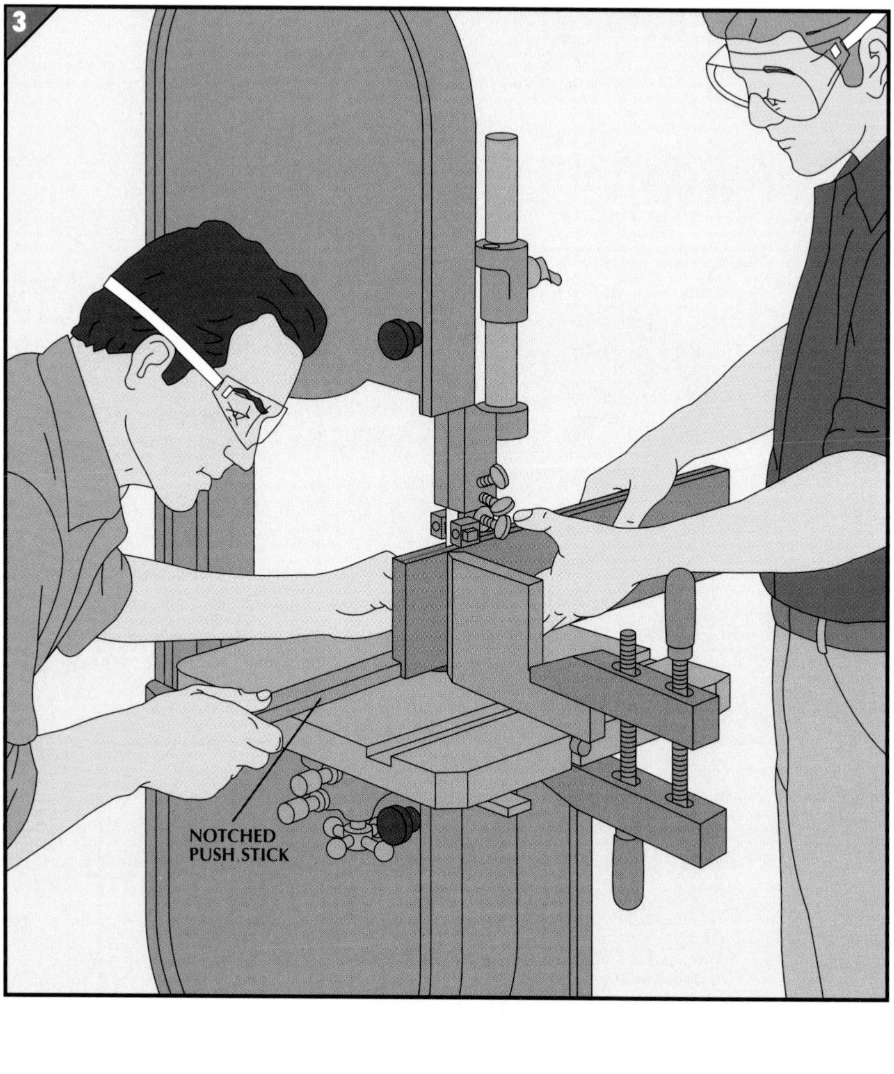

3. Finishing the cut.

◆ Cut a notch from one end of a wood scrap to make a push stick.

◆ As you near the end of the cut, use the notched push stick to guide the stock past the blade *(left)*. Maintain pressure against the side of the stock with your left hand, but move this hand forward with the stock to avoid any danger of touching the blade at the end of the cut. Have a helper support the leading end of any piece too unwieldy for you to hold as it comes off the table. If you do not have a helper, stop feeding the workpiece 3 to 4 inches from the end of the cut; then, walk around the table and pull the wood past the blade from the opposite side.

Dimensioning Stock with Hand Planes

To bring a board to its final dimensions, no tool will leave a smoother surface than a hand plane. Even if you use a power planer and a jointer for big jobs, you will need to make a final pass with a hand plane to remove the power tools' machining marks.

Adjusting a Plane: A 14-inch-long jack plane is adequate for sizing most lumber. But you can flatten surfaces more thoroughly with a jointer plane—its long 20- to 24-inch body will straddle and erase imperfections on the surface of a board rather than follow them. With its shallow blade angle, the 6-inch block plane excels at smoothing the ends of boards.

Whichever type of plane you use, adjust the blade depth to slice thin shavings. To set the cutting edge parallel with the mouth of the plane—essential for straight cuts—sight down the length of the plane's sole and use the lateral adjusting lever located on top of the tool.

To keep a hand plane in top working order, clean the sole with mineral spirits and lubricate it with paraffin; store the plane on its side to protect the blade.

Dimensioning a Board: Always plane with the grain *(page 10)*. If you are unsure of the grain direction, make a few end-to-end test strokes in each direction—the plane will lift a thin curl of wood with little effort when it is moving in the grain direction.

Start by flattening one face *(page 22)*, then an edge so it is perpendicular to the face *(page 23)*. Then, mark the desired width of the board on one face with a combination square and a pencil or with a marking gauge, and plane the remaining edge to the line. Finally, mark the final thickness on both edges and plane the rough face down to the lines. Once the faces and edges are the required size, smooth the ends with a block plane *(page 24)*.

TOOLS

- Bench dogs
- Jack plane
- Straightedge
- Combination square
- Clamps
- Block plane

THE INDISPENSABLE WORKBENCH

A solid work surface is a must for many woodworking tasks—particularly planing. A workbench *(below)* with an end vise can hold boards for planing edges and ends. For face planing, boards are secured between a pair of square bench dogs that fit in the tail vise and in one of a row of holes along the bench. Benches are available—usually partially assembled—through woodworking suppliers, but you can also buy plans and hardware to make your own. In a pinch, any sturdy table can be used, provided boards can be clamped in place. For example, you can improvise end stops by clamping plywood scraps, thinner than the board you are planing, to the work surface at each end of the board.

SMOOTHING BOARDS TO SIZE

1. Leveling the first face.

◆ With the aid of a workbench vise, secure the board on a flat work surface with bench dogs or end stops. Set it concave side down if it is cupped; if the board is twisted, steady it by shimming the higher corners.

◆ With a jack or jointer plane adjusted for a fine cut, guide the tool along the surface from end to end, working in the grain direction *(right)*. Making passes that overlap slightly, try to flatten the surface uniformly; check your progress by eye.

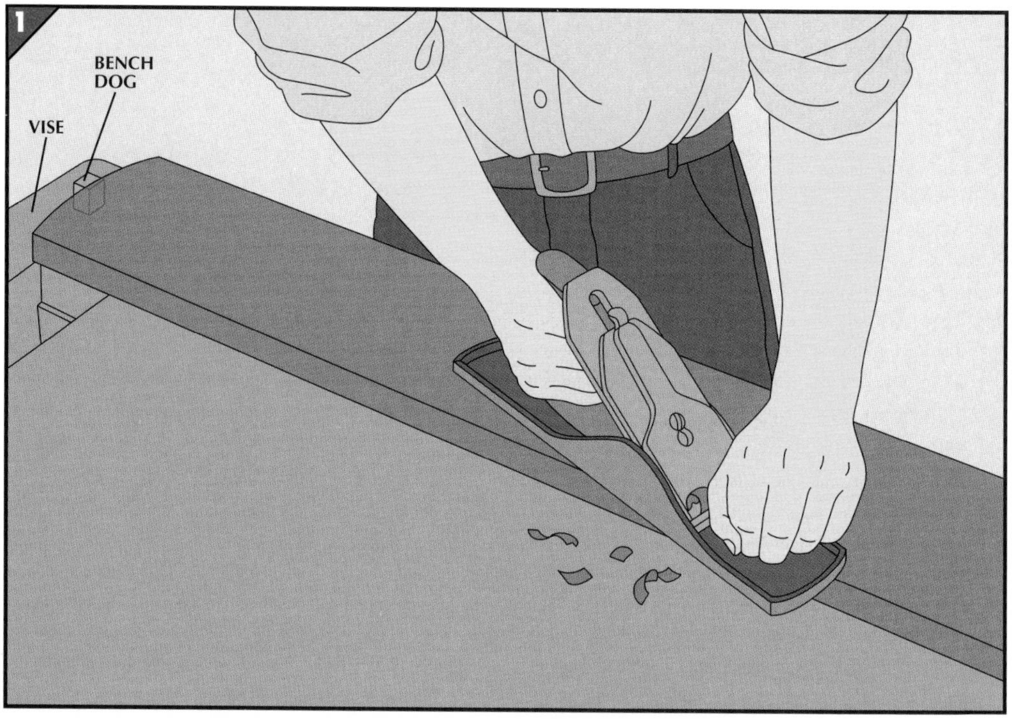

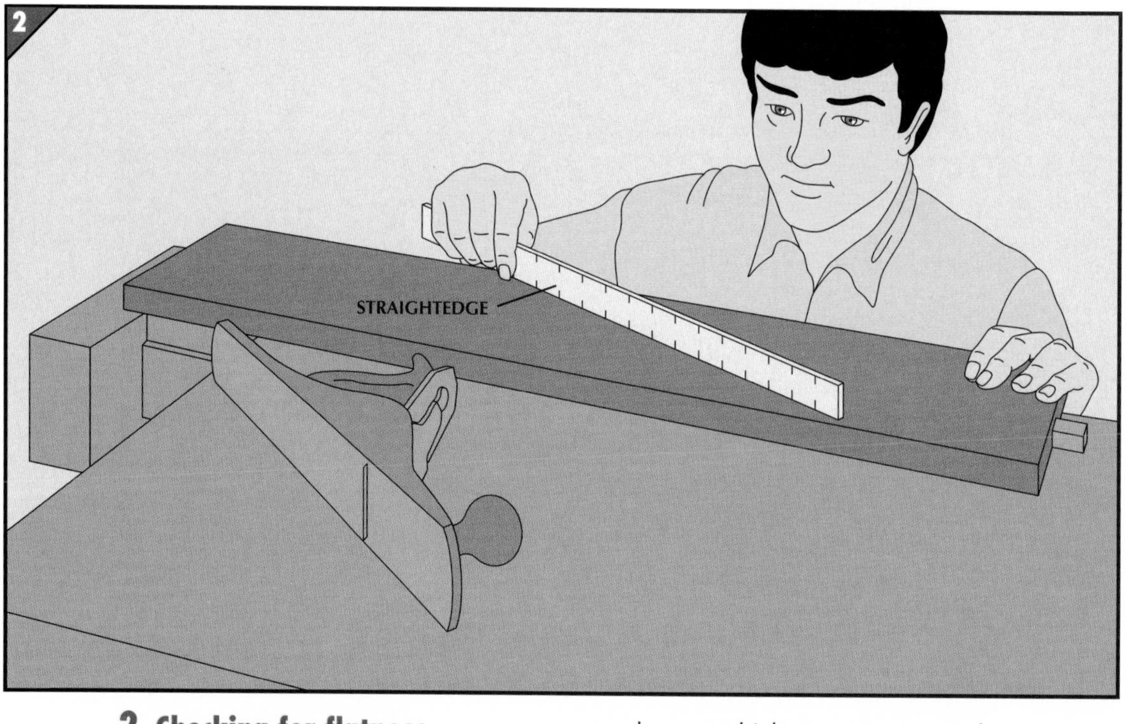

2. Checking for flatness.

◆ Set a straightedge on edge diagonally across the planed surface.

◆ Sighting from just above the surface, slide the straightedge toward you *(above)*—light will be visible between the straightedge and the board at any low areas between high spots. Repeat with the straightedge at various angles, marking high spots on the board as you go.

◆ Plane down the high spots.

◆ Make a series of final smoothing passes with the plane flat on the board but at a slight angle to the edges.

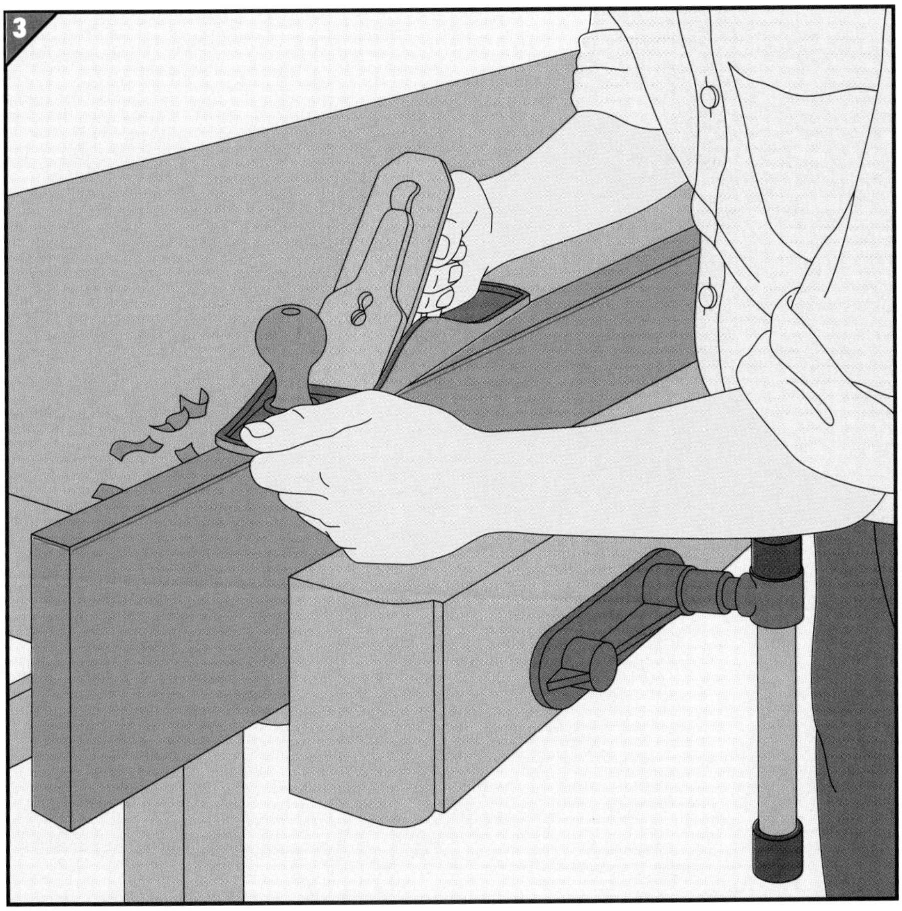

3. Planing an edge.

◆ With a straightedge, mark a reference line along each face of the board, about $\frac{1}{16}$ to $\frac{1}{8}$ inch from the same edge. Then, clamp the board in a vise so the smooth face is out.

◆ Holding the plane flat on the edge of the board and slightly angled to one side with the cutting edge centered on the surface, guide the tool from one end to the other. Keep the plane centered and flat on the surface by pressing your thumb down on the toe of the plane and sliding your knuckles along the smooth face of the board *(left)*.

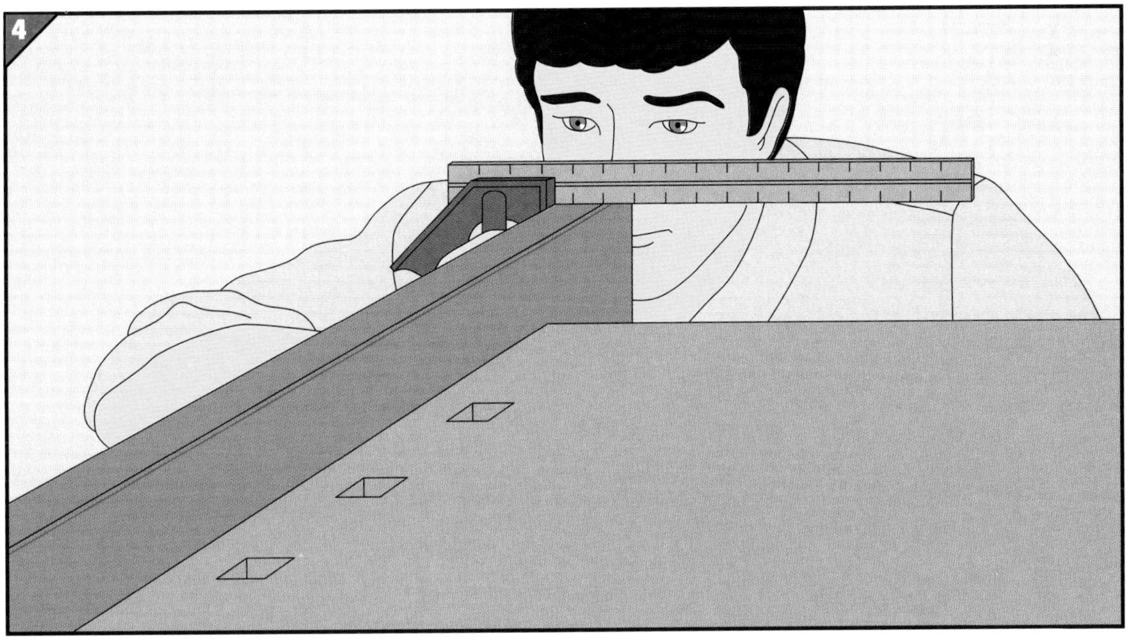

4. Squaring the edge.

◆ When you have planed to within a few strokes of the reference lines, check the edge for square by placing a combination square on the board so the head rests flat against the smooth face; then, slide the square along the edge, looking for and marking gaps *(above)*.

◆ Continue planing to the lines, making sure to keep the tool flat on the marked areas.

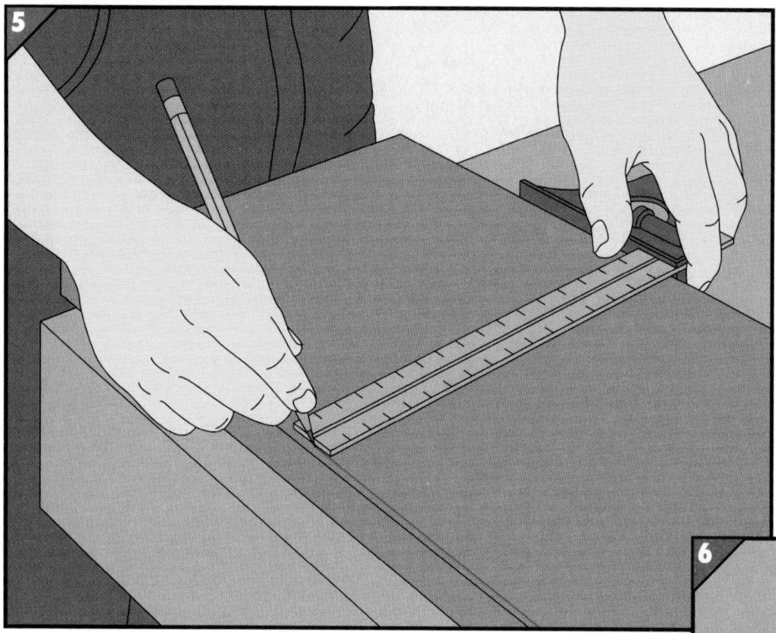

5. Planing the board to width.

◆ Unclamp the board and set it flat.
◆ Extend the ruler of a combination square to the desired final width of the board and lay the square on the face so the head sits against the planed edge. Holding a pencil at the end of the ruler, slide the square and pencil together along the length of the board, marking a line parallel to the planed edge *(left)*. Turn the board over and repeat to mark a line on the opposite face.
◆ Plane the rough edge to the lines as in Step 3.

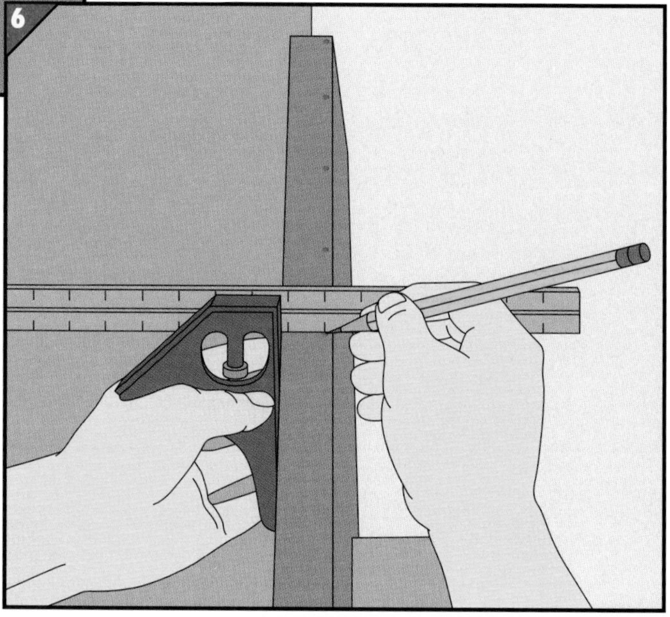

6. Planing to thickness.

◆ Clamp the board in a vise.
◆ Mark the final thickness of the board on an edge with the head of a combination square flat against the planed face and the ruler on the edge. Starting near one end, mark the edge with a dot, guided by the ruler *(right)*. Slide the square along the board, adding a dot every few inches, until you reach the opposite end. Then, connect the dots into a line with a straightedge and repeat on the other edge.
◆ Plane the rough face of the board to the line *(Step 1)*, checking frequently for flatness *(Step 2)*.

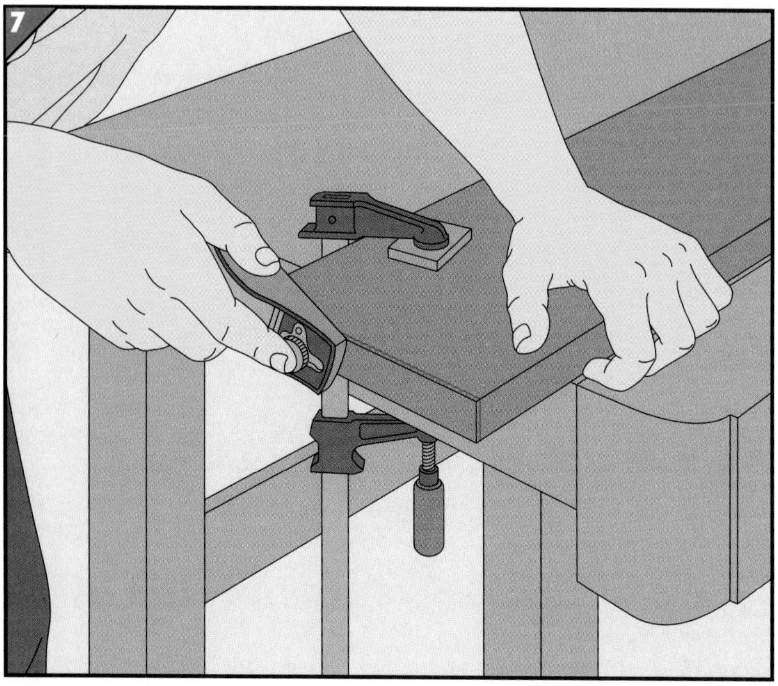

7. Smoothing the end grain.

◆ Mark reference lines across all four sides of the board at one end, using a combination square to make the lines perpendicular to the edges.
◆ Protecting the board with wood pads, clamp it flat to the workbench so one end overhangs the bench top by a few inches.
◆ With a block plane set for a shallow cut, push the tool at a slight angle across the grain with short, even strokes *(left)*. To prevent chipping when you reach an edge, plane from one edge only to the middle; then turn the board over and work from the opposite edge to the middle. Check for squareness *(Step 4)*.
◆ Repeat the process on the opposite end.

Preparing Wood with Power Tools

The duo of jointer and planer can smooth, square, and size a large number of boards in a short time. Both tools excel at shaving wood from lumber rapidly and uniformly. The usual sequence is to smooth one face and one edge on the jointer, and then shave the board to the desired thickness on the planer.

The Versatile Jointer: As with hand planes, jointer blades trim faces and edges smoothly only when cutting in the direction of the wood grain *(below and pages 26-27)*, although the tool can also handle end grain *(page 27)*. Adjust a jointer for a shallow depth of cut—no more than $\frac{1}{8}$ inch—and feed stock into the blades slowly.

The jointer can flatten warped lumber *(page 28)*, and with minor adjustments, it can even produce bevels, chamfers, and rabbets *(page 41)*.

The Stationary Planer: Although jointers can be used to trim boards to a given thickness, the best tool for this job is the planer *(page 29)*. The largest home-shop jointers aren't designed to handle stock wider than 6 inches; planers can generally take on boards up to 12 inches wide. Larger stock can be planed at a millwork shop.

Tool Maintenance: Clean jointer and planer knives periodically with mineral spirits. When the shavings produced by a machine become limp, uneven, or appear burnished, hone the knives in place with a few light strokes from a flat oilstone, removing as little steel as possible.

After three or four sharpenings, have the knives ground by a professional. To reinstall them properly afterward, use a commercial jig, available from woodworking supply houses.

TOOLS
- Jointer
- Push blocks
- Hammer
- Level
- Utility knife
- Stationary planer

MATERIALS
- Scrap wood
- Common nails
- Wedge-shaped shims
- Wood glue

SAFETY TIPS

Put on goggles when operating a power tool.

THE INNER WORKINGS OF A JOINTER

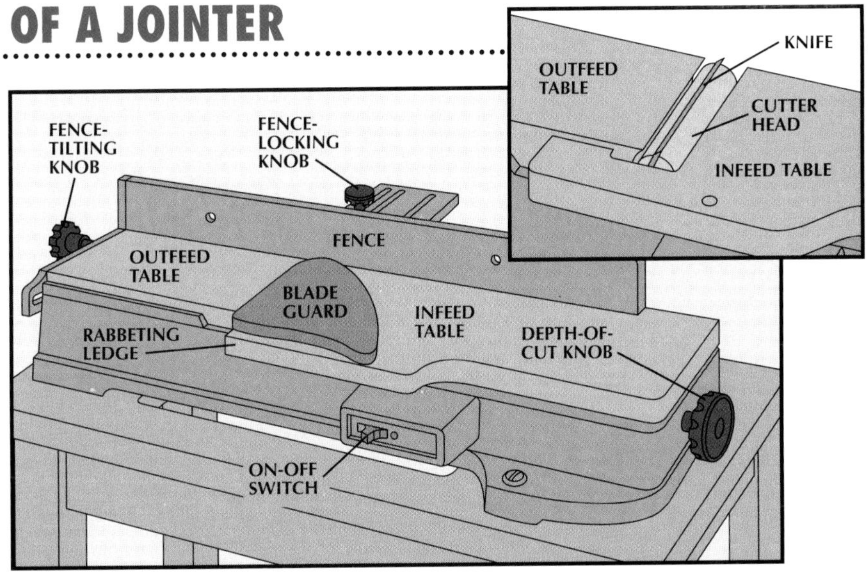

Anatomy of a jointer.

Mounted on a stationary base, a jointer is composed of two tables—infeed and outfeed—separated by a cutter head *(right and inset)*. The spring-activated blade guard, which normally covers the cutter head, is nudged aside momentarily when a board is fed across the tables. Set at a 90-degree angle to the tables for standard jointing, the fence can be locked at angles from 45 to 135 degrees to cut chamfers and bevels. The rabbeting ledge enables the jointer to cut rabbets *(page 41)*; the blade guard must be removed for rabbeting operations.

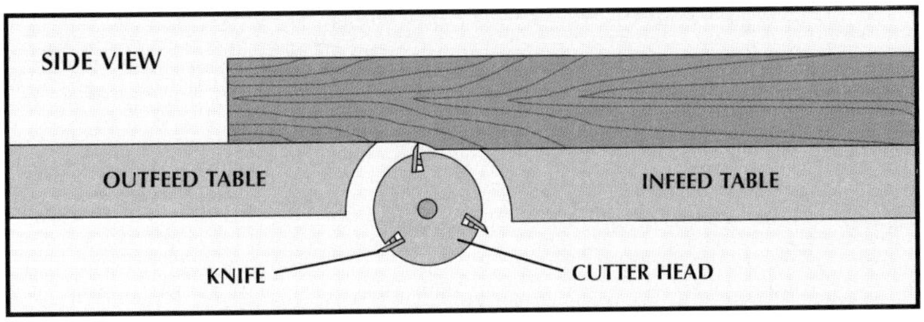

Adjusting the cutting depth.

The tables are adjusted independently, with the outfeed table usually set at the same level as the highest reach of the knives. The height of the infeed table in relation to the outfeed table determines the depth of cut *(right)*.

Safe Jointer Operation

In addition to the safety rules for power tools listed on page 14, observe these precautions:

✔ Unplug the machine before adjusting the fence and tables or sharpening the knives.

✔ Remove the blade guard only when making a rabbet cut.

✔ Do not joint pieces of wood less than 12 inches long. If you need short pieces, prepare a long board, then cut it to the needed lengths.

✔ Do not joint the face of a board that is thinner than $\frac{1}{4}$ inch.

✔ Use push blocks to feed any board less than 3 inches thick.

THREE SQUARING CUTS

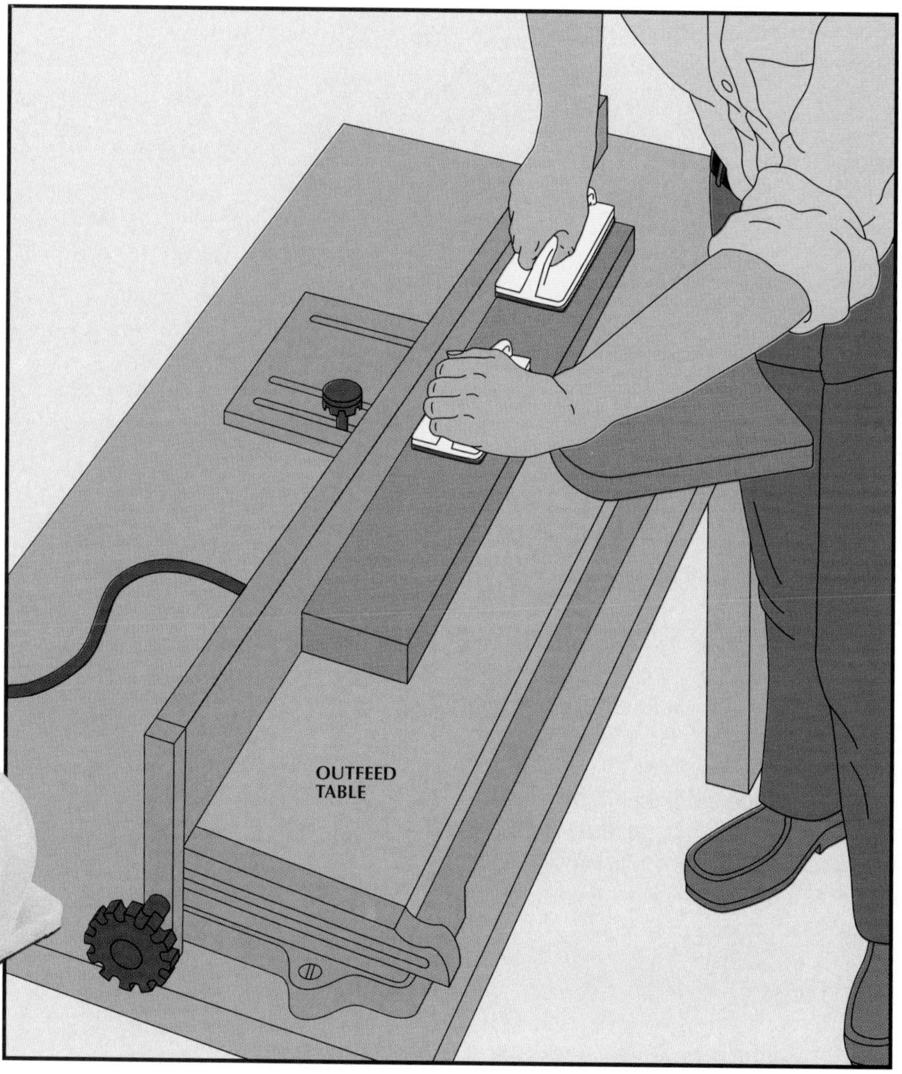

Jointing a board face.

◆ Set the board on the infeed table, edge against the fence, with its end a few inches from the blade guard.

◆ Turn on the jointer's motor and, pressing down on the stock with a push block *(photograph)* in each hand, guide the board forward slowly and steadily over the knives, keeping the edge flush against the fence *(right)*.

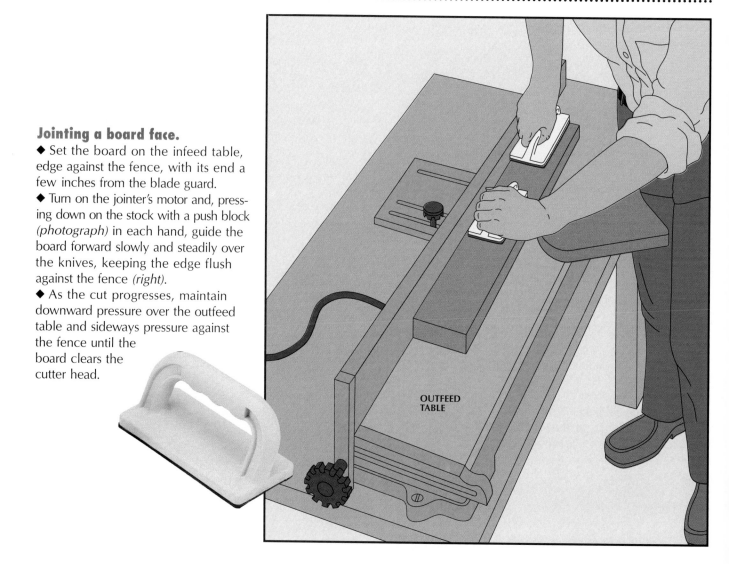

◆ As the cut progresses, maintain downward pressure over the outfeed table and sideways pressure against the fence until the board clears the cutter head.

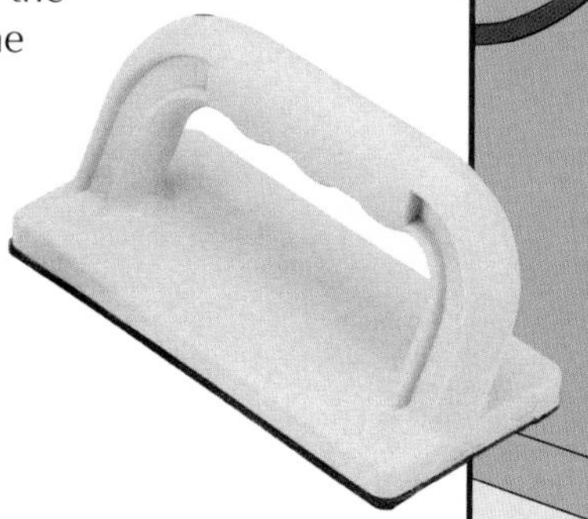

Jointing an edge.

◆ Place your hands on the top edge of the board, your left hand at the front end and your right at the back. Pressing the face of the board against the fence, push the board slowly and steadily across the tables *(left)*.

◆ As the cut progresses, press the board down on the outfeed table and up against the fence with your left hand; move the board forward with your right. Keep both hands well away from the cutter head, and do not relax the pressure or change the feed rate until the cut is finished and both hands are well beyond the cutter head.

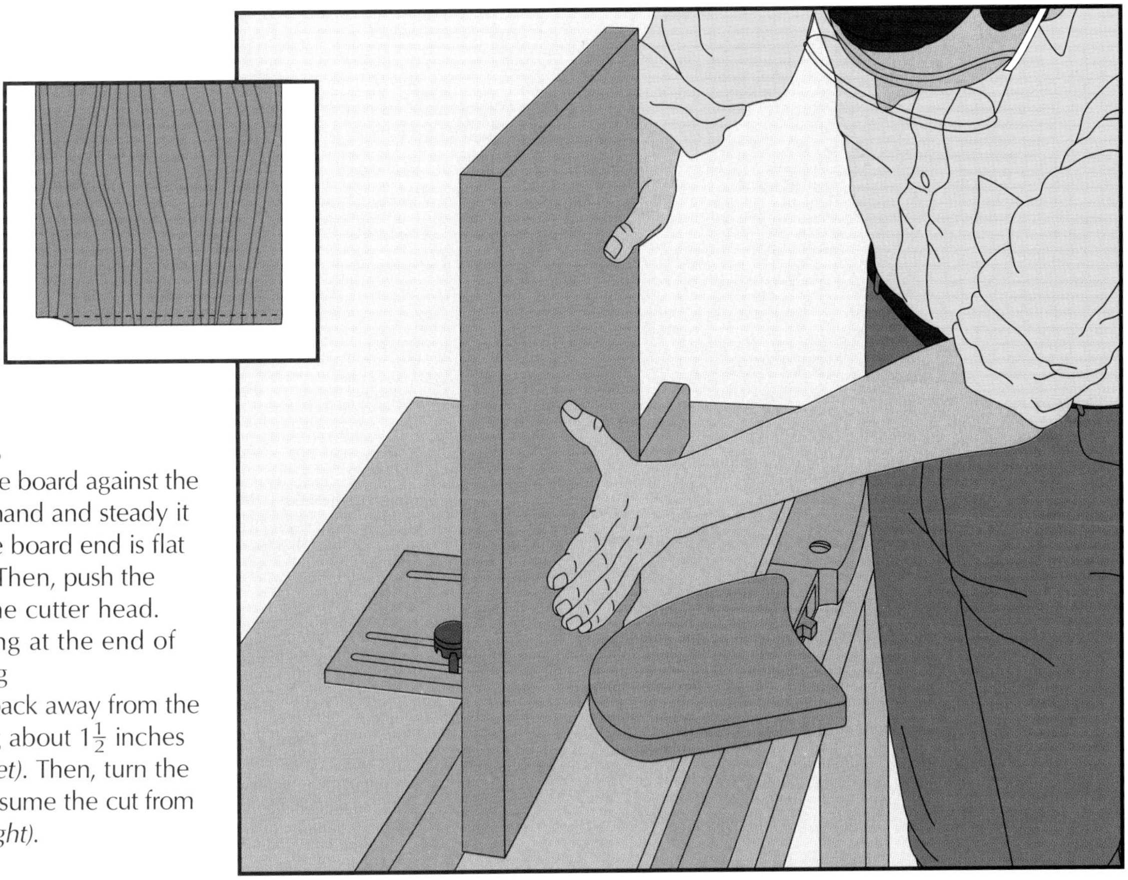

Trimming an end.

◆ Hold the face of the board against the fence with your left hand and steady it with your right so the board end is flat on the infeed table. Then, push the board forward into the cutter head.

◆ To avoid splintering at the end of the cut, stop feeding the board and tilt it back away from the knives after trimming about $1\frac{1}{2}$ inches of the end grain *(inset)*. Then, turn the board around and resume the cut from the opposite edge *(right)*.

Salvaging a cupped board.

◆ Place the board concave side down on the infeed table and pass it over the cutter head *(page 26)*. Repeat this procedure until the high points along the edges are leveled and the face is flat *(right, top)*. Then, turn the jointer off.

◆ The easiest way to flatten the opposite side is with a planer *(opposite)*. If you don't have one, you can finish the job on the jointer: Turn the board over and press the edge firmly against the fence. Then, holding a wood scrap against the opposite edge, mark the scrap at the level of the top of the board *(right, bottom)*. Move the board and the scrap to a worktable and tack the scrap to the board edge, using the mark to align the pieces; drive the nails as close to the top of the board as possible. The scrap will help keep the board from rocking as it is fed across the jointer. Feed the board and scrap across the cutter head repeatedly until the second face is flat.

(In the illustrations at right, the blade guard has been removed for clarity.)

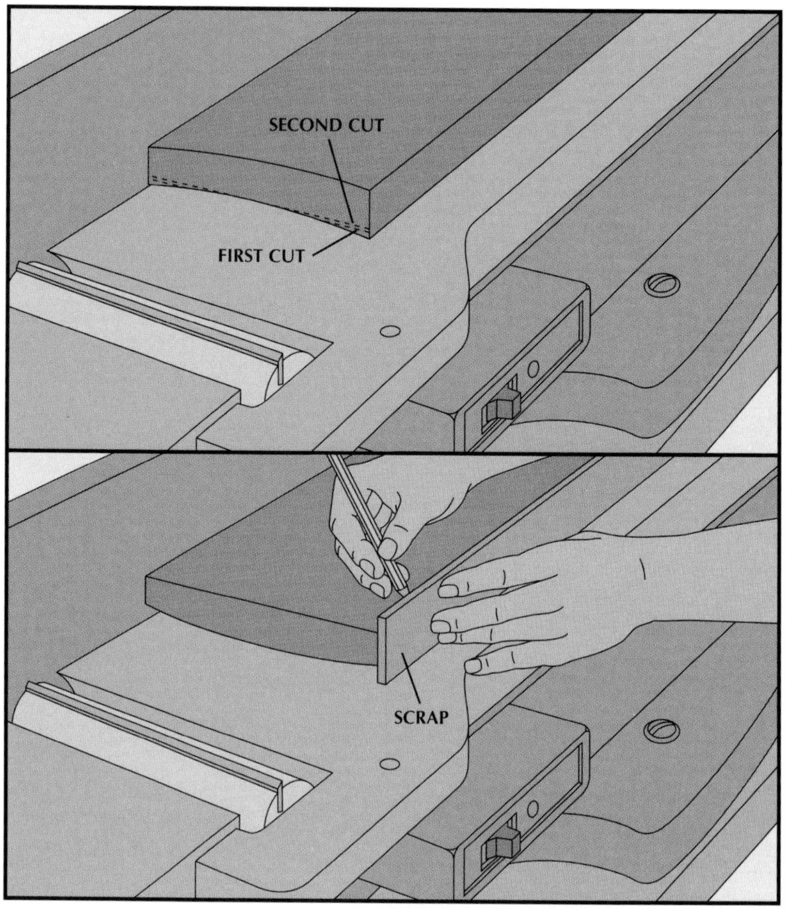

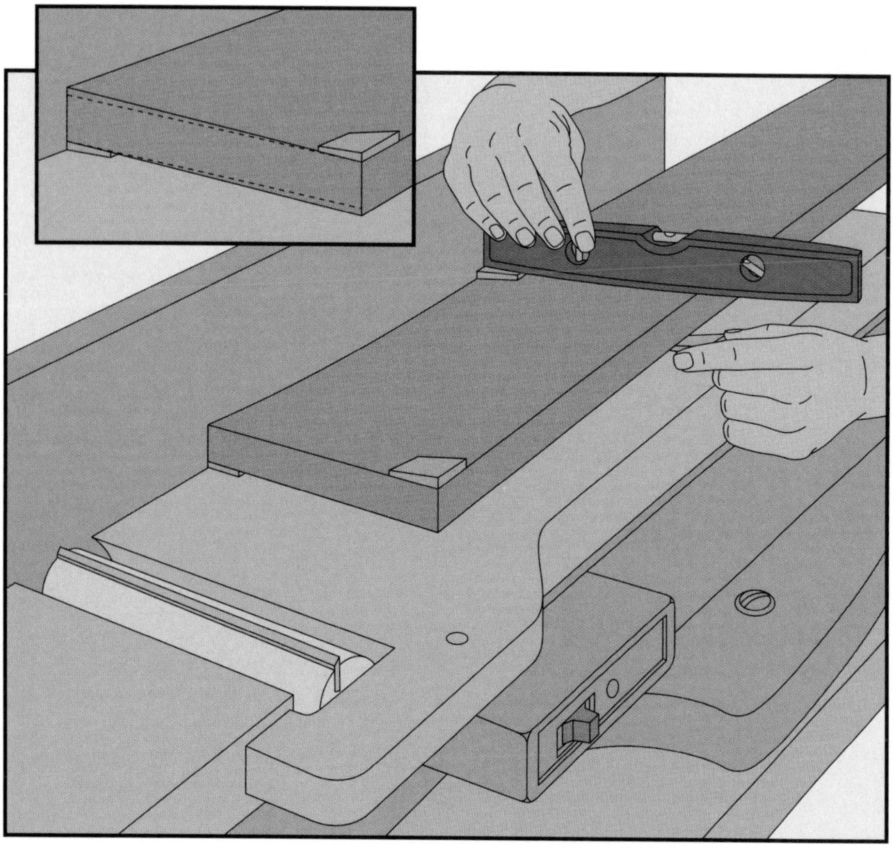

Jointing a twisted board.

◆ Lay the board on the infeed table and, checking with a carpenter's level, glue a wedge-shaped shim on each low spot on both sides of the piece to create a level surface *(left)*. The shims will enable you to make enough passes across the jointer to flatten the board, as represented by the dashed lines in the inset.

◆ Once the glue is dry, trim the shims even with the edges of the board using a utility knife.

◆ Joint one face of the board repeatedly until the shims on it have been completely cut away and the face is flat. Repeat the shimming and shaving process on the opposite side on the jointer.

(In the illustration at left, the blade guard has been removed for clarity.)

THINNING BOARDS ON THE PLANER

How a planer works.
A board fed into the machine is pulled along the table by the infeed roller; table rollers reduce friction. As the cutter head knives shave wood from the board's top surface, the chipbreaker helps prevent tearout and the pressure bar holds the board down. The outfeed roller keeps the board moving until it clears the machine.

Although a planer will make one face of a board parallel to the opposite one, it cannot flatten warped stock if both sides are not straight—it merely makes the piece thinner. You can salvage warped stock by flattening one face on the jointer *(opposite)*, then running the board through the planer to flatten the opposite side.

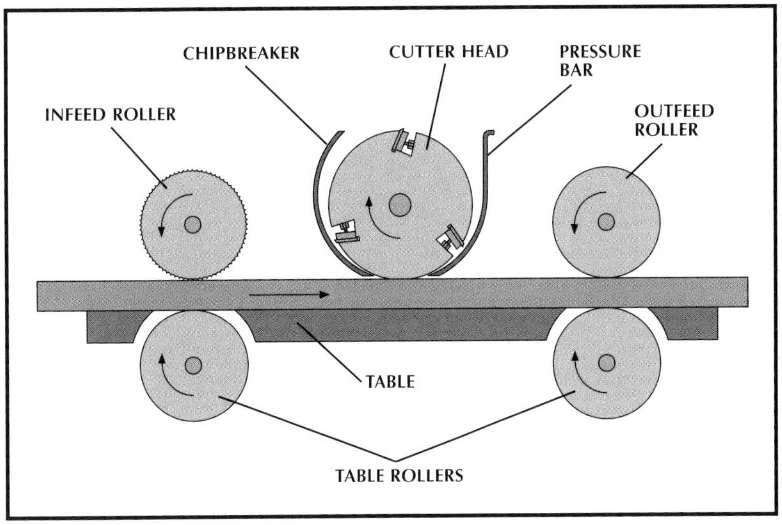

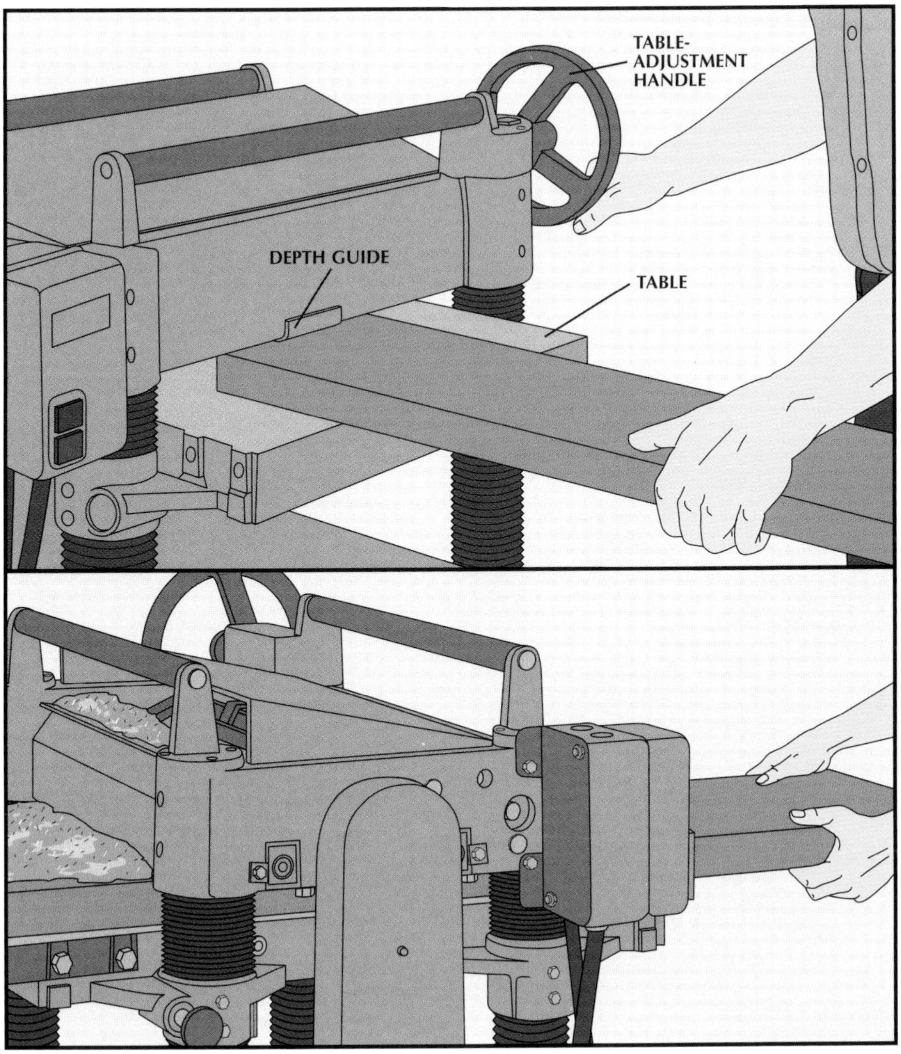

Planer Safety

In addition to the safety rules for power tools listed on page 14, observe these precautions:

- ✔ Always feed wood into the knives following the direction of grain.
- ✔ Although the maximum depth of cut for most planers is $\frac{1}{8}$ inch, limit each pass to $\frac{1}{16}$ inch.
- ✔ Do not plane boards thinner than $\frac{3}{16}$ inch, or the minimum thickness specified by the manufacturer.

Planing a board.
◆ To set the cutting depth, lay the workpiece on the table and align its end with the depth guide. Turn the table-adjustment handle for a $\frac{1}{16}$-inch cut *(above, top)*.
◆ Stand to one side of the board and feed it into the planer with both hands *(above, bottom)*. Support the trailing end until the board emerges from the opposite side of the planer. As the trailing end reaches the table, move to the other side of the machine and support the front of the board as it clears the outfeed roller.

Fashioning Panels From Individual Boards

Before plywood came into common use in the 1930s, wood panels were formed by joining boards edge to edge. Still used in fine cabinetwork, this method relies for success on careful planning and correct technique.

Selecting and Preparing Boards: To reduce the risk of a panel warping after it is glued, use well-seasoned boards no wider than 6 inches, arranging them so the growth rings visible at the ends of adjoining boards curve in opposite directions. To create the illusion that the panel is a single piece of wood rather than a composite, choose boards with similar grain patterns, and experiment with layouts until you find one that is visually pleasing.

Board edges must be straight and square along their entire lengths before they are glued together, and adjoining edges must fit together precisely. Any gaps between boards will greatly reduce the glue's holding power and ruin the appearance of the panel. You can prepare board edges on a jointer *(page 27)*. To do the job by hand, the best tool is a jointer plane *(opposite)*. Its 22- to 24-inch-long sole will help ensure straight edges without any bumps and dips.

Clamping: Bar clamps with two adjustable jaws are best for gluing panels. You'll need one clamp for every 12 to 18 inches of board length. Place thin wood scraps between the boards and the clamp jaws to avoid damaging the wood. To prevent the metal bars from staining the panel, lay sheets of wax paper on the bars before placing the boards on them.

TOOLS

- Straightedge
- Circular saw
- Jointer plane
- Bar clamps
- Rubber mallet
- C-clamps
- Bench dogs

MATERIALS

- Wood glue
- Lumber for cauls ($\frac{3}{4}$")
- Wedge-shaped shims

MATCHING GRAIN AND EDGES

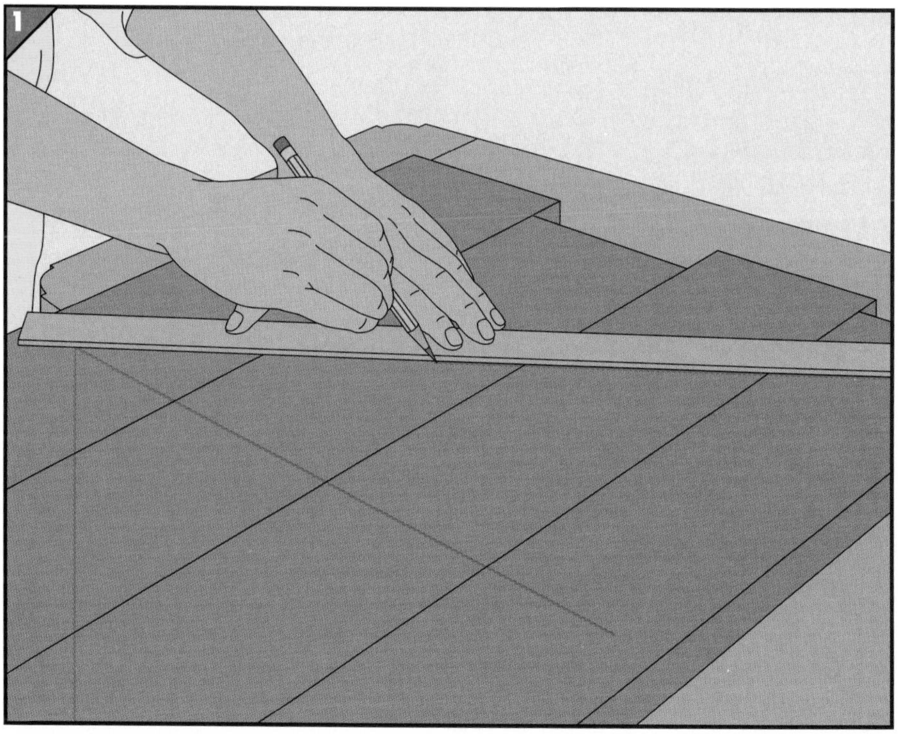

1. Laying out the panel.

◆ Place the boards on a flat surface and arrange them so they combine to produce an attractive grain pattern. Make sure the growth rings at the ends of adjacent boards curve in opposite directions.

◆ With a pencil and a straightedge, mark a three-line crow's-foot from one side of the assembly to the other *(right)*, so you will be able to restore the boards to this arrangement after jointing their edges.

◆ Mark the ends of the boards at a point about 3 inches beyond the planned length of the finished panel, and trim the boards there.

2. Jointing the board edges.
A power jointer makes quick work of this step *(page 27)*. To do the work by hand, proceed as follows:
◆ Clamp one of the outside boards in a vise so its inside edge faces up.
◆ Holding a jointer plane on the board edge at a slight angle to the faces, guide the tool along the surface from one end to the other *(right)*.
◆ Check the edge for square *(page 23, Step 4)*, then make another pass with the plane, if necessary.
◆ Joint the mating edge of the next board in the same way.

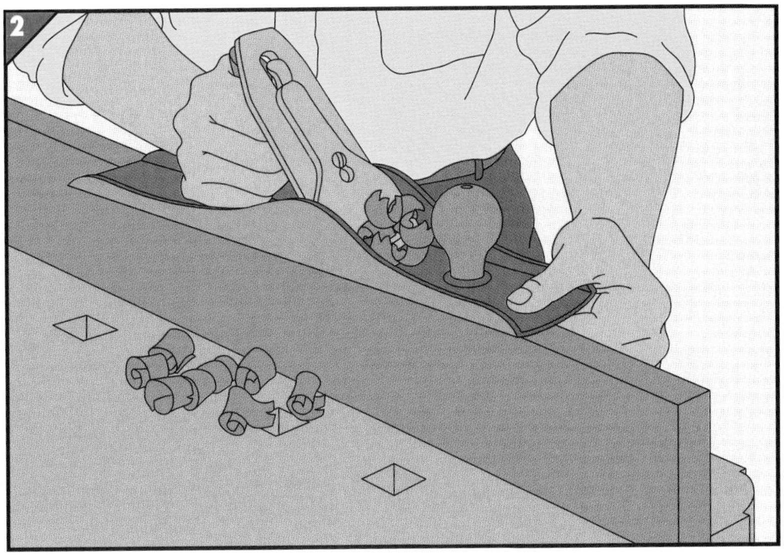

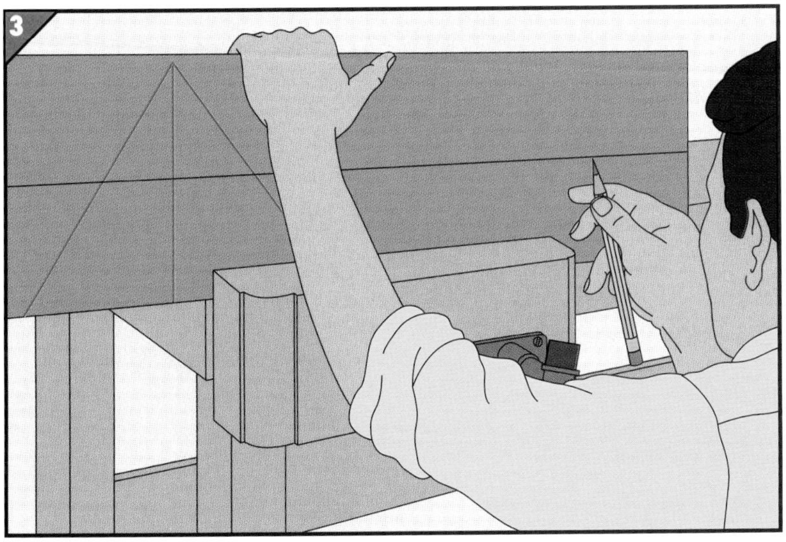

3. Testing mating edges.
◆ With the second board in the vise, set the planed edge of the first board on top of it and align the crow's-foot marks.
◆ Check the joint for gaps—no light should pass through the seam at any point. Mark any areas with chinks *(left)*, then plane the affected surface and recheck the joint.
◆ Pass the remaining edges across the jointer and test the edge-to-edge joints as described in Steps 2 and 3.

TRICKS OF THE TRADE

A Shooting Board for Straight Edges

A shooting board is a simple jig that guides a plane along a straight line and allows it to trim a wood surface evenly. To make this jig, cut a straight 1-by-6 and a piece of $\frac{1}{8}$-inch tempered hardboard to the length of the board to be planed. Rip the hardboard to a width of 4 inches, with one perfectly straight edge. Align the two pieces so the straight edge of the hardboard divides the width of the 1-by-6, then screw the hardboard in place as a depth stop.

Place the workpiece against the shooting board so the edge to be planed sits evenly above the depth stop, then clamp the assembly in a vise. Joint the board with the side of the plane's sole against the shooting board. To reduce friction, rub paraffin on the sole of the plane. The top edge of the workpiece will be shaved to the same level as the depth stop.

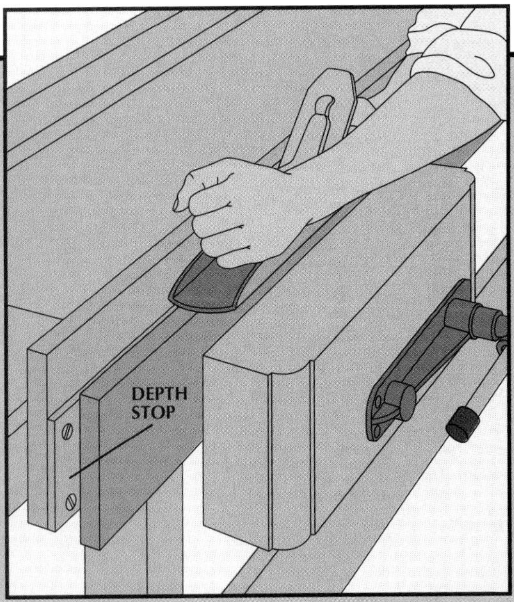

1. Assembling the panel.

◆ Set two bar clamps on a flat surface, drape wax paper on the metal bars, and place the boards side by side on them, matching the crow's-foot marks *(above)*. Slip wood pads between the boards and clamp jaws.

◆ Stand each board—except the one closest to you—on edge. Spread a layer of wood glue on each edge, then lay the boards flat.

◆ Slide each pair of boards together to work glue into the pores of the wood. Align the crow's-foot marks perfectly.

2. Adjusting the assembly.
Tighten the bar clamps lightly against the boards. If any board sits above the others, gently tap it down into place with a rubber mallet until the surface of the assembly is flat *(right)*.

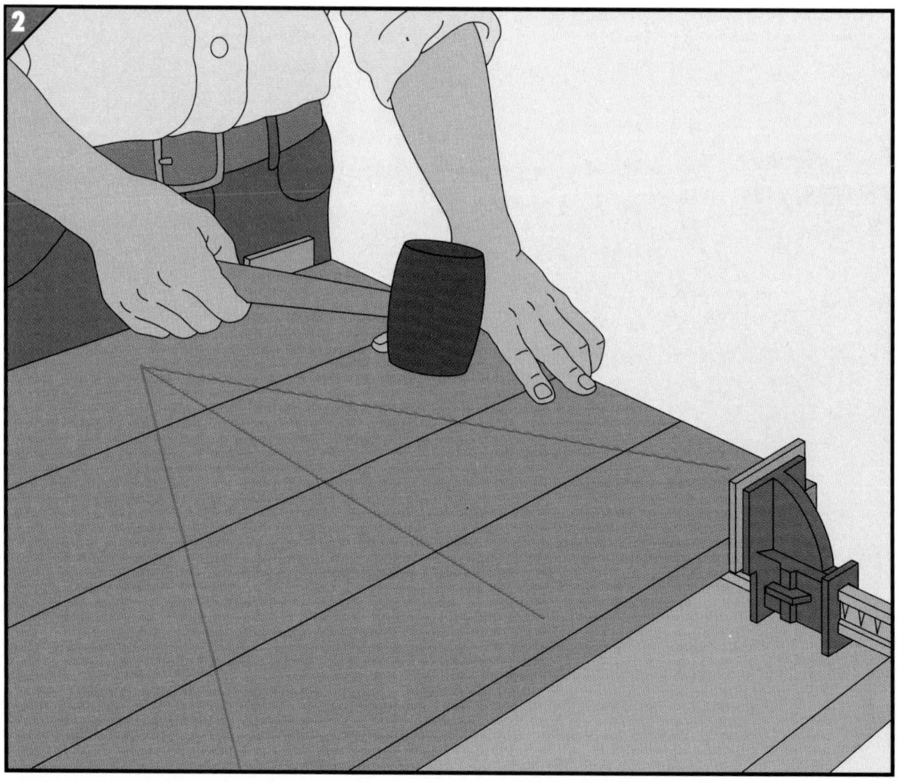

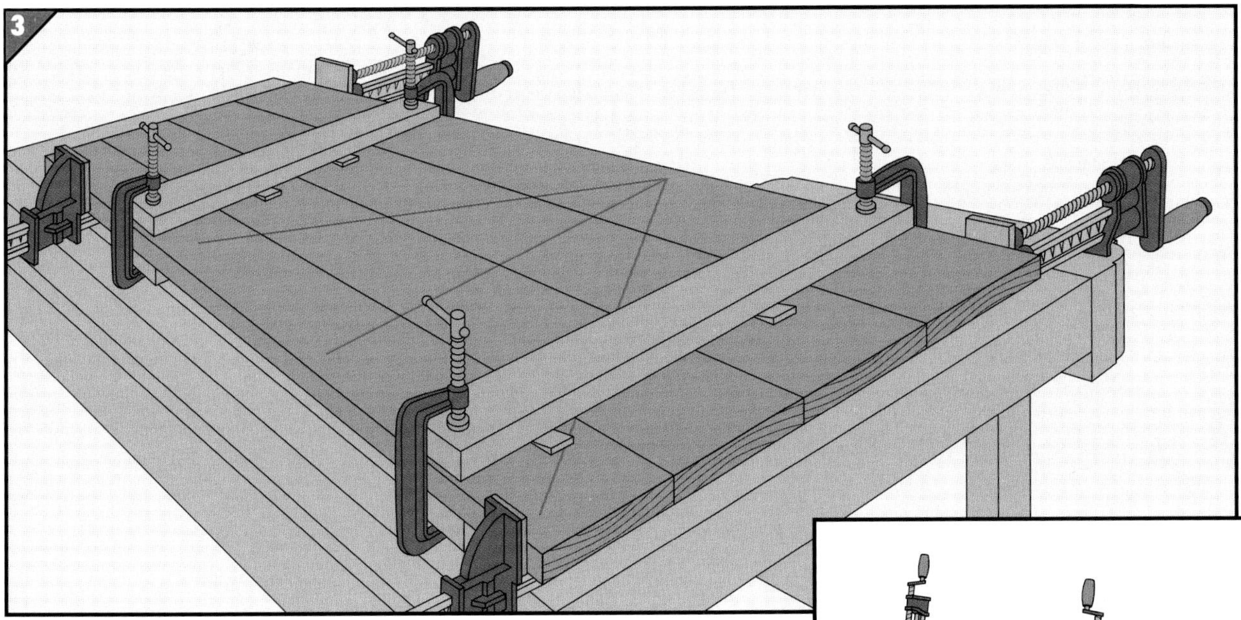

3. Tightening the clamps.

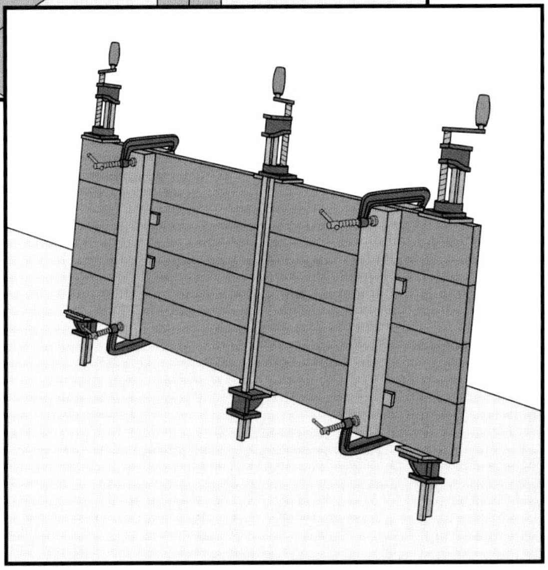

◆ To keep the panel flat, make four cauls—boards of $\frac{3}{4}$-inch stock cut to the width of the panel. Place two cauls across the panel near each end, one on each side, holding them in place with C-clamps. Tap wedge-shaped shims between the cauls and the panel to press protruding boards into alignment *(above)*.

◆ Add another bar clamp across the top of the panel, centered between the bottom clamps at the ends of the panel. Tighten all the bar clamps evenly until a thin bead of glue squeezes out of each joint. Wipe up extruded glue immediately with a damp rag.

◆ As the glue is drying, keep the panel flat; you can also prop the assembly against a wall, but rest the ends of the bar clamps against both the wall and the floor to keep the panel from twisting *(inset)*.

◆ Let the glue dry.

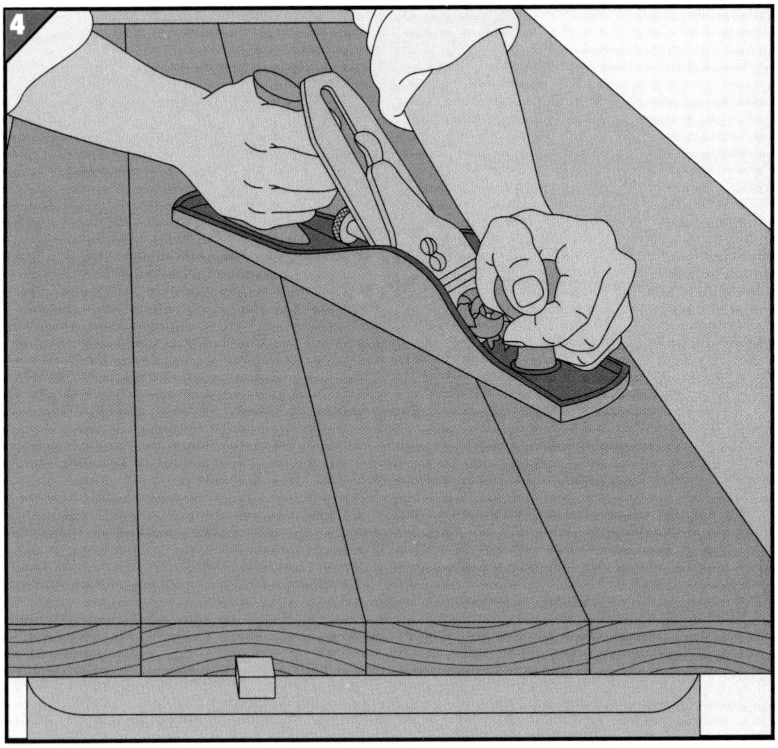

4. Planing the panel surface.

◆ Remove the clamps and cauls, then check with a straightedge whether the panel is flat *(page 22, Step 2)*; plane down any high spots *(page 31, Step 2)*.

◆ Mark the desired thickness of the panel around its edges.

◆ Secure the panel on a workbench between bench dogs, then plane it to the marked line *(page 23, Step 3)*.

2 A Choice of Connections

More than just a means of locking together pieces of wood, a joint can merge component parts with grace or set them off in fine contrast to each other. Delicate dovetails speak of the skill of the maker, while a half-blind lock joint is nearly invisible. This chapter introduces a wide range of woodworking joints—and helps you select and produce the best ones for your projects.

Assembling a dovetail joint →

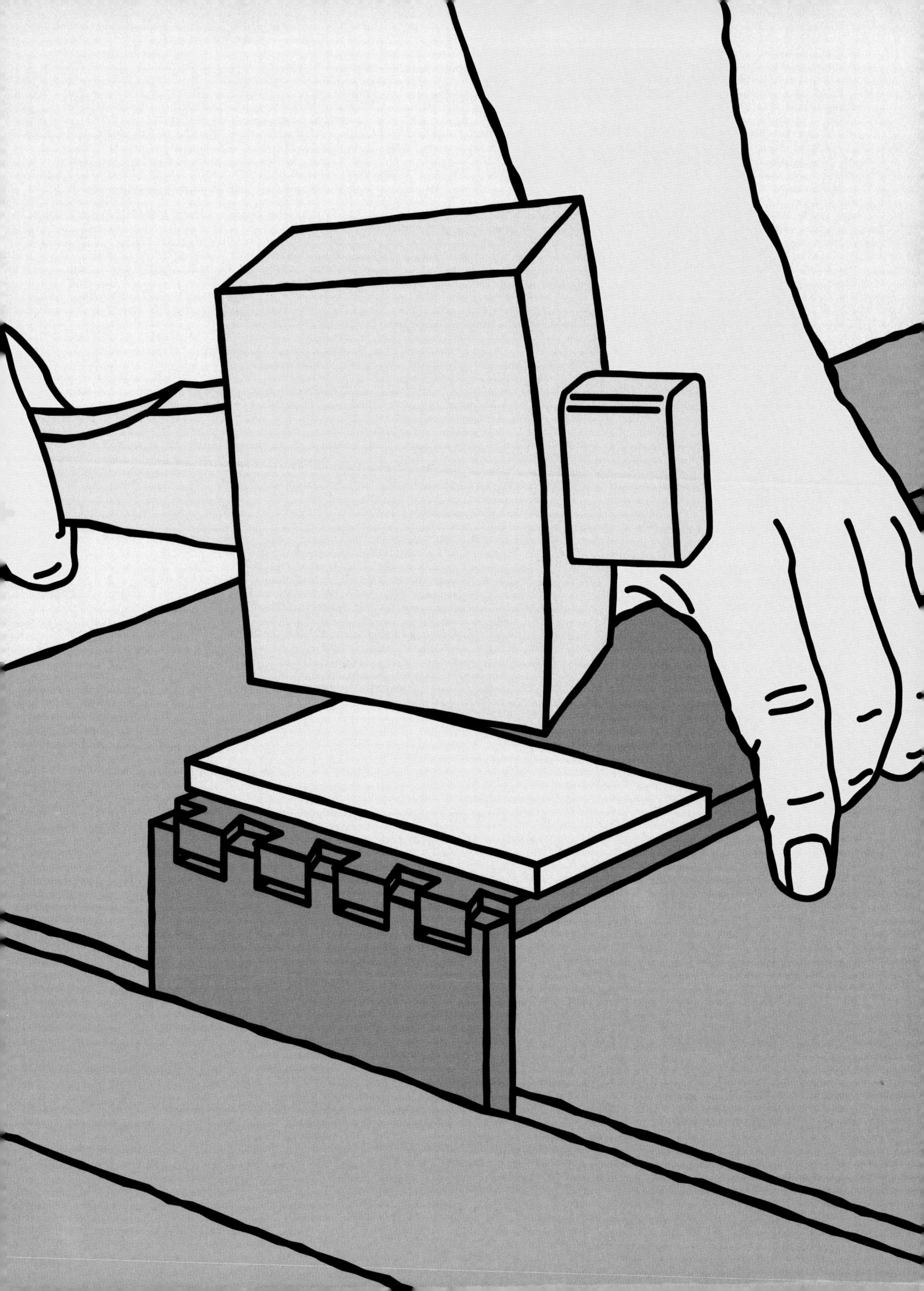

The Family of Tongue-and-Groove Joints

Fitting a tongue on one board into a groove in another is one of the best ways to make a strong wood joint. The tongue and groove and its variations *(below)* owe their strength to large gluing surfaces and to a structure that resists stress.

Dadoes, Rabbets, and Tongues: Two relatively simple cuts, the dado and the rabbet, form the basis of all these joints. A dado is a rectangular channel cut across the grain of a board—it is sometimes called a groove when the cut follows the grain. A rabbet is a steplike cut made along the end or edge of a board. Tongues are formed by cutting two parallel rabbets along each side of a board edge or end, leaving a projection at the center.

Cutting Methods: The tools most commonly used for making these cuts are the router *(opposite and page 38)* and the table saw *(pages 39-40)*; but you can also use a jointer to cut rabbets *(page 41)*. A table saw equipped with a dado head—a special saw blade designed to cut dadoes up to 1 inch wide—will do the job most efficiently. But if you are cutting dadoes and rabbets in wide boards, plywood sheets, or irregularly shaped pieces, the router is a better choice, since the wood remains stationary as the tool makes its cut.

Whichever tool you choose, take the time to measure your cuts and set them up carefully. Test tool settings on scrap wood before starting.

Use power tools safely *(page 14)*, following the safety precautions for the table saw *(page 15)*, the jointer *(page 26)*, and the router *(opposite)*.

TOOLS

- Circular saw
- Router
- Straight bit
- Three-wing slotting cutter
- Rabbeting bit
- Carpenter's square
- Screwdriver
- Straightedge
- Clamps
- Table saw
- Dado head
- Combination square
- Jointer
- Push blocks

MATERIALS

- Lumber for router jig
- $\frac{3}{4}$" lumber for auxiliary fence
- Wood screws (No. 6, No. 8)

SAFETY TIPS

Goggles protect your eyes when you are operating a power tool.

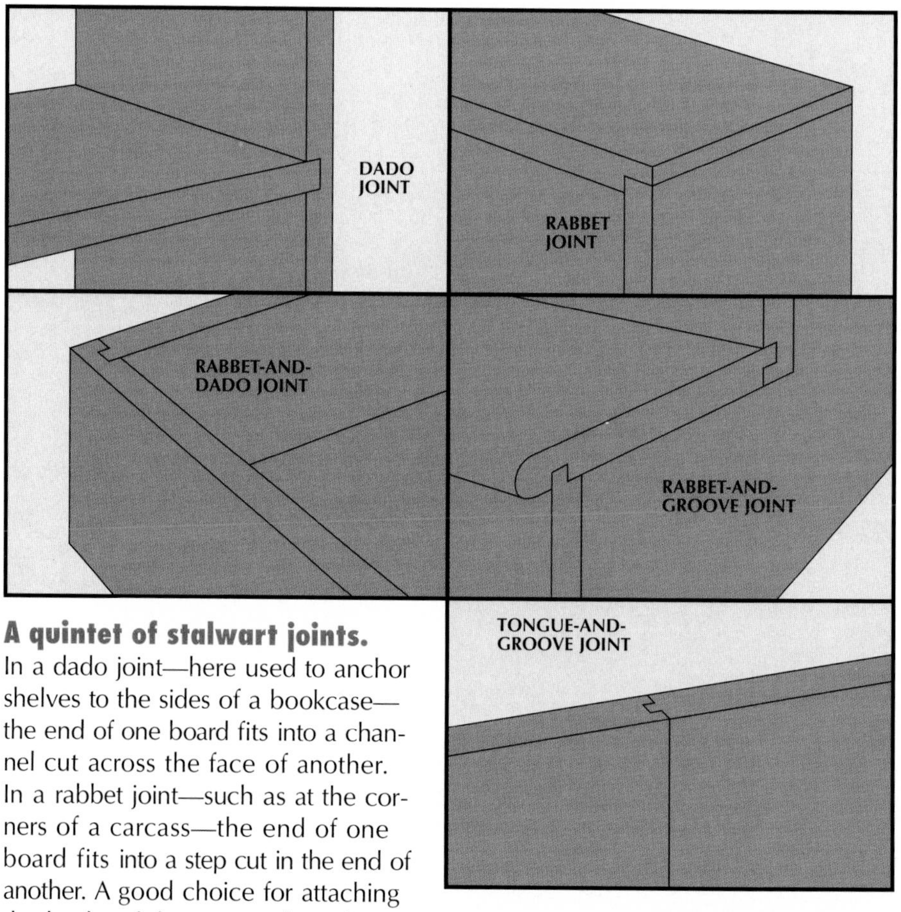

A quintet of stalwart joints. In a dado joint—here used to anchor shelves to the sides of a bookcase—the end of one board fits into a channel cut across the face of another. In a rabbet joint—such as at the corners of a carcass—the end of one board fits into a step cut in the end of another. A good choice for attaching the backs of drawers to the sides, a rabbet-and-dado combines these two joints, with the rabbeted end of one board meshing with a dado in the mating piece. The similar rabbet-and-groove joint is often used to attach stair treads to risers. A common method of joining boards side by side in flooring and paneling is the tongue-and-groove joint.

Preventing Tearout

To reduce torn fibers along the edges of the cut when routing a dado in plywood, score its outline with a utility knife and a carpenter's square *(right)*. The incision will sever the wood fibers, keeping the edges of the cut clean.

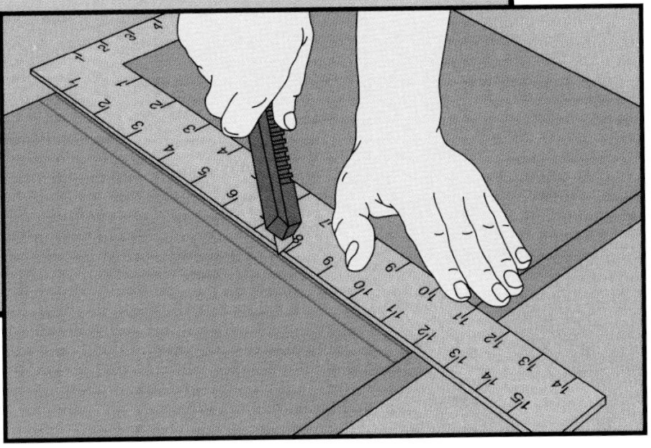

ROUTING DADOES AND GROOVES

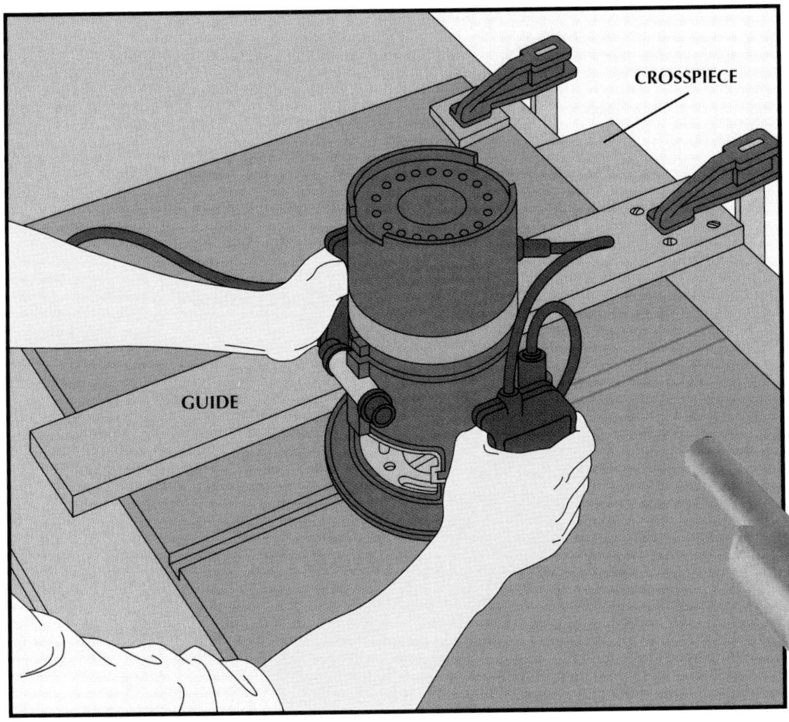

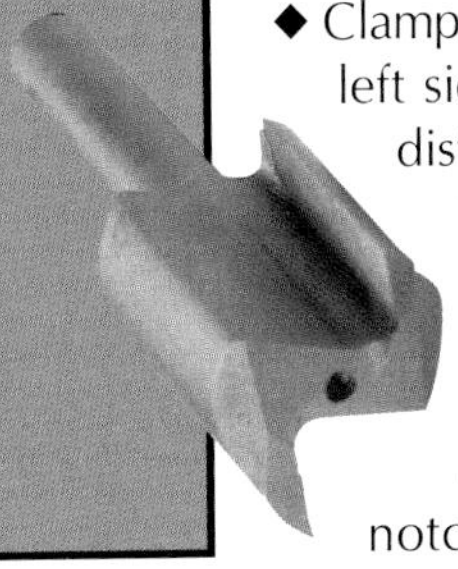

Plowing a cross-grain channel.

◆ First, make a T-shaped jig from two 3-inch-wide boards as thick as the one being dadoed: Cut a guide long enough to span the workpiece, and fasten it to a crosspiece with No. 8 wood screws, using a carpenter's square to ensure the boards form a right angle.

◆ Protecting the wood with pads, clamp the workpiece to a work surface.

◆ Outline the dado on the face and mark its depth on the edges.

◆ Fit a straight bit *(photograph)* in your router and adjust the bit to the marked depth.

◆ Clamp the jig to the table parallel to and on the left side of the dado outline, offset by the distance between the edge of the bit and the router base plate.

◆ Turn on the router, and feed the bit into the edge, holding the tool flat on the surface and flush against the jig *(left)*. Lift the bit clear once it cuts a notch into the jig's crosspiece.

Router Safety

In addition to the safety rules for power tools listed on page 14, observe these precautions:

✔ Unplug the tool before installing or removing a bit, and tighten the chuck securely once the bit is in place.

✔ Anchor work securely with clamps or nails, leaving both hands free to guide the router.

✔ Let the bit reach full speed before beginning a cut, and lift it from the work before switching the router off.

✔ When cutting a dado that is wider than the bit, make the first pass along the right side of the channel, then move the guide and cut the left-hand channel.

Creating an edge groove.

◆ Use a special router bit called a piloted three-wing slotting cutter *(photograph)*. At its tip, the cutter has a pilot bearing—a cylindrical guide that rolls along a board edge to ensure that the groove will be of uniform depth. These cutters typically come with a set of pilot bearings in varying diameters.

◆ Fit the cutter with a bearing of the correct diameter for the groove depth, and install it in the router.

◆ Outline the groove on the board and clamp the board to a worktable.

◆ With the router flat on the board, set the cutter's height even with the outline.

◆ To prevent splintering, begin the cut about 1 inch from the left end; guide the router along the board, keeping the pilot bearing pressed against the edge *(below)*.

◆ Finish the groove by cutting from right to left.

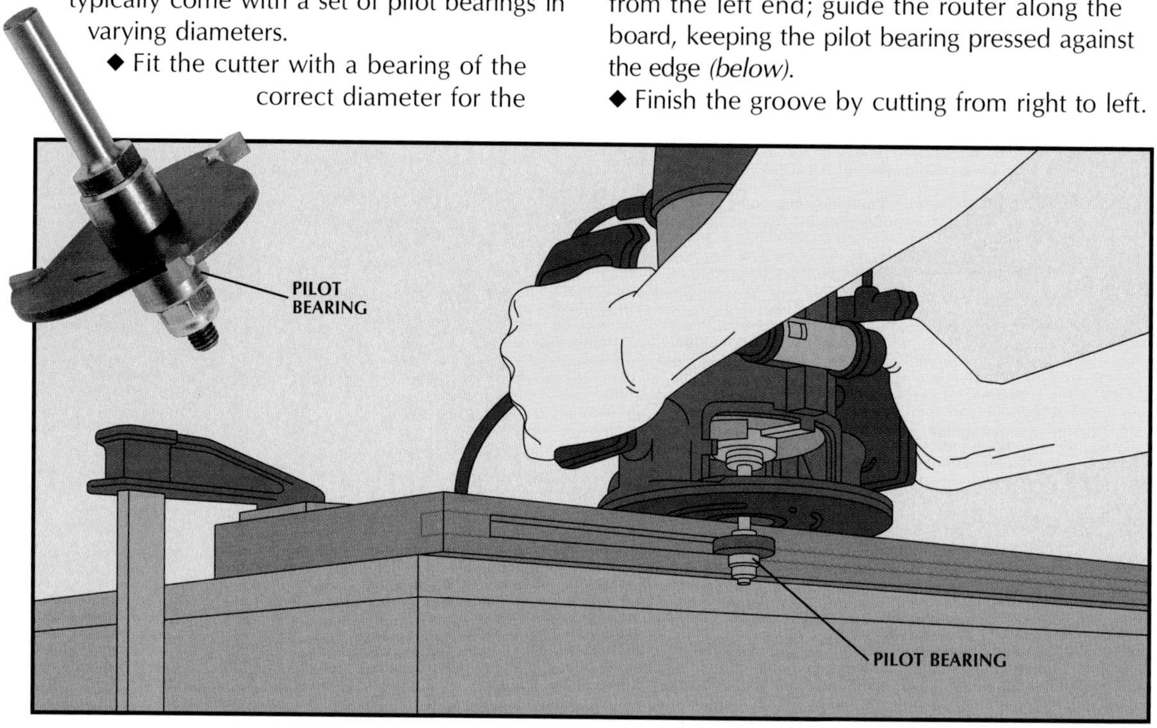

Cutting rabbets and tongues.

◆ A rabbeting bit equipped with a pilot bearing *(photograph)* is used in the same way as the slotting cutter above. Fit the bit with a bearing of the correct diameter for the rabbet width—usually between $\frac{1}{4}$ and $\frac{1}{2}$ inch wide.

◆ Set the bit to the desired depth up to $\frac{3}{8}$ inch; for deeper rabbets, make two or more passes, increasing the cutting depth each time.

◆ Set the router on the board and, with the bit clear of the edge, turn on the tool. Ease the bit into the edge about 1 inch from the left end and move the router along the face, keeping the bearing against the edge *(right)*. To complete the rabbet, feed the router from right to left.

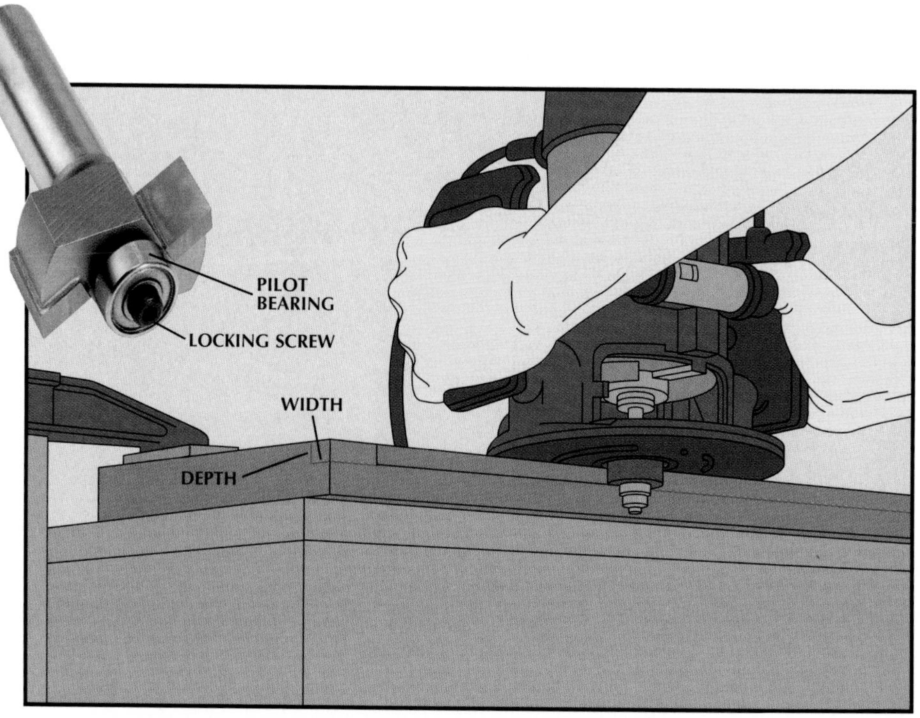

To create a tongue on the edge of a board, first cut a rabbet, then turn the board over and rout an identical rabbet on the opposite side so the tongue is centered and has the desired thickness. For a tongue-and-groove joint, cut the tongue $\frac{1}{16}$ inch narrower than the depth of the groove into which it will fit.

CLEARING CHANNELS ON A TABLE SAW

1. Installing a dado head.

◆ Remove the standard blade from its arbor and slide the first dado blade on the arbor, orienting the blade according to the instructions printed on it. Add chippers and the second blade to cut a dado of the desired width, arranging the chippers so they are evenly spaced and their tips are framed by the gullets of the blades. Lock the dado head in place with the arbor washer and nut.

◆ Measure the dado head from the outside tips of the teeth, removing or adding chippers, if necessary. If this procedure does not produce the dado width you need, space out the blades and chippers with paper washers.

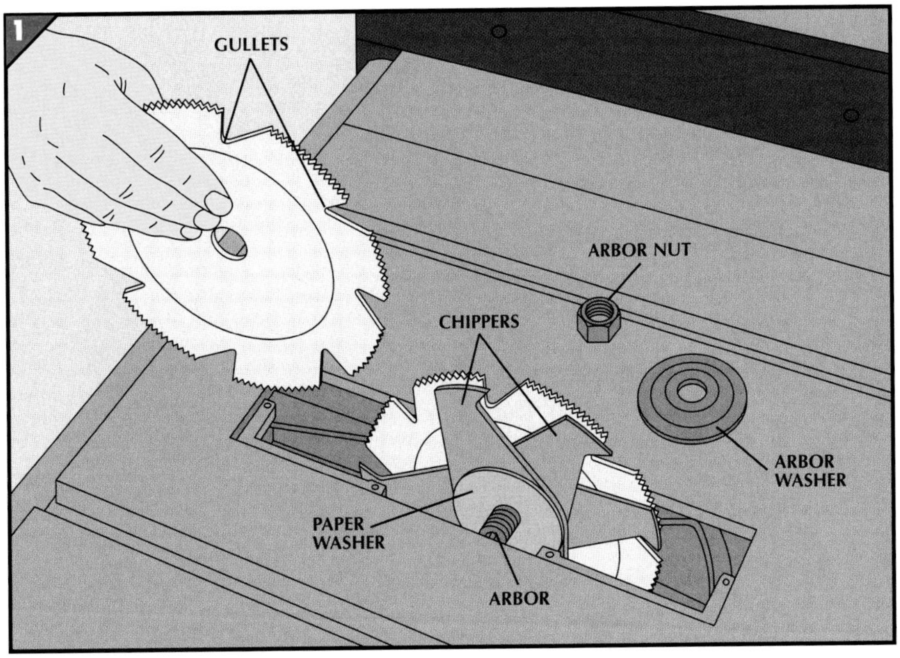

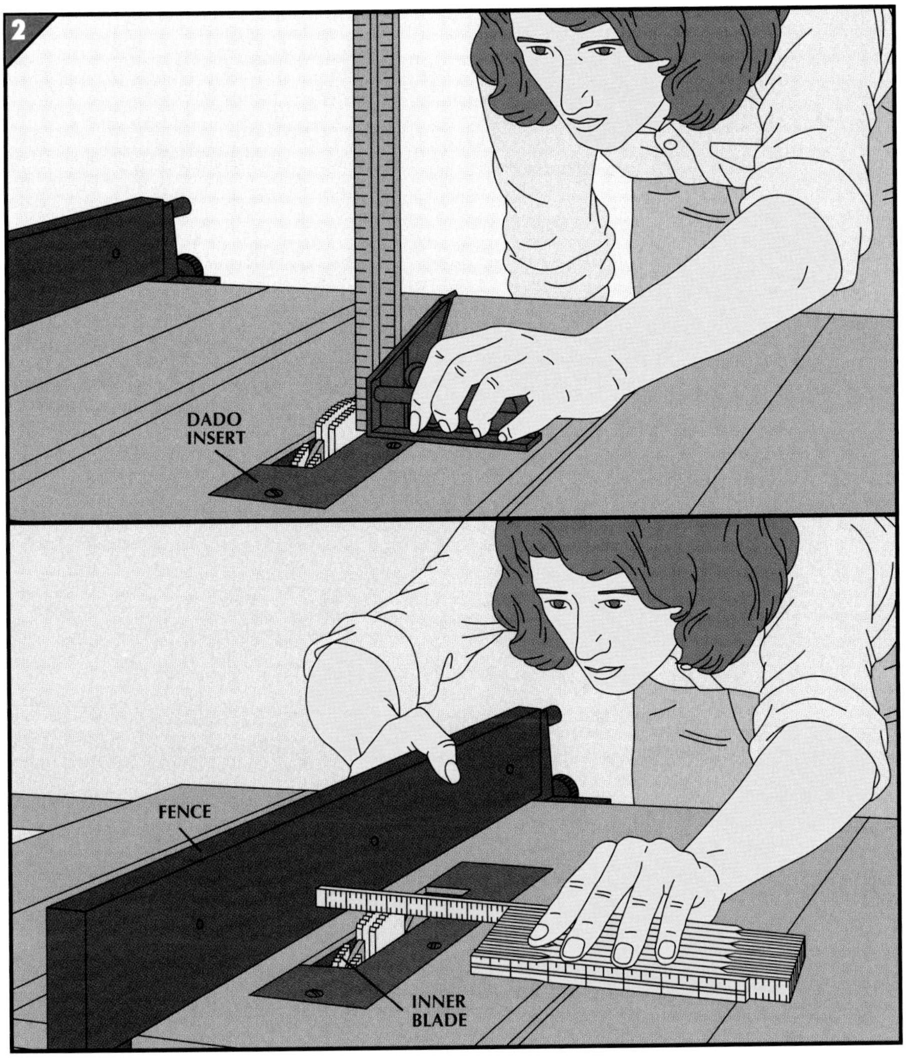

2. Setting up the cut.

◆ Install a dado insert in the opening of the saw table.

◆ With a combination square, check the height of the dado head, setting it about $\frac{1}{16}$ inch lower than the desired dado depth *(left, top)*.

◆ Make a test cut *(page 40, Step 3)*. Adjust the height and width of the dado head, if necessary, and retest until the cut has the correct dimensions.

◆ Position the fence so the distance between it and the dado head equals the desired distance between the edge of the workpiece and the dado *(left, bottom)*. If the tips of the blade teeth angle inward and outward, measure from the fence to the closest tooth edge. You can also position the fence by aligning the dado outline on the workpiece with the dado head and butting the fence against the board.

◆ Lock the fence in place.

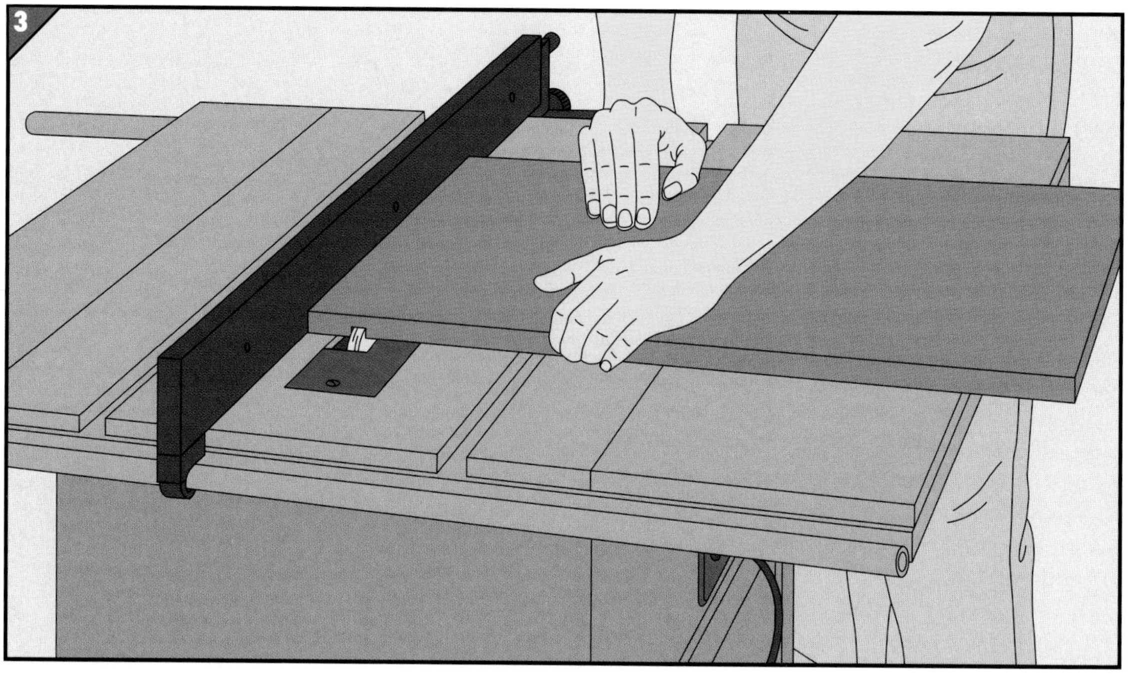

3. Cutting the dado.

◆ Set the workpiece on the saw table, end against the fence, so the dado outline is even with the dado head.

◆ Holding the workpiece down and against the fence, feed it steadily across the table *(above)*. Feeding too rapidly can result in cuts with rough edges, and may cause kickback; feeding too slowly burns the wood. Feed a short board with a push stick to keep your hands well away from the dado head.

SAWING RABBETS

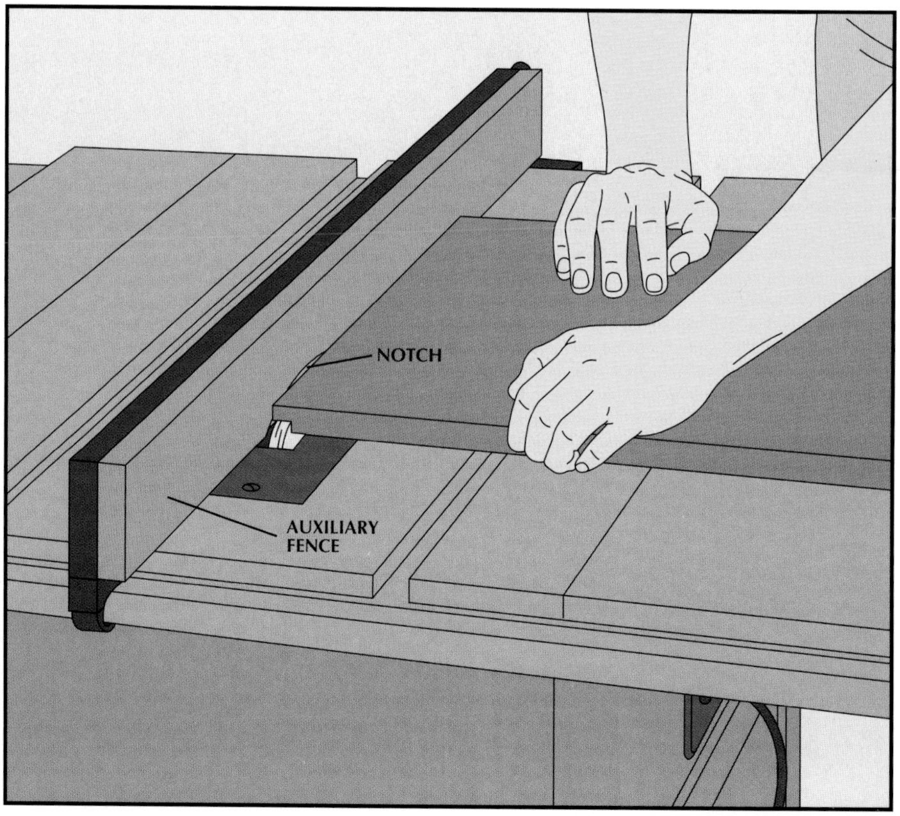

Using an auxiliary fence.

◆ Install a dado head *(page 39, Step 1)* about $\frac{1}{8}$ inch wider than the desired width of the rabbet. Lower it below the table surface.

◆ Cut a wooden auxiliary fence from a straight, flat $\frac{3}{4}$-inch board, and fasten it to the table saw's fence with No. 6 screws driven from the left side of the fence through the predrilled holes. Position the fence so it overlaps the dado head by about $\frac{1}{4}$ inch. Turn on the saw and slowly raise the dado head slightly higher than the thickness of the workpiece to make a notch in the auxiliary fence.

◆ Adjust the fence and the blade height for the desired depth and width of cut *(page 39, Step 2)*, then saw the rabbet as for a dado *(above, Step 3)*.

To make a tongue, cut two identical rabbets on opposite sides of workpiece.

A JOINTER VARIATION

Making an edge rabbet.

◆ Mark the width and depth of the rabbet on the leading end of the workpiece.
◆ Remove the blade guard from the jointer to provide access to the rabbeting ledge, as shown on page 25.
◆ Line up the width mark with the corner of one of the cutterhead knives, then lock the fence against the board.
◆ Adjust the height of the infeed table to set the cut no deeper than $\frac{1}{4}$ inch.
◆ Feed the workpiece along the rabbeting ledge with your right hand while pressing it against the fence with your left hand.
◆ If additional passes are necessary to reach the rabbet's full depth, lower the infeed table no more than $\frac{1}{4}$ inch at a time *(right)*.

CAUTION *When cutting rabbets on a jointer* (right and below), *keep your hands well away from the exposed cutterhead on both sides of the fence.*

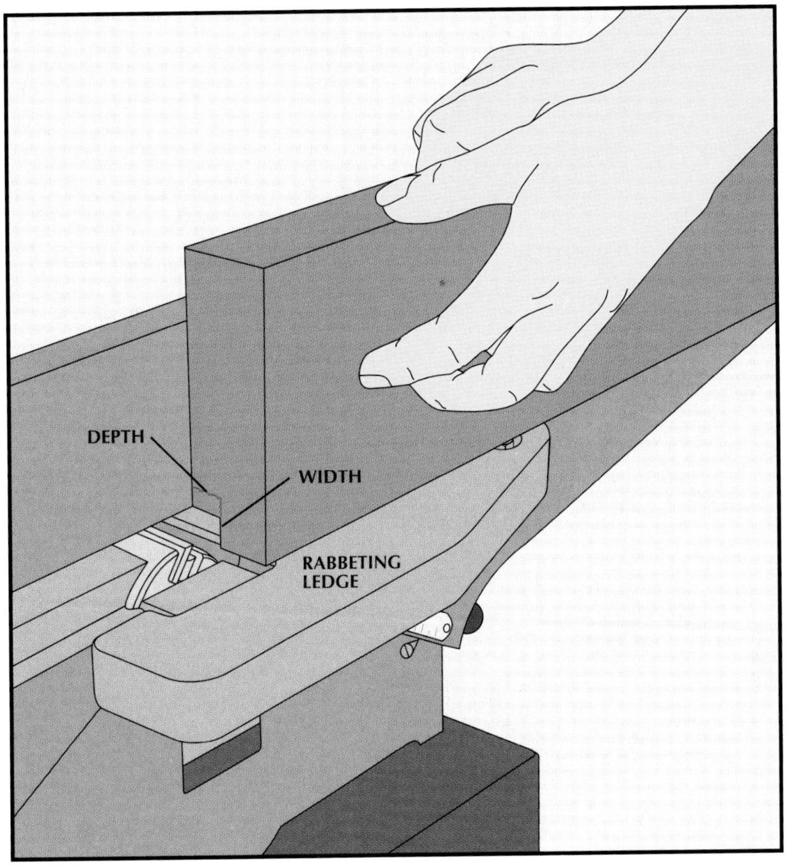

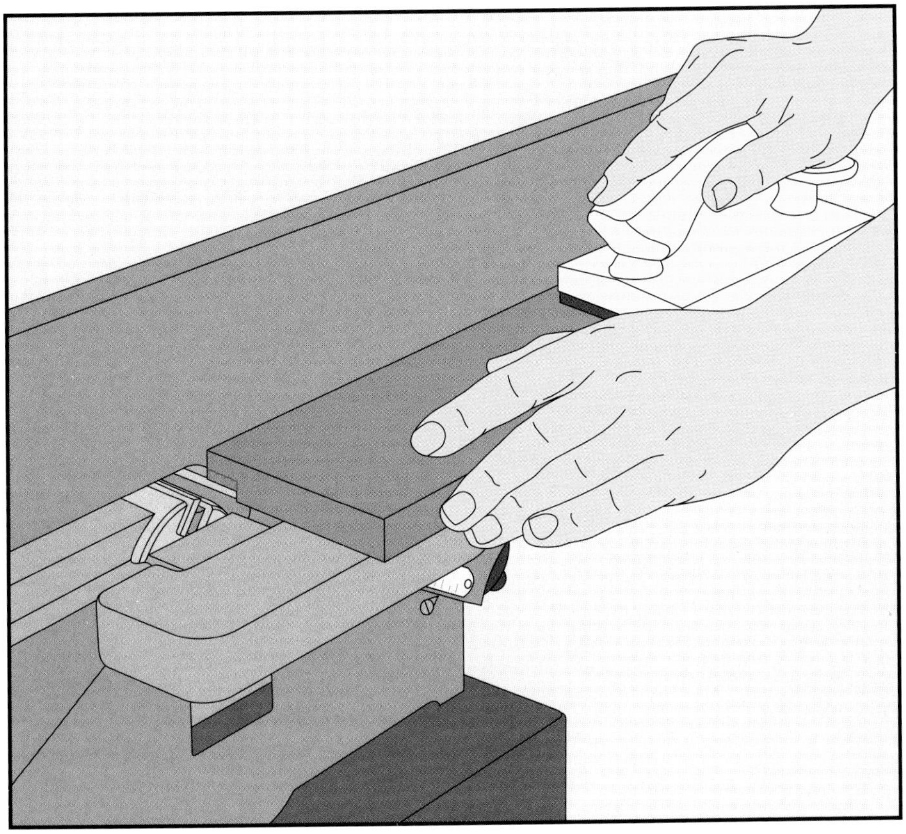

Cutting a rabbet along a face.

◆ Remove the guard and adjust the jointer fence and infeed table as described above.
◆ Holding the workpiece against the fence with your left hand, use a push block to slowly feed it forward and keep it flat on the table.
◆ To make additional passes, increase the cutting depth by a maximum of $\frac{1}{4}$ inch at a time *(left)*.

The Half-Blind Lock Joint

The strategic combination of dadoes and tongues in the half-blind lock joint gives strength to a corner joint by increasing its glue area while locking the pieces in every direction but one. It is a favorite for attaching drawer fronts, since the joint is hidden from view and resists being pulled apart as the drawer is opened. Though not quite as strong as a dovetail *(page 48-53)*, it is easier to produce and, unlike dovetails, can be formed from plywood. Made completely on the table saw, the joint demands precision craftsmanship.

Planning Ahead: Choose boards that are straight, smooth, and squarely cut. Check your stock carefully and rectify any flaws *(pages 21-29)*. To help you keep track of the joint as it takes shape, label the inside and outside faces of the mating pieces. Outline each cut as the project progresses and adjust your table saw carefully, always testing with scrap wood pieces that are the same thickness as the work, fitting the mating parts together before making any final adjustments on the saw.

TOOLS

Table saw
Dado head
Tenoning jig
C-clamp
Bar clamps

MATERIALS

Stock for auxiliary fence
Wood glue

SAFETY TIPS

Put on goggles when operating power tools.

A CORNER OF INTERLOCKING TONGUES AND DADOES

1. Anatomy of the joint.

The front piece has a wide dado centered between two tongues of equal width. The front tongue extends across the side piece to hide its end grain, and the rear tongue fits into a narrow dado in the inside face of the side piece to lock the joint securely. The tongues are one-sixth to one-third the thickness of the board.

The cuts are made in the sequence shown in the inset: First comes the dado in the front piece *(1)*. It forms the reference point for determining the position of the narrow channel *(2)* and the length of the short rear tongue *(3)*.

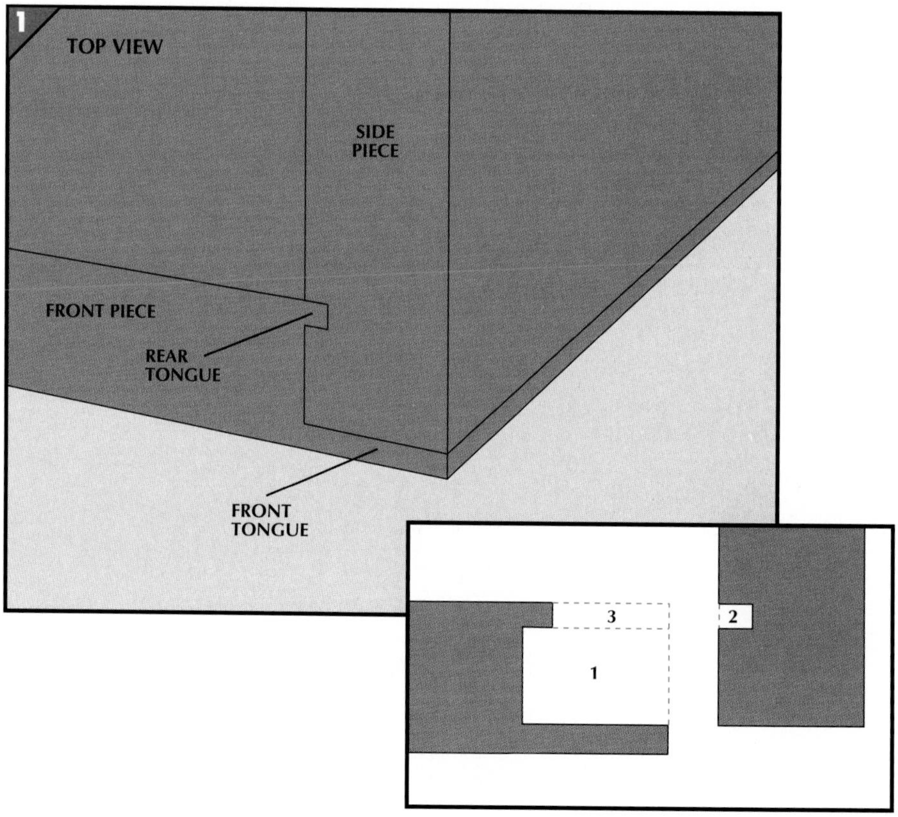

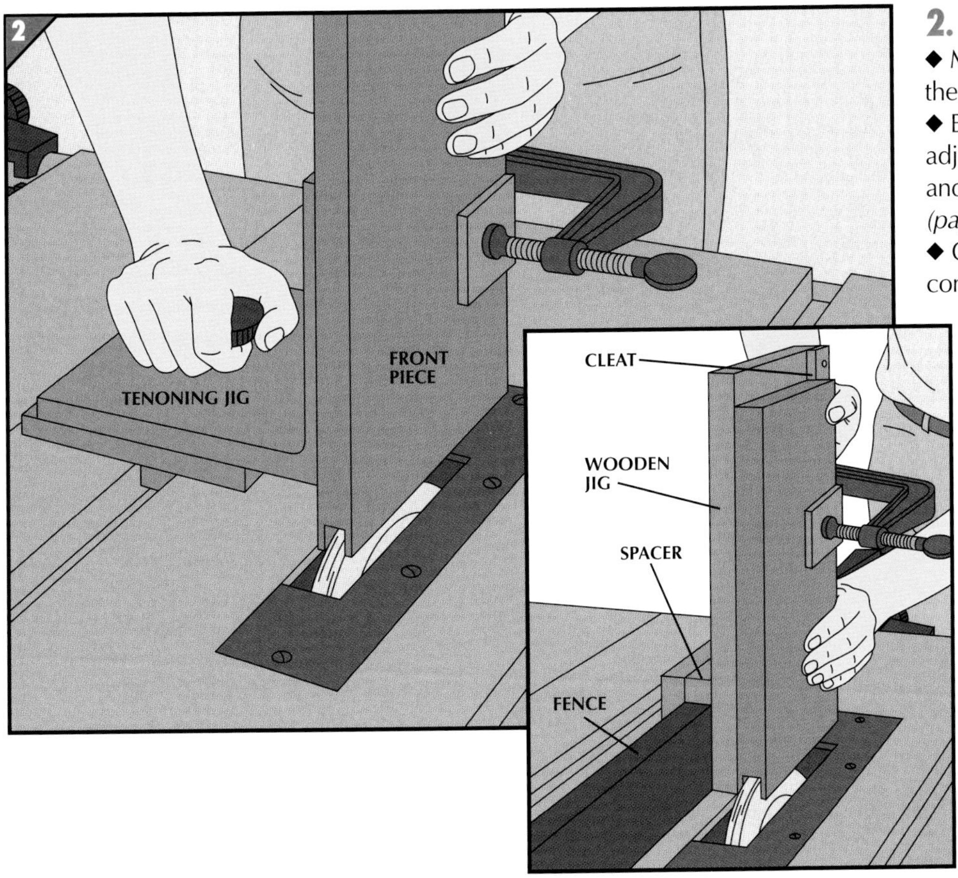

2. Cutting the wide edge dado.

◆ Mark the wide dado on the end of the front piece.

◆ Equip a table saw with a dado head, adjusting it for the width of the dado and setting its height for the dado depth *(page 39, Steps 1 and 2)*.

◆ Clamp the drawer front on end in a commercial tenoning jig—the model shown slides in the miter slot—and adjust the jig to align the dado outline with the dado head.

◆ With one hand pushing the jig and the other steadying the front, feed the assembly across the saw table, cutting the dado *(left)*.

To make a wooden tenoning jig, screw two pieces of $\frac{3}{4}$-inch plywood to a spacer the same thickness as the fence, forming an "h" shape. Fasten a thin board vertically as a cleat along one edge of the jig. Clamp the workpiece to the jig, edge flush against the cleat, and cut the dado *(inset)*.

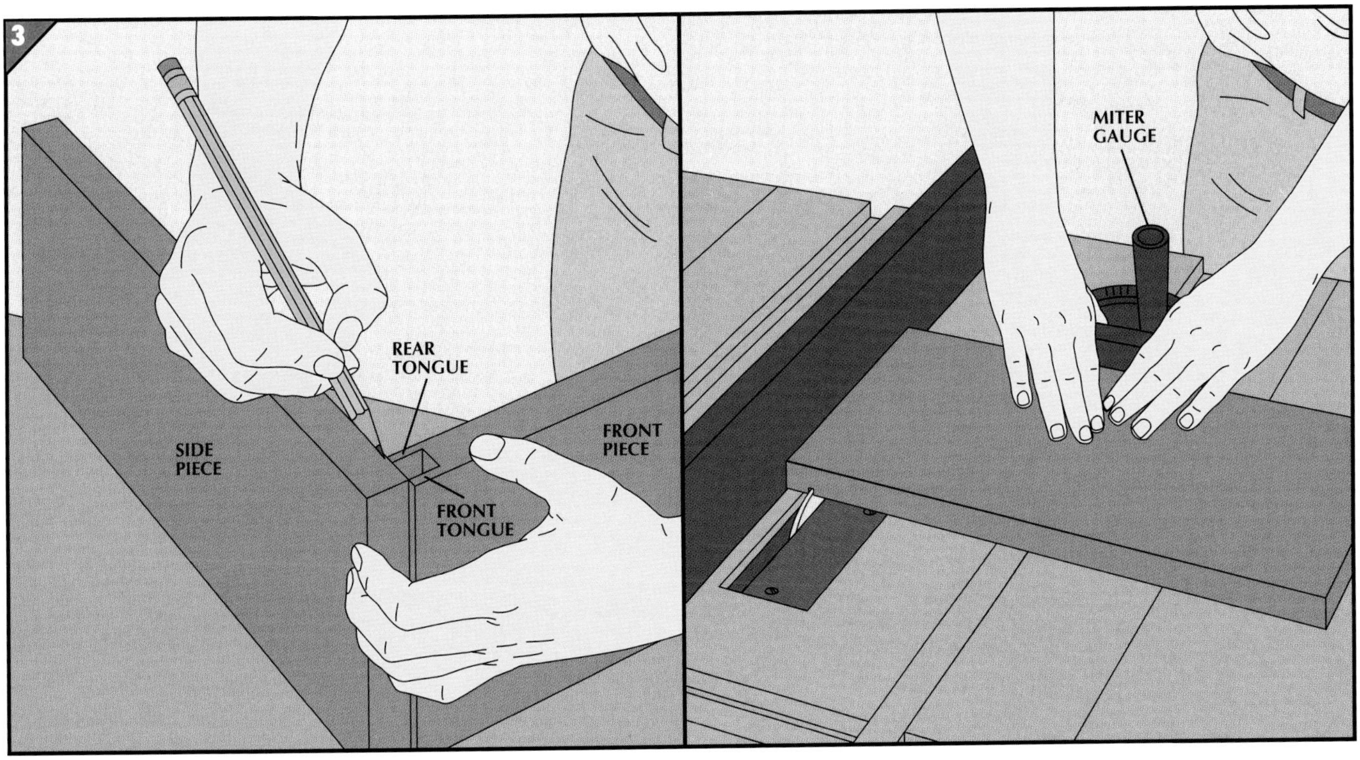

3. Sawing the second dado.

◆ Stand the front piece on edge and butt the side piece against it, aligning the inside of the front tongue with the end of the side piece. Outline the rear tongue on the side piece *(above, left)*.

◆ Install on the saw a blade that leaves a $\frac{1}{8}$-inch kerf; if you need a wider kerf, plan to make additional passes. Adjust the blade height to cut about one-quarter the thickness of the side piece in depth.

◆ Place the side piece on the saw table, align the dado outline with the blade, and lock the fence up against the board. With the miter gauge, guide the piece across the table, keeping it pressed against the fence *(above, right)*.

4. Marking the rear tongue.

◆ Stand the front piece on edge and set the side piece on it so the second dado lines up with the rear tongue and the inside face of the side piece is even with the bottom of the first dado.

◆ Holding the side piece in position, insert a pencil in the second dado and make a mark across the rear tongue at the bottom of the dado *(right)*.

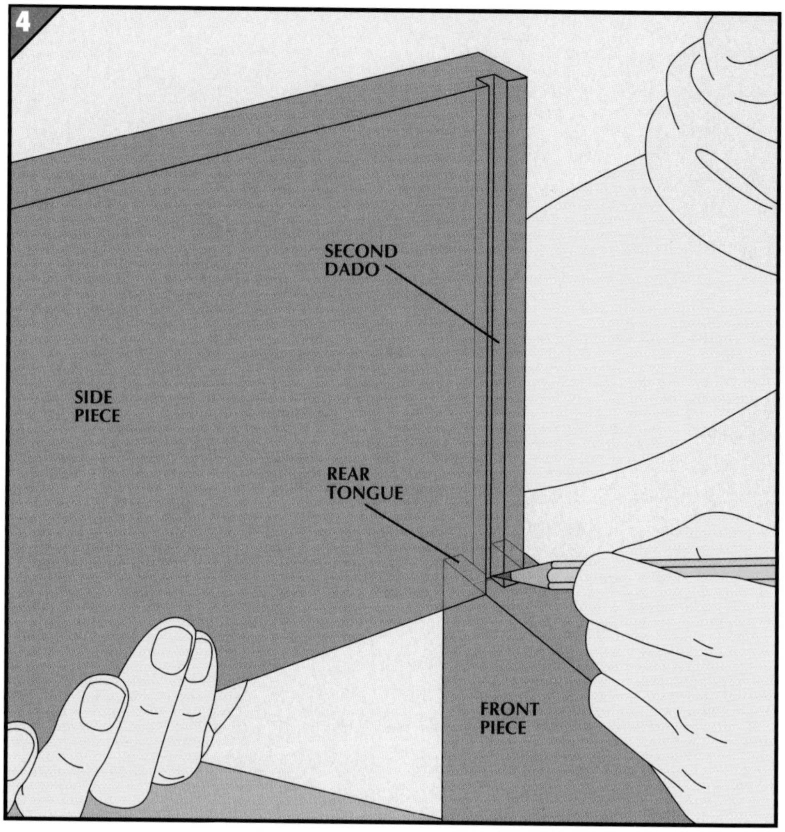

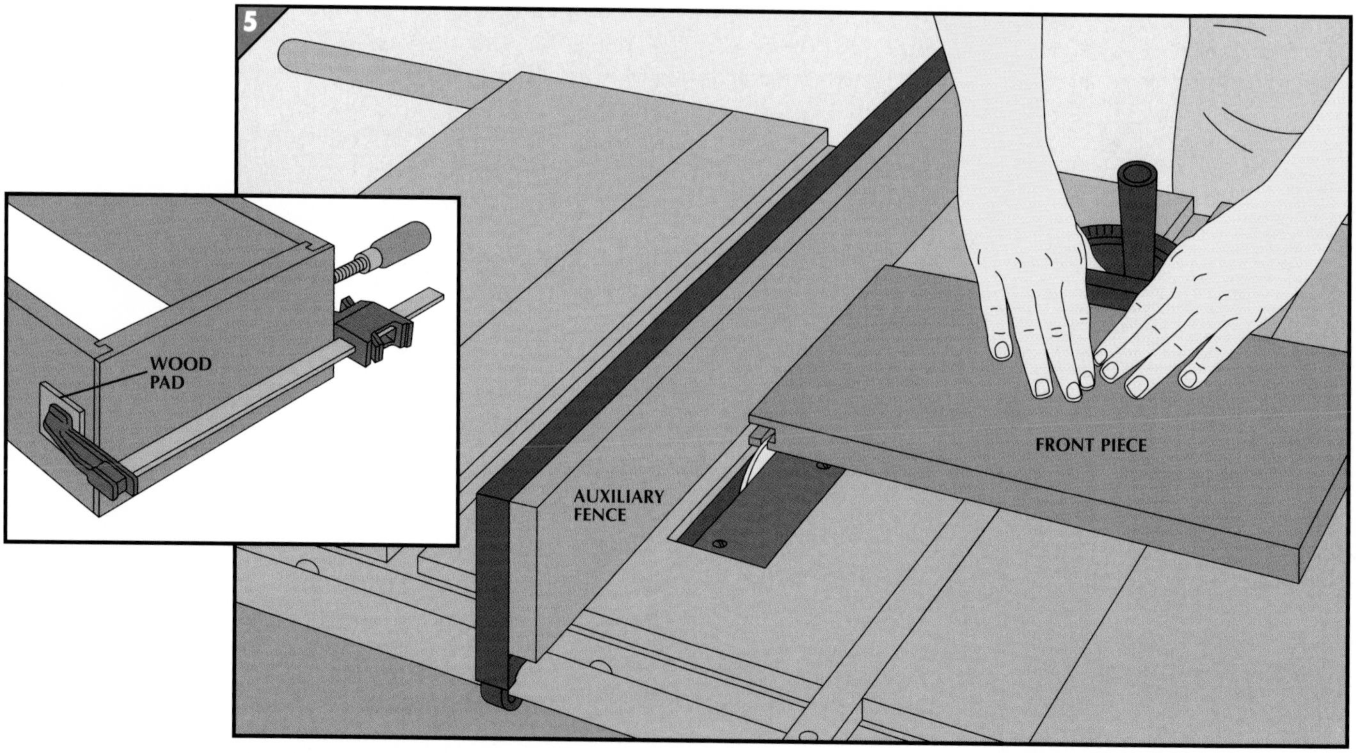

5. Trimming the rear tongue.

◆ Fasten a wooden auxiliary fence to the rip fence *(page 40)* so it sits $\frac{1}{4}$ inch above the saw table.

◆ Place the front piece flat on the table, align the tongue mark with the blade, and lock the fence up against the board.

◆ Feed the piece with the miter gauge, sliding its end along the fence *(above)*.

◆ Cut the remaining corners of the drawer, then spread wood glue on all the contacting surfaces of the joints. To secure them while the glue dries, place a bar clamp across the front and back pieces, protecting the wood with pads *(inset)*.

◆ Wipe away any extruded glue.

The Box Joint

Before the advent of plastic and cardboard packaging, many products were sold in inexpensive pine boxes. The popularity of the quickly made, machine-cut box joint dates from that period. Its straight-sided fingers and slots may lack the holding power of the dovetail joint with its splayed pins and tails *(pages 48-53)*, but the joint is still surprisingly strong. Its many fingers provide a gluing surface as much as three times as long as the joint.

Planning the Joint: Box joints are best cut on a table saw equipped with a dado head and with the help of an indexing jig that helps keep the fingers identical and evenly spaced. To create a symmetrical joint, frame the top and bottom of the corner with a full-size finger. Simply divide the width of the boards by the total number of fingers and notches at each end, and use the result to set the thickness of the dado head.

Cutting the Notches: Adjust the height of the dado head about $\frac{1}{16}$ inch higher than the thickness of the boards. Although this will result in fingers that extend slightly beyond the corners, the excess wood is sanded away after the joint is assembled. To account for this excess, make each board $\frac{1}{8}$ inch longer than needed.

When you have cut the four corners of the box, glue and clamp it as you would a dovetailed one *(page 51)*.

TOOLS

Table saw
Dado head
Electric drill
Countersink bit
Screwdriver

MATERIALS

Plywood ($\frac{3}{4}$")
Wood screws (No. 6)

SAFETY TIPS

Put on goggles when operating power tools.

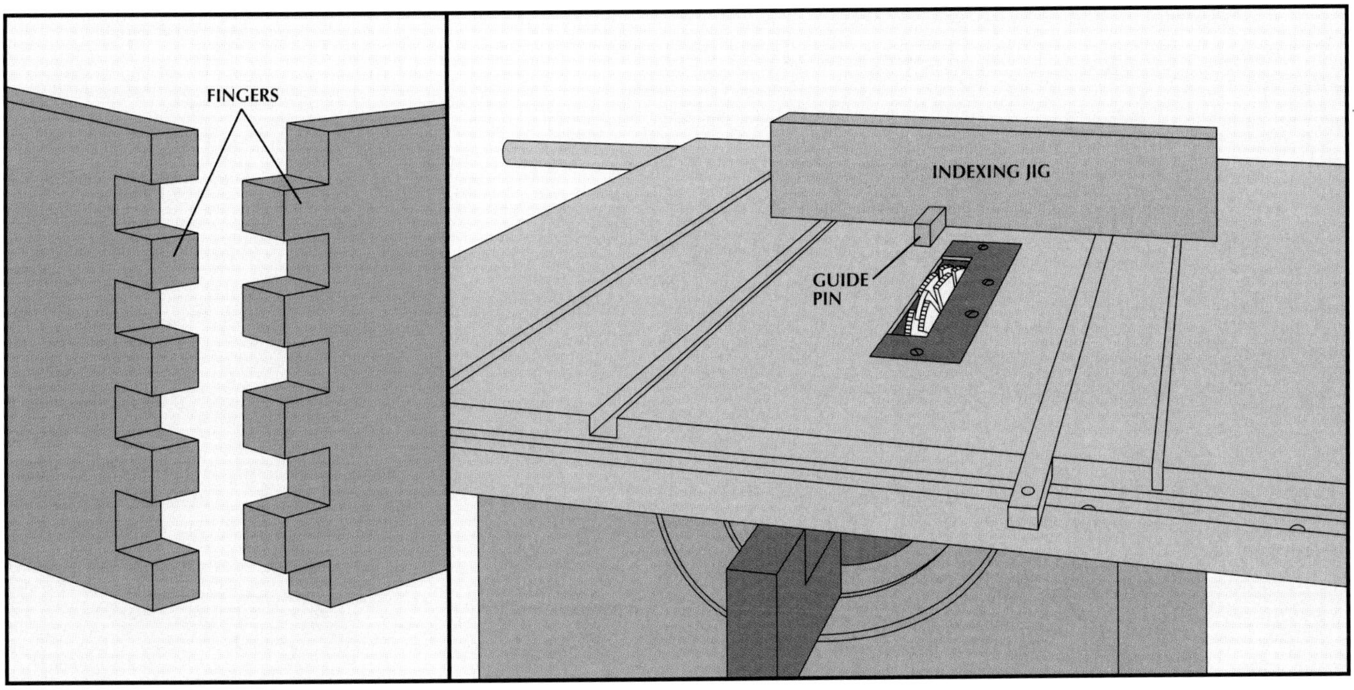

A jig for making box joints.

The width of the fingers and notches is identical *(above, left)*—usually about $\frac{1}{8}$ to $\frac{1}{2}$ inch less than the thickness of the wood being joined. A table-saw indexing jig *(above, right)*, fastened to the miter gauge, ensures that the fingers and notches are evenly spaced. The jig begins as a piece of $\frac{3}{4}$-inch plywood, cut 4 inches high and about 20 inches long.

Once the dado head is assembled for the width of the notches and its cutting height is set to $\frac{1}{16}$ inch higher than the board thickness *(page 39, Step 1)*, a notch is made near the center of the plywood. A guide pin is cut to fit in the notch and is fixed in place with a countersunk No. 6 wood screw. The plywood is then screwed to the miter gauge with a gap between the pin and the dado head equal to the width of one notch.

CUTTING SLOTS AND FINGERS

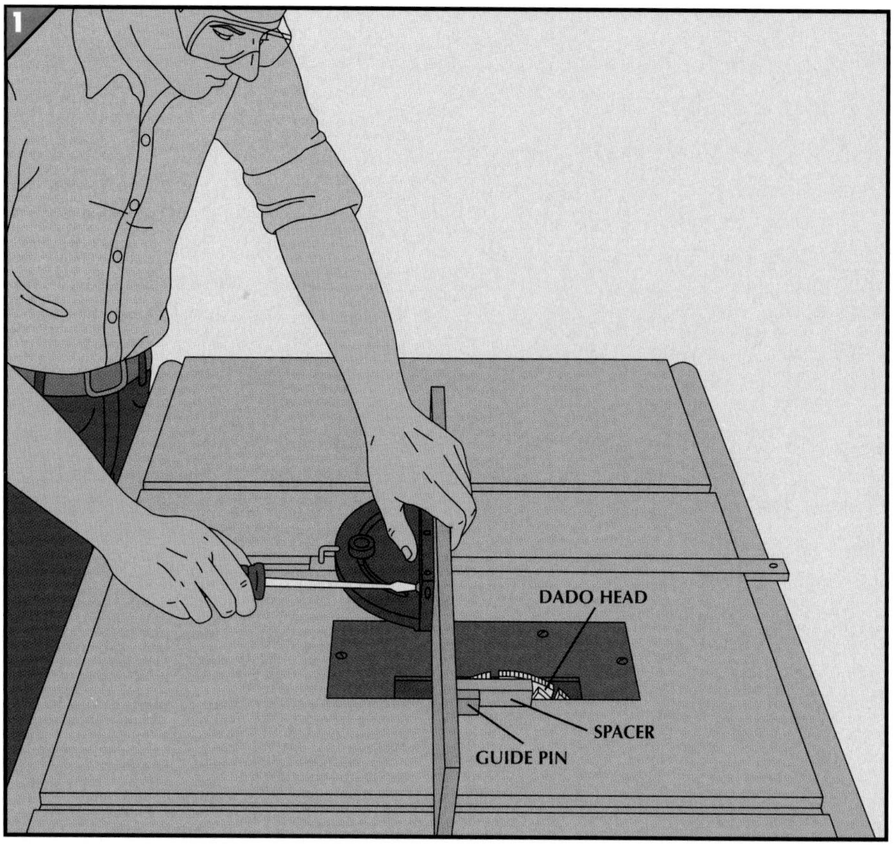

1. Setting up the indexing jig.

◆ Hold the jig, with the guide pin in place, against the miter gauge, and slide the assembly forward until the jig almost touches the dado head.

◆ Place a wooden spacer the same thickness as the guide pin against the side of the dado head, and slide the jig sideways along the miter gauge until the pin presses the spacer against the dado head.

◆ Holding the jig in this position, fasten it to the miter gauge with No. 6 wood screws *(left)*.

2. Making the first notch.

◆ Using both hands, hold the first board on end, with the inside face against the jig and an edge butted against the guide pin.

◆ Switch on the saw, and push the jig and board slowly across the dado head, cutting a notch through both the board and the jig *(right)*. Switch off the saw and wait for the blade to stop spinning, then return the jig to its starting position.

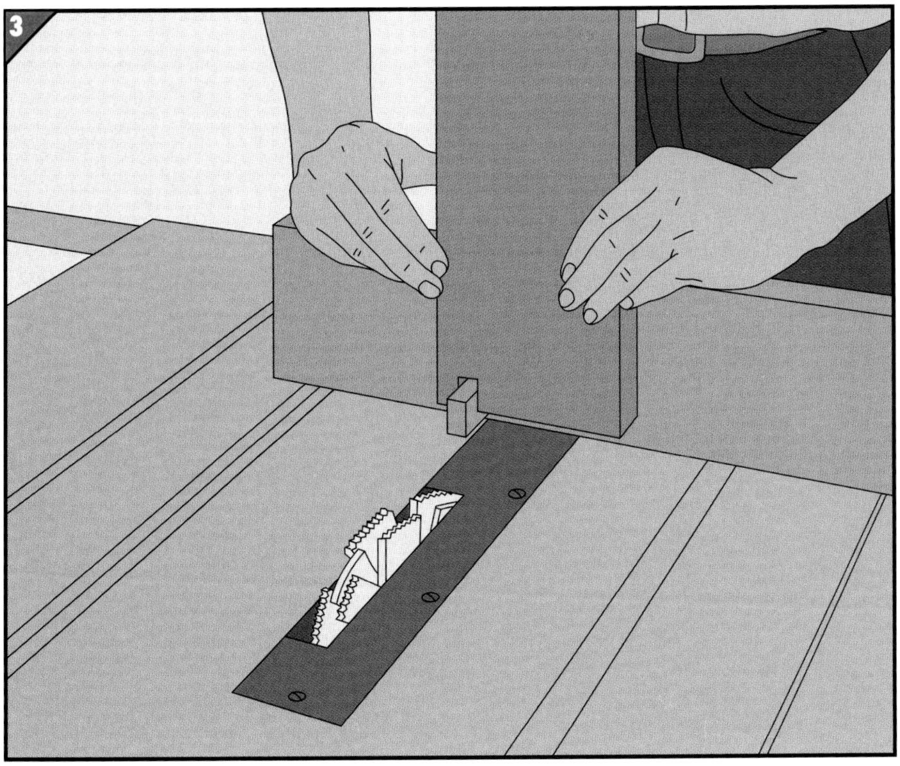

3. Cutting the remaining notches.

◆ Reposition the board by slipping the notch you just cut over the guide pin *(left)*. Holding the board firmly against the jig, cut another notch.

◆ Cut the subsequent notches in the same way, slipping the newly cut notch over the pin before each pass.

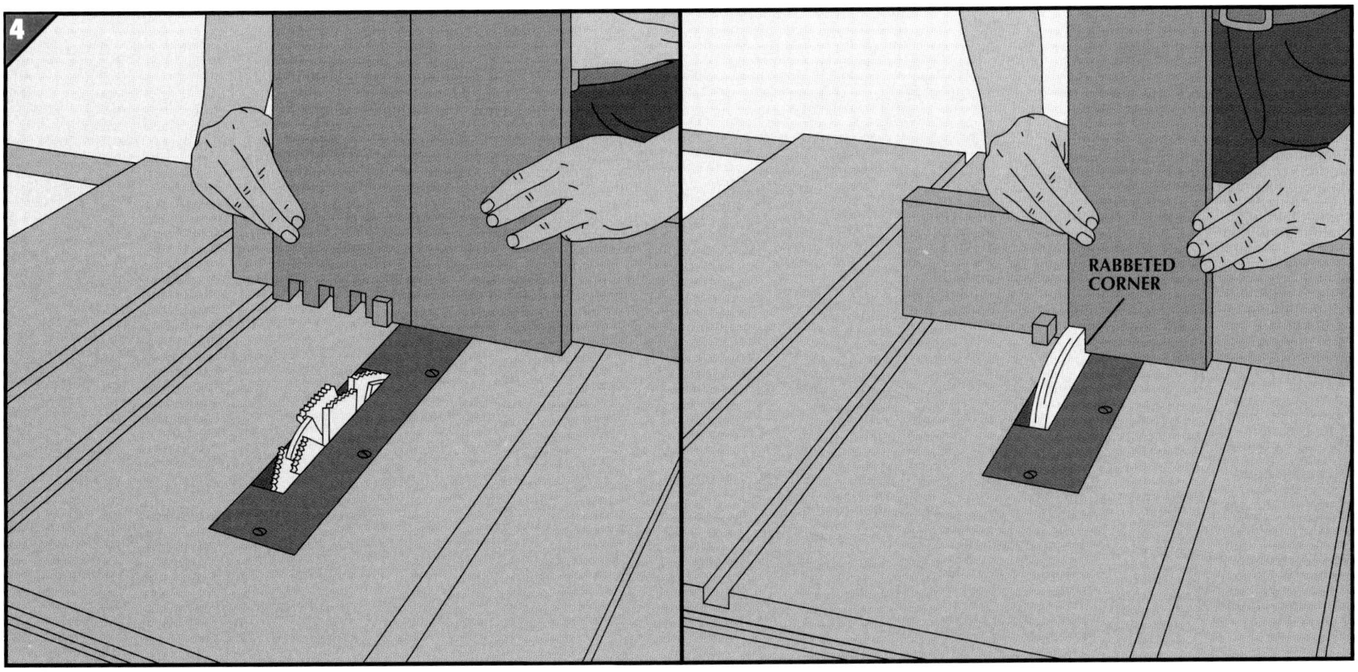

4. Sawing on the matching board.

◆ Position the first board with its outside face against the jig and the first notch over the guide pin. Butt the edge of the matching board against it, with its inside face against the jig *(above, left)*.

◆ Hold the matching board firmly against the jig and remove the first board. Push the board across the saw table to cut a rabbet at the corner *(above, right)*.

◆ Slip the rabbet over the guide pin and continue cutting additional notches across the board as in Step 3, ending with a rabbet at the opposite corner.

Dovetail Joints

Often used for decorative effect at the corners of boxes or cabinets, dovetails are equally useful hidden away on the sides of drawers since they are among the strongest of joints. Although dovetails can be made quickly with a router *(page 52)*, hand-cutting permits a wider variety of sizes and shapes *(pages 49-53)*.

Cutting the Pins and Tails: Whether you are making through or lap dovetails *(below)*, the joint requires well-honed tools and precise methods. Tight-fitting tails and pins begin with accurate measuring, marking, and cutting.

First, label the mating pieces at each corner of the joint for easy identification as your work progresses. Any pencil lines you mark must be sharp. With its fine teeth, a dovetail saw excels at making smooth, accurate cuts *(pages 50 and 52)*.

Always saw along the waste side of cutting lines; you can always shave away a bit of wood to make a tight fit better, but there is no good way of adding wood to a loose joint. Absolute accuracy is not essential in cutting tails; when you cut the sockets and pins, however, there is no margin for error.

Assembling Dovetails: Cut and fit the four corners of the project before gluing and clamping them. For a drawer needing a bottom panel or a carcass with a back panel that will be set in a groove, cut the groove after the dovetails have been cut, then install the panel when gluing and clamping the joint.

TOOLS

- Protractor
- T-bevel
- Marking gauge
- Try square
- Dovetail saw
- Coping saw
- Hand-screw clamp
- Wood chisels
- Mallet
- Bar clamps

MATERIALS

- Scrap wood
- Wood glue

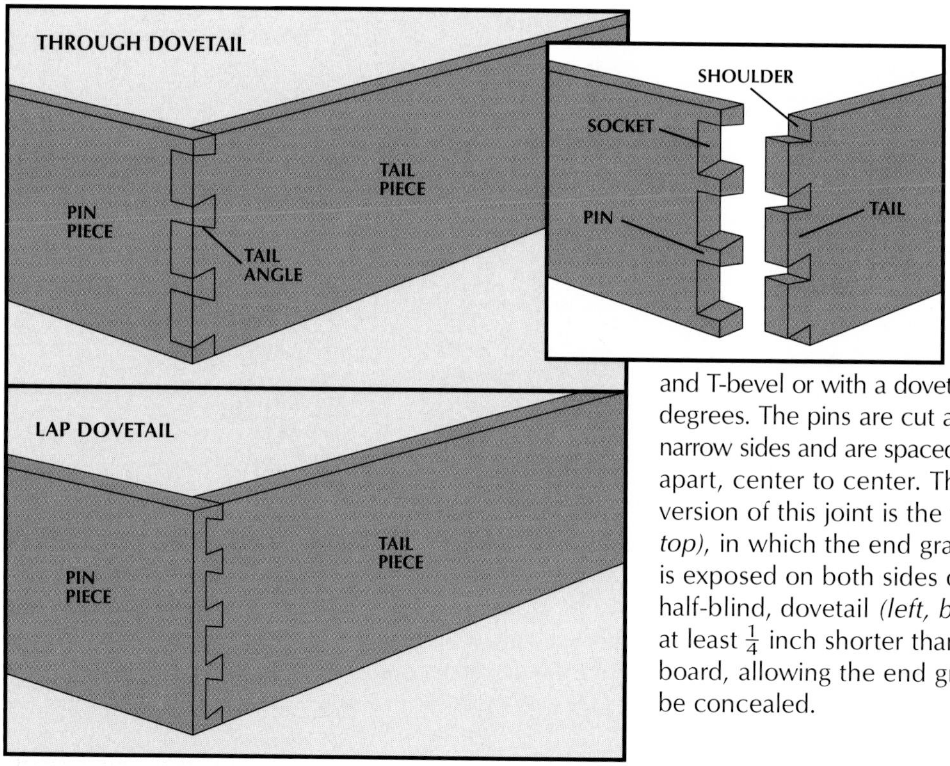

Two tailed joints. The superior holding power of the dovetail joint derives from the interlocking of angled tails on one board with tapered pins and sockets on another *(inset)*. The angle of the tails, set with a protractor and T-bevel or with a dovetail square, measures 80 degrees. The pins are cut at least $\frac{1}{4}$ inch wide on their narrow sides and are spaced no more than 3 inches apart, center to center. The simplest and strongest version of this joint is the through dovetail *(left, top)*, in which the end grain of the mating boards is exposed on both sides of the joint. In the lap, or half-blind, dovetail *(left, bottom)*, the tails are cut at least $\frac{1}{4}$ inch shorter than the thickness of the pin board, allowing the end grain of the tail piece to be concealed.

CUTTING A THROUGH DOVETAIL

1. Marking the shoulder lines.
◆ Set a marking gauge to the thickness of the pin board and scribe a line on all sides of the tail piece *(right)*.
◆ Adjust the gauge to the thickness of the tail piece and scribe a line on both faces of the mating end of the pin board.

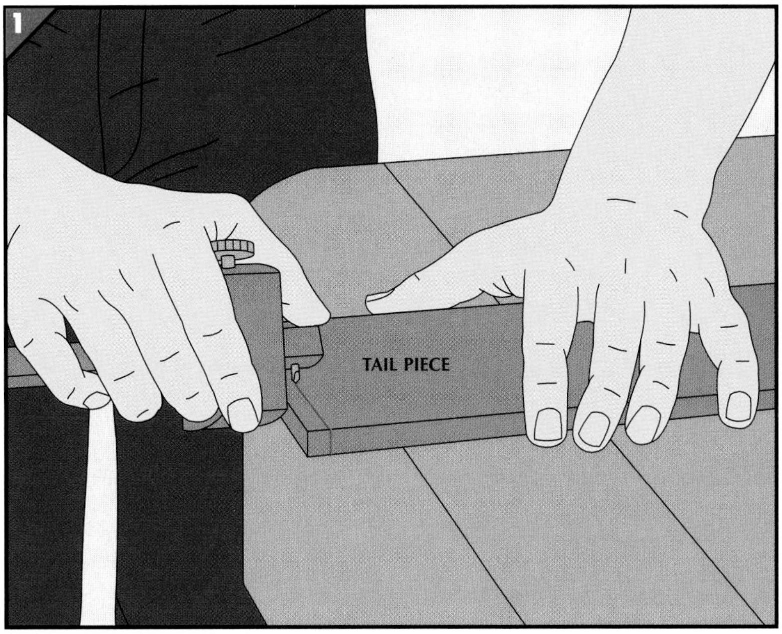

TRICKS OF THE TRADE

Sharpening a Marking-Gauge Pin

Most marking gauges have a pin with a conical point that tears wood fibers when drawn across the grain. For the pin to cut a sharp line, file it to a knife edge angled slightly toward the gauge fence *(right)*. In use, the angled edge helps hold the fence against the edge of the workpiece.

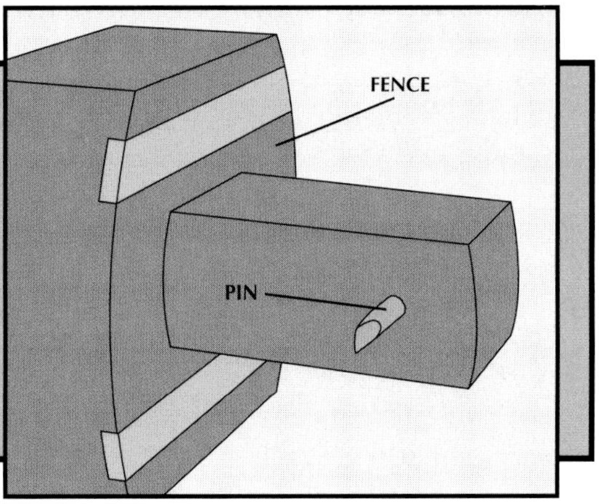

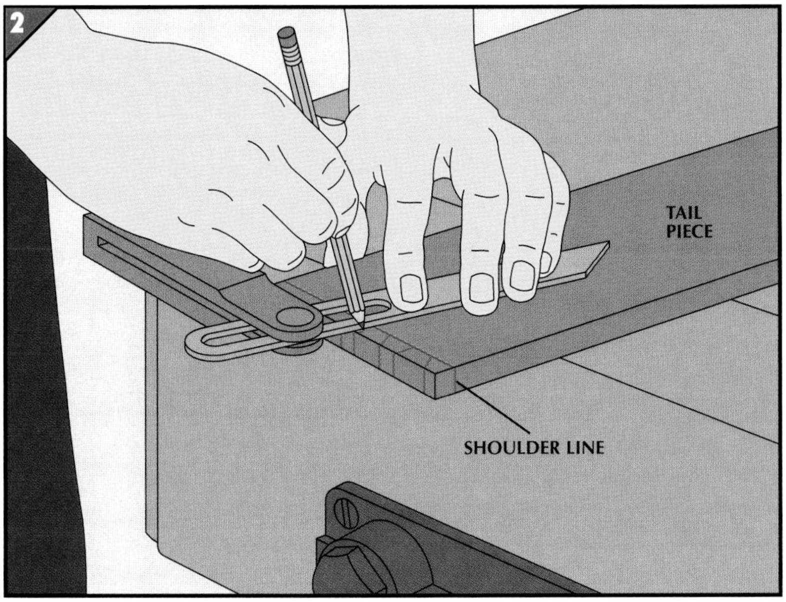

2. Outlining the tails.
◆ With a try square, mark two lines across the end of the tail piece, parallel to the edges and offset from each edge by a distance equal to half the thickness of the pin board.
◆ Divide the space between the two lines into equal segments for the tails, leaving at least $\frac{1}{4}$ inch between the tails for pins, and mark the positions of the ends of the tails on the board end.
◆ With a T-bevel set to the tail angle, or using a dovetail square, extend the lines along the face of the board to the shoulder line *(left)*.

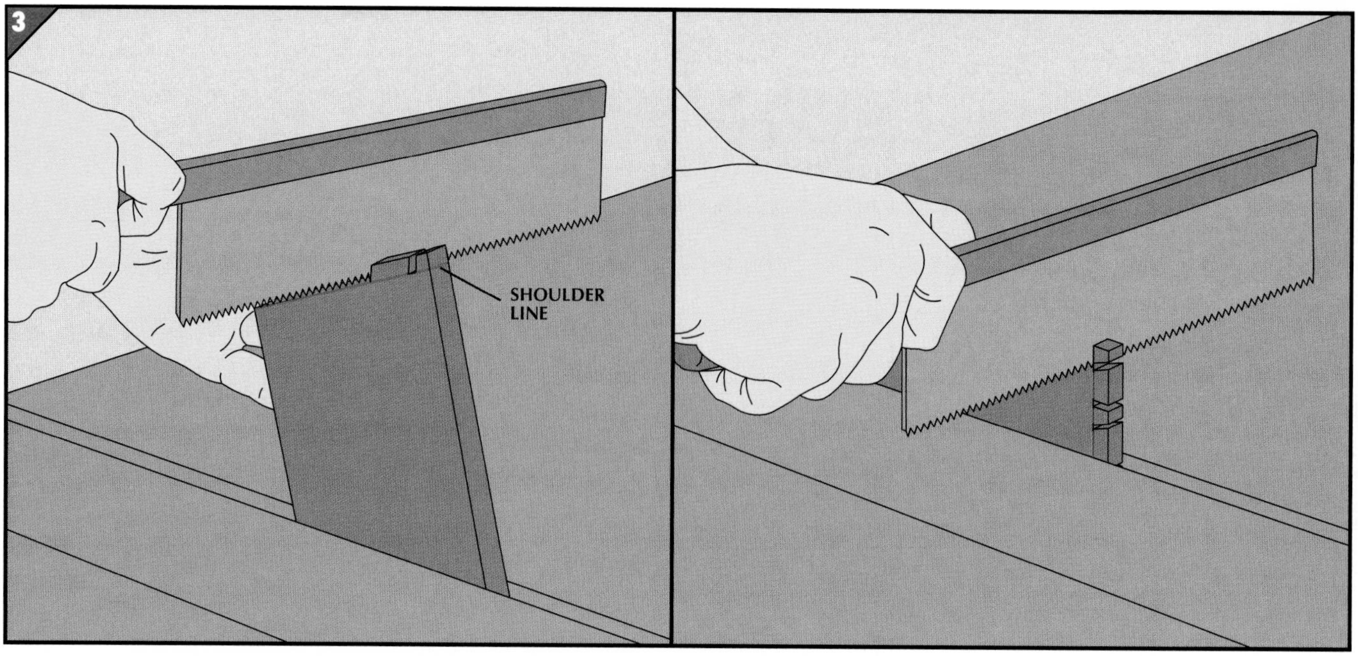

3. Cutting the tails and shoulders.

◆ Clamp the tail piece in a vise so the marked lines defining one side of the tails are vertical.

◆ With a dovetail saw, cut down each vertical line to the shoulder line *(above, left)*.

◆ Reposition the board in the vise so the lines defining the other side of the tails are vertical, and cut along the lines in the same way.

◆ Clamp the board so the shoulder line is vertical and saw along it from the edge of the piece to the cut at the base of the first tail *(above, right)*.

◆ Rotate the piece in the vise and cut the shoulder line in the same way.

4. Cutting out the waste.

◆ Clamp the tail piece vertically in the vise.

◆ With a coping saw, cut out as much of the waste wood between the tails as possible. Begin each cut by slipping the blade into a kerf made by the dovetail saw and cutting along the shoulder line to the kerf alongside the adjacent tail; work carefully to avoid cutting below the shoulder line *(right)*.

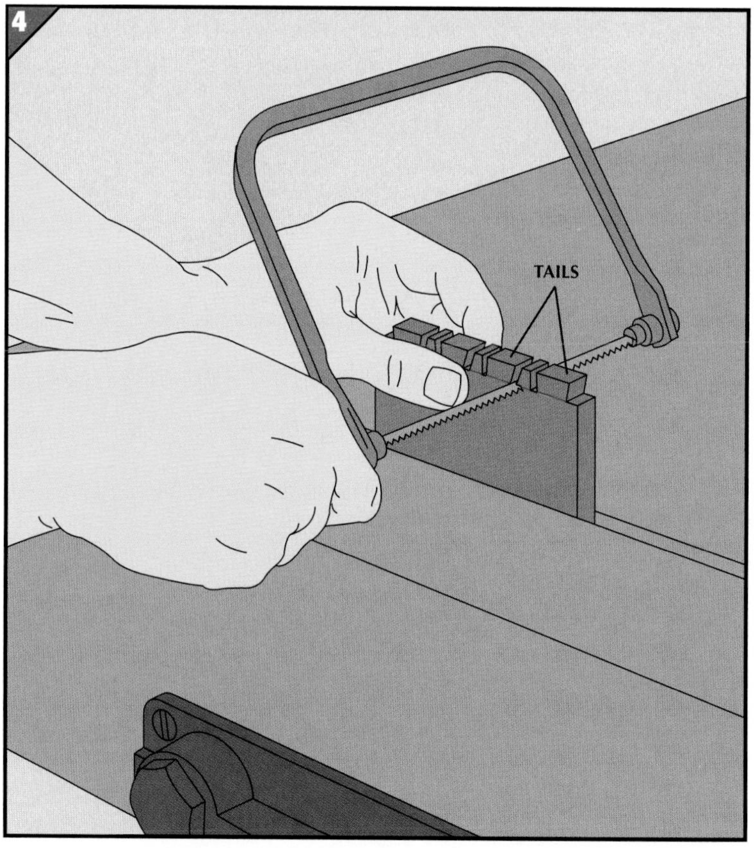

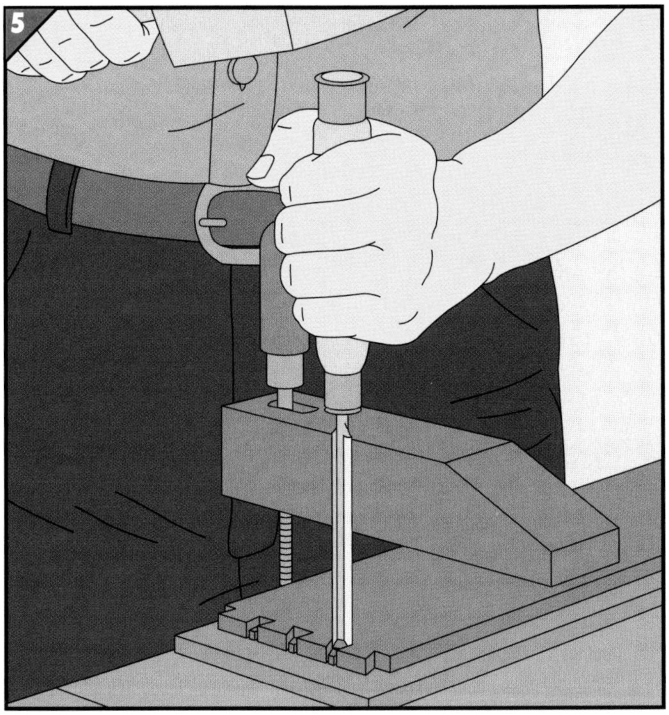

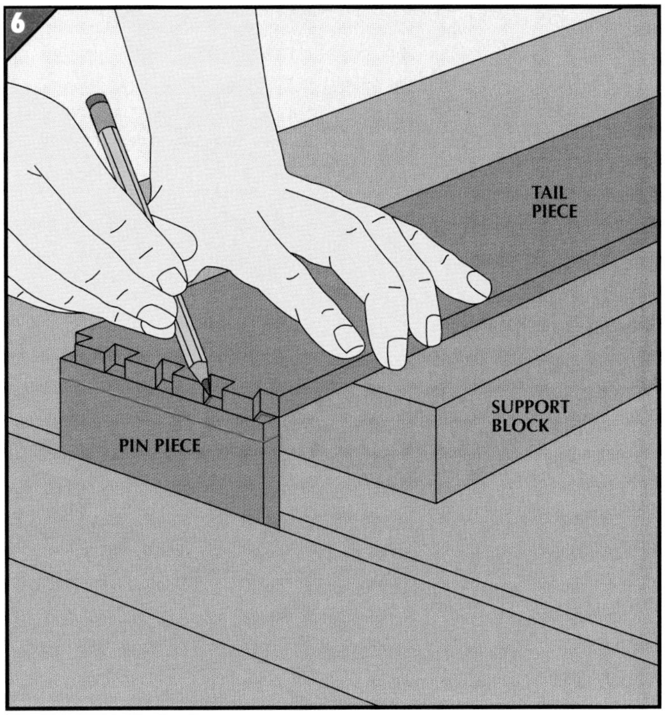

5. Chiseling out remaining waste.

◆ Clamp the tail piece atop scrap wood on a worktable.
◆ Holding a chisel no wider than the space between the tails vertically, with its cutting edge at the shoulder line, and its bevel facing the waste, tap the handle lightly with a mallet. Then, holding the chisel horizontally, cut a thin shaving of waste wood from between the tails to the chisel cut at the shoulder line.
◆ Continue making vertical and horizontal cuts in the same way until the waste has been removed from about half the thickness of the board, then repeat the process to remove waste beside the other tails.
◆ Turn the tail piece over and clamp it, then chisel out the remaining waste beside the tails in the same way *(above)*.

6. Marking the pin piece.

◆ Clamp the pin piece in a vise and place the tail piece at a right angle to it on a scrap wood block. Holding the tail piece so its end aligns with the outside face of the pin piece and the edges of the two boards line up, outline the tails on the end of the pin board *(above)*.
◆ With a try square, extend the lines along each face of the pin board to the shoulder lines.
◆ Cut along the marked lines with a dovetail saw, stopping at the shoulder line. Remove the waste beside the pins with a coping saw *(Step 4)* and a chisel *(Step 5)*.

7. Finishing the joint.

◆ With the pin board in the vise, position the tail piece against it, fitting the pins and tails together by hand.
◆ Protecting the wood with a scrap board, tap the tail piece lightly with a mallet to close the joint *(right)*. If the fit is too tight, separate the boards and shave the edges of the tails with a chisel. Check the fit again.
◆ Cut and test the dovetails for the remaining boards that make up the assembly.
◆ When all the joints fit well, spread wood glue on their contacting surfaces.
◆ Assemble the joints and, protecting the tail pieces with scrap wood, install a bar clamp along the face of each pin board *(inset)*.

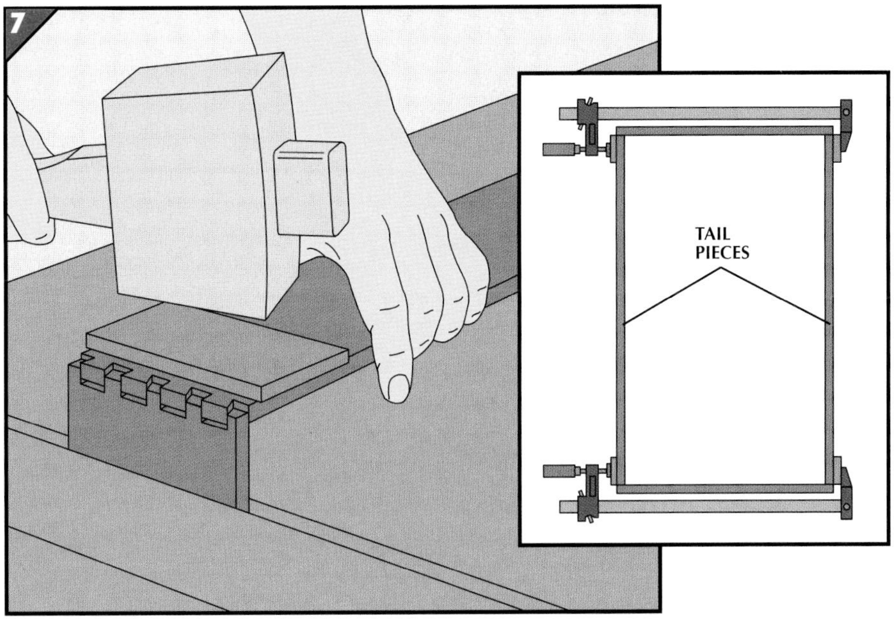

DOVETAIL JIGS FOR SPEEDY JOINTS

Paired with a router, a commercial dovetail jig can rapidly cut perfect and identical joints. Some jigs produce only through dovetails, but the model shown below can cut lap dovetails as well. The device can also be set up quickly: Once the template is adjusted for the desired tail spacing, the tail board is clamped to the jig and the template is secured in position. The router, fitted with a special dovetail bit, moves in and out of the template fingers, shaping the tails. The procedure is repeated on the pin board, this time with a straight bit in the router.

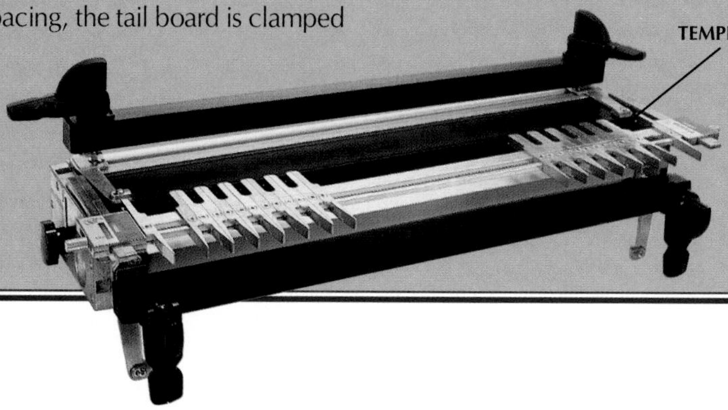

FASHIONING A LAP DOVETAIL

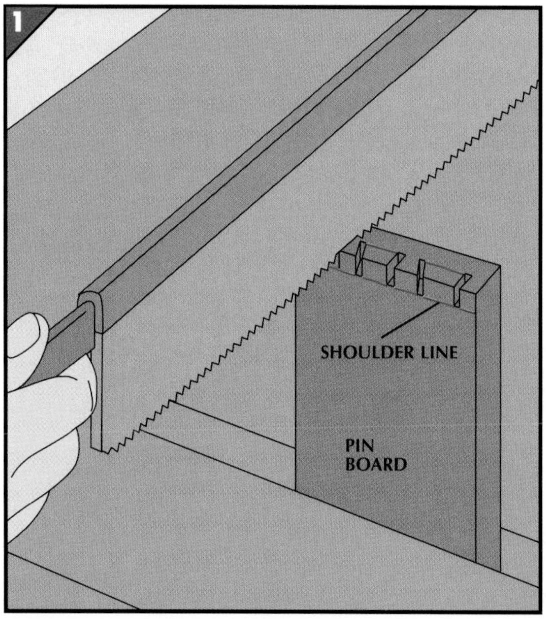

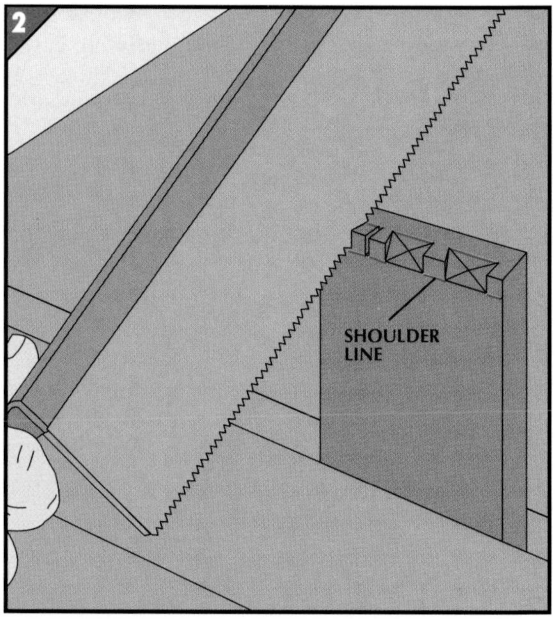

1. Sawing the tails and pins.

◆ Cut the tails as for a through dovetail *(pages 49-51, Steps 1-5)*, but locate the shoulder line so the tails' length will be three-quarters the thickness of the pin board.

◆ Outline the tails on the pin piece *(page 51, Step 6)*, being sure to align the base of the tails with the inside face of the pin board.

◆ Holding a dovetail saw at an angle that parallels the pin-edge marks, cut the edges of the pins *(above)*.

2. Removing the waste.

Place the saw blade on the middle of the socket between the first two pins and cut at an angle to the bottom edge of one of them, stopping at the shoulder line. Make each pin cut in the same way, then saw out the waste between the remaining pins *(above)*.

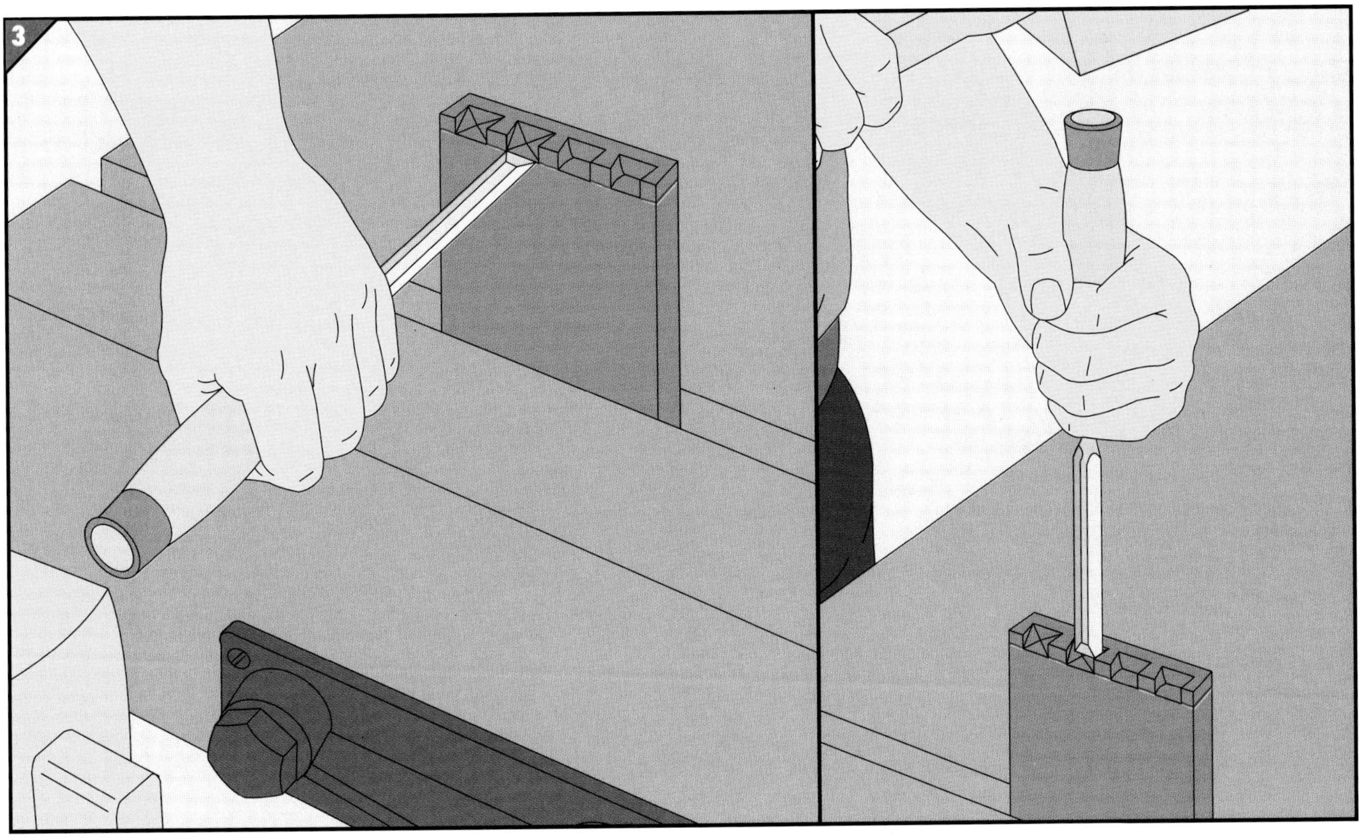

3. Chiseling out remaining waste.

◆ Center a chisel horizontally on the shoulder line between the first two pins, bevel side up, then tap it lightly with a mallet, shaving waste wood from the shoulder. Avoid gouging the angled sides of the pins.

◆ Repeat the chisel cut, but with the tool held vertically against the back of the socket, bevel side toward the waste.

◆ Continue these horizontal *(above, left)* and vertical *(above, right)* cuts to chip out the waste from between the remaining pins.

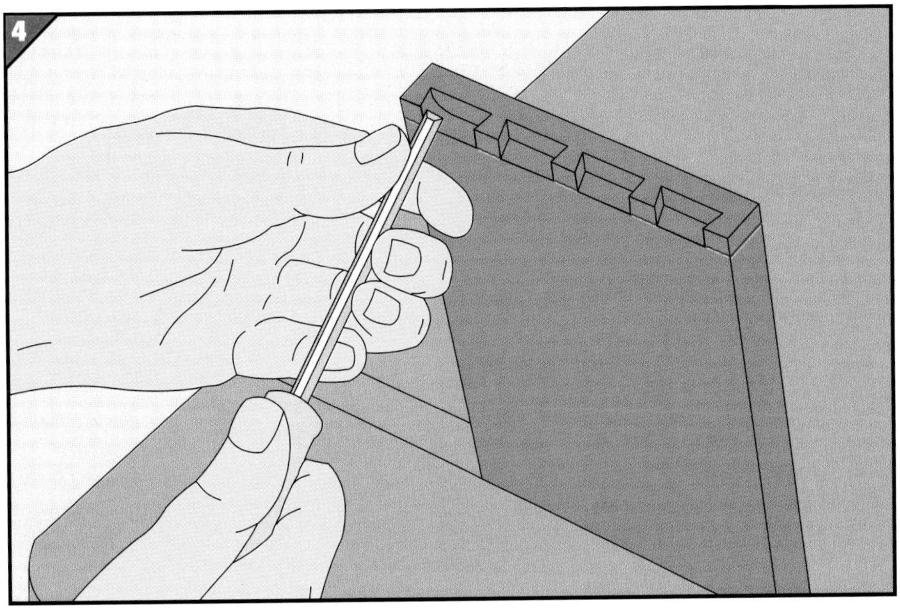

4. Clearing out the corners.

◆ Guiding a narrow bevel-edge chisel by hand, flat side down, shave the remaining waste from the corners of the sockets *(above)*.

◆ Test the joints, then cut the tails and pins in the remaining boards and glue the assembly *(page 51, Step 7)*.

Reinforcing Joints with Dowels

The blind dowel joint *(below and opposite)*—in which wooden pins are buried between the pieces being joined—is both sturdy and easy to make. Less durable than many joints, it is still a reliable choice for assembling cabinet frames.

Planning: Use dowels with a diameter one-third to one-half the thickness of the stock being assembled; and cut them $\frac{1}{8}$ inch shorter than the combined depth of the holes you drill for them. Grooved dowels are best; they allow excess glue to escape from the holes as the dowels are inserted.

Aligning Dowel Holes: Drill dowel holes at a 90-degree angle to the wood surface. You can achieve this precision on a drill press, or with an electric drill guided by a doweling jig *(opposite)*. The jig also ensures that the holes in mating boards will align. But you can also use dowel centers—metal cylinders with raised points—for this purpose.

After drilling the holes in one board, insert a dowel center into each hole, then press the boards together in position. The points will indent the wood, providing drilling locations for the mating holes.

TOOLS

Try square
Doweling jig
Electric drill
Stop collar
Screwdriver
Bar clamps

MATERIALS

Dowels
Wood glue
Scrap wood

SAFETY TIPS

Protect your eyes with goggles when using a power tool.

MAKING A BLIND DOWEL JOINT

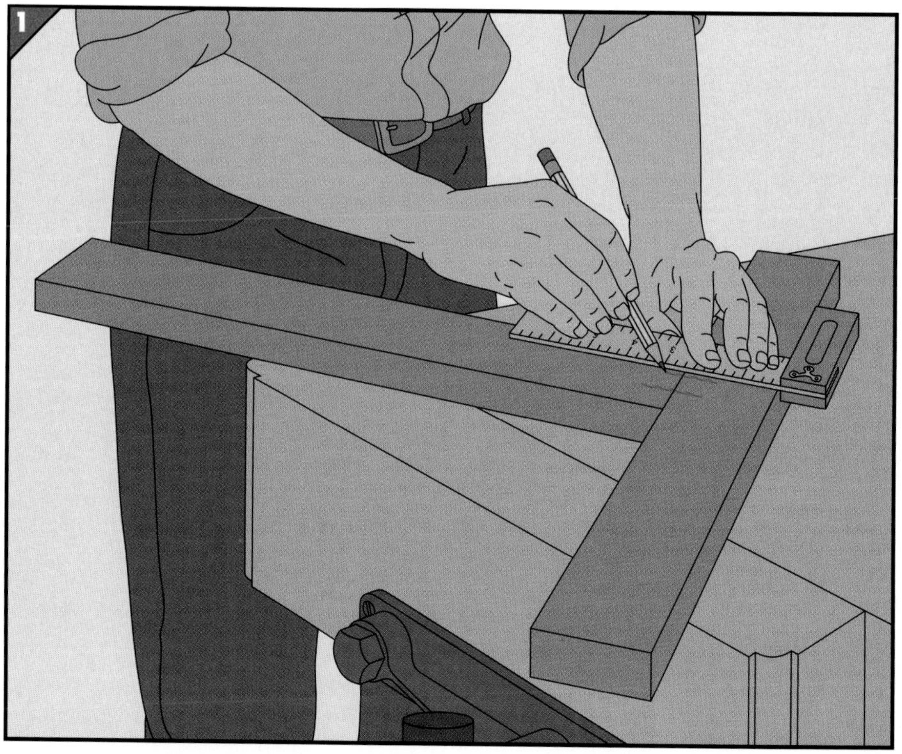

1. Marking the dowel locations.

◆ Place two boards to be joined on a worktable and hold them together in their final position.

◆ With a try square, mark two dowel-location lines across the boards, offsetting the marks from the edges of the vertical piece by one-quarter the width of the stock *(right)*.

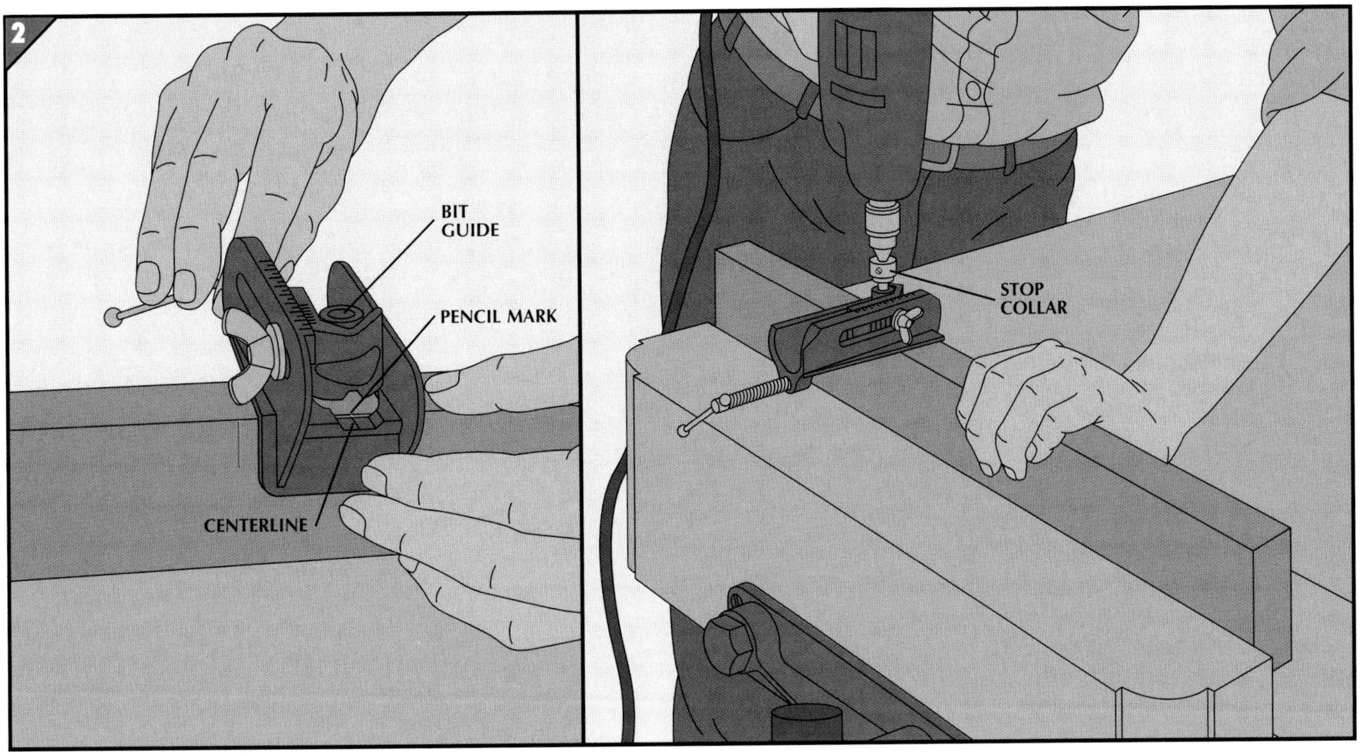

2. Drilling the dowel holes.

◆ Fix one of the boards in a vise and clamp a doweling jig on its edge, aligning the jig's centerline with one of the dowel locations *(above, left)*.
◆ Center the jig's bit guide over the board edge.
◆ Fit a stop collar around the drill bit to stop it at the correct depth, insert the bit in the guide, then drill the hole *(above, right)*.
◆ Reposition the jig to drill the other hole in the board, then clamp the mating board in the vise and drill holes at its dowel-location marks.

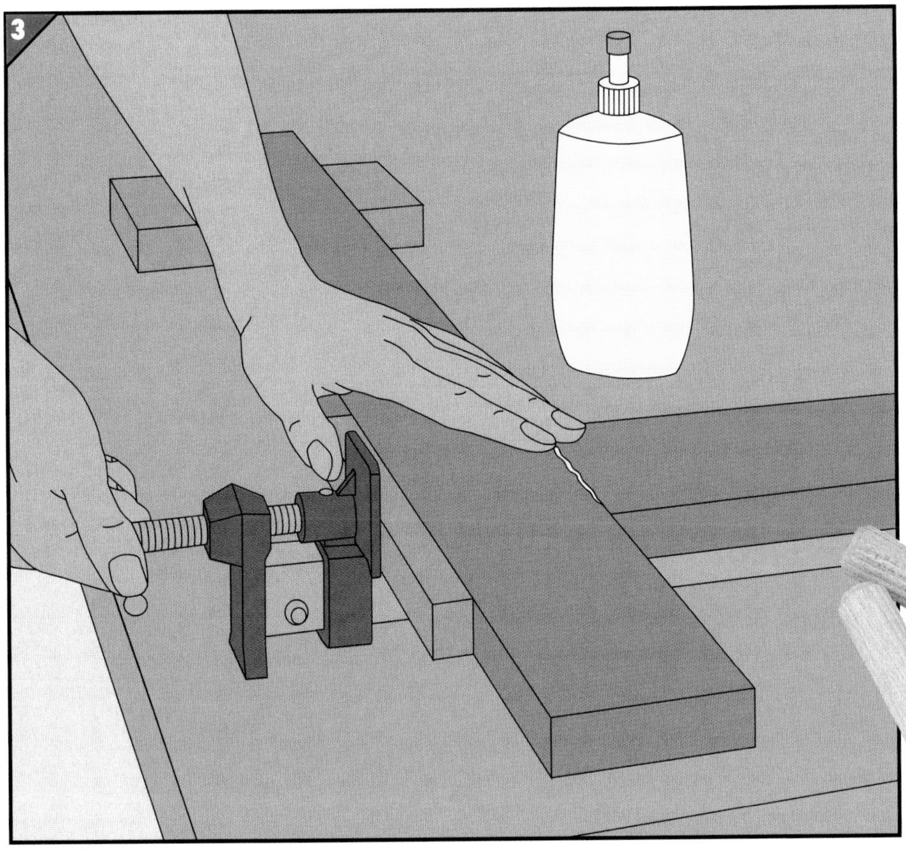

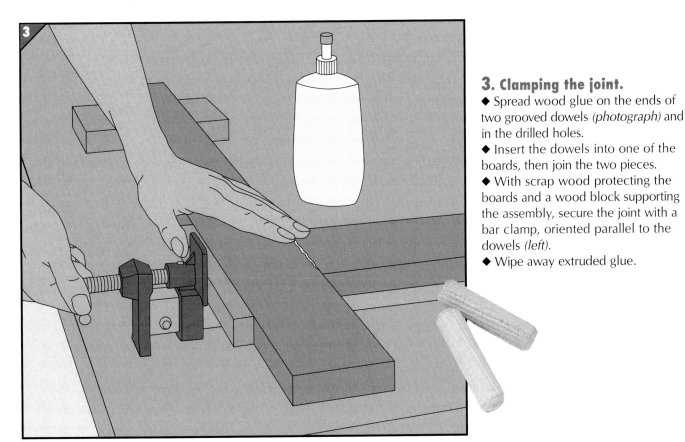

3. Clamping the joint.

◆ Spread wood glue on the ends of two grooved dowels *(photograph)* and in the drilled holes.
◆ Insert the dowels into one of the boards, then join the two pieces.
◆ With scrap wood protecting the boards and a wood block supporting the assembly, secure the joint with a bar clamp, oriented parallel to the dowels *(left)*.
◆ Wipe away extruded glue.

Mortise-and-Tenon and Lap Joints

Mortise-and-tenon joinery is based on a simple premise: Hollow out a space in one piece, and shape a projection on the second piece to fit into it. There are several versions of the joint to suit the orientation of the parts or the desired look *(below)*. A variation called the lap joint allows boards to cross each other in situations where strength is less crucial.

Making Mortises: Outline and cut out the mortise first *(opposite and pages 58-59)*, because it is easier to fine-tune a tenon to fit a mortise than the reverse. Make the width of the mortise one-third to one-half the thickness of the stock.

Mortises can be created with an electric drill or drill press for roughing out the waste and a chisel for squaring the corners *(page 58)*. For a quicker method, use a drill press equipped with a mortising attachment. This accessory combines a drill bit with a square cutter that together hollow out a four-sided hole. A router will plow out mortises with smooth sides and rounded ends *(page 59)*. You can then either square the cavities with a chisel or produce tenons with rounded ends.

Cutting Tenons: You can use a handsaw to fashion tenons, but a table saw will get the job done more rapidly *(pages 60-61)*.

TOOLS

- Try square
- Marking gauge
- Drill press
- Forstner bit
- C-clamps
- Wood chisel
- Mallet
- Router
- Edge guide
- Straight bit
- Table saw
- Dado head
- Rasp
- Tenoning jig

MATERIALS

- Scrap wood
- Dowels
- Wood glue
- Sandpaper

SAFETY TIPS

Shield your eyes with goggles when chiseling or using power tools.

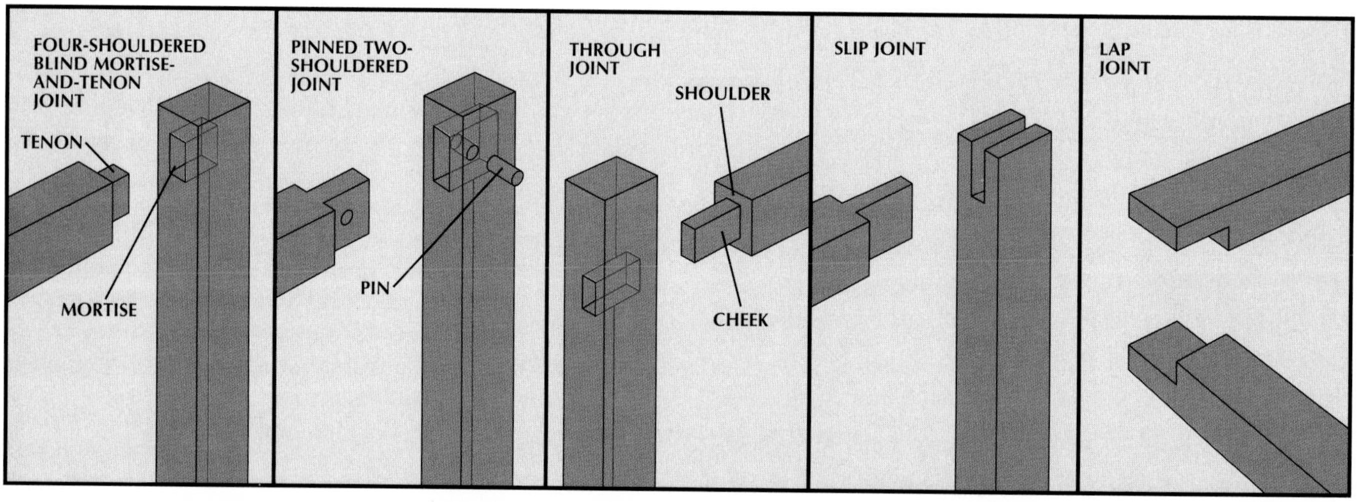

Five versions of the mortise and tenon. When a mortise is cut only partway through a board, hiding the mating tenon, the resulting joint is a blind mortise and tenon. For added strength, a tenon can be pinned *(page 61)*. A mortise cut straight through the piece, revealing the end grain of the tenon, produces a through mortise-and-tenon joint. For any of the varieties of mortise-and-tenon joints, the tenon can be trimmed on all four sides, producing four cheeks and four shoulders, or on only two sides. Used to assemble frames, the slip joint—also called the bridle joint—can be made relatively quickly, since the tenon is housed in a slot, instead of a mortise *(page 62, top)*. Essentially two one-sided tenons bonded together, the lap joint can be made very efficiently, since both boards are cut in the same way *(page 62, bottom)*.

OUTLINING A MORTISE FOR A FOUR-SHOULDERED TENON

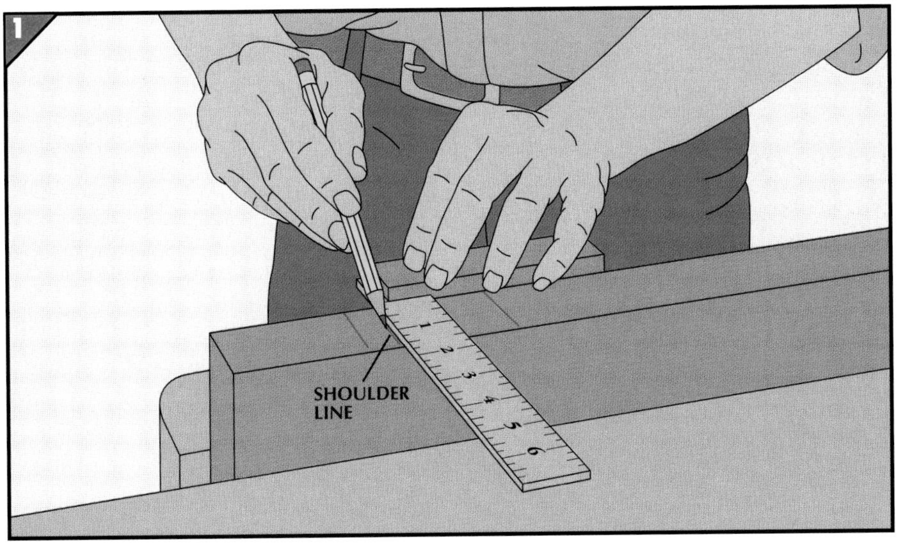

1. Marking the shoulder lines.
◆ Clamp the mortise piece in a vise, then position the tenon piece against it. Mark the edges of the tenon piece on the surface.
◆ With a try square, make a parallel mark inside each tenon-piece line to define the two narrow shoulders of the tenon *(right)*.

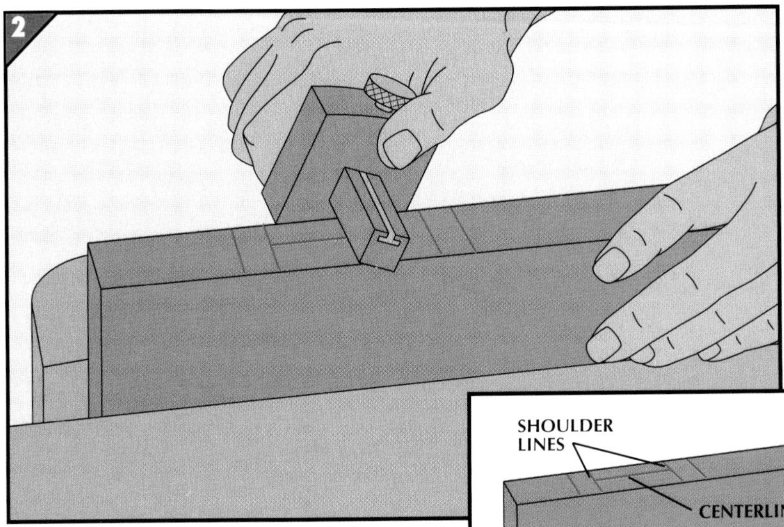

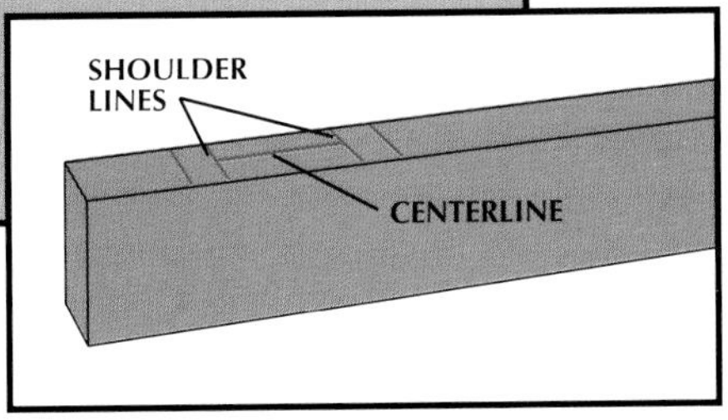

2. Centering the mortise.
◆ To find the center of the board edge, position the pin of a marking gauge near the middle with the fence up against the face and press the pin into the wood, leaving a mark. Repeat with the fence on the opposite face. If the marks don't coincide, reposition the fence on the bar and mark the edge again.
◆ With the gauge fence pressed against the board face, draw the pin along the edge between the marked shoulder lines *(left and inset)*.

TRICKS OF THE TRADE

Marking the Center of a Board

You can find the center of a board quickly using only a ruler and a pencil. Position the 1-inch mark of the ruler at one edge of the board and angle the tool until a measurement that can be divided easily in half is aligned with the other edge of the board—in this case, 2 inches, or the 3-inch mark. The center of the board will be at the mark halfway in between—in the example shown, the ruler's 2-inch mark *(right)*.

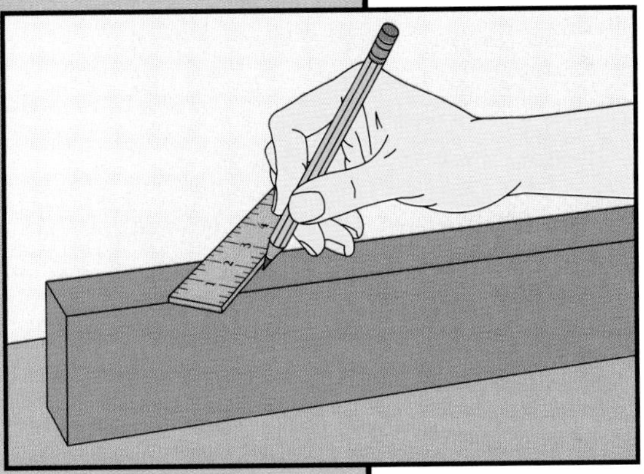

USING A DRILL PRESS AND CHISEL

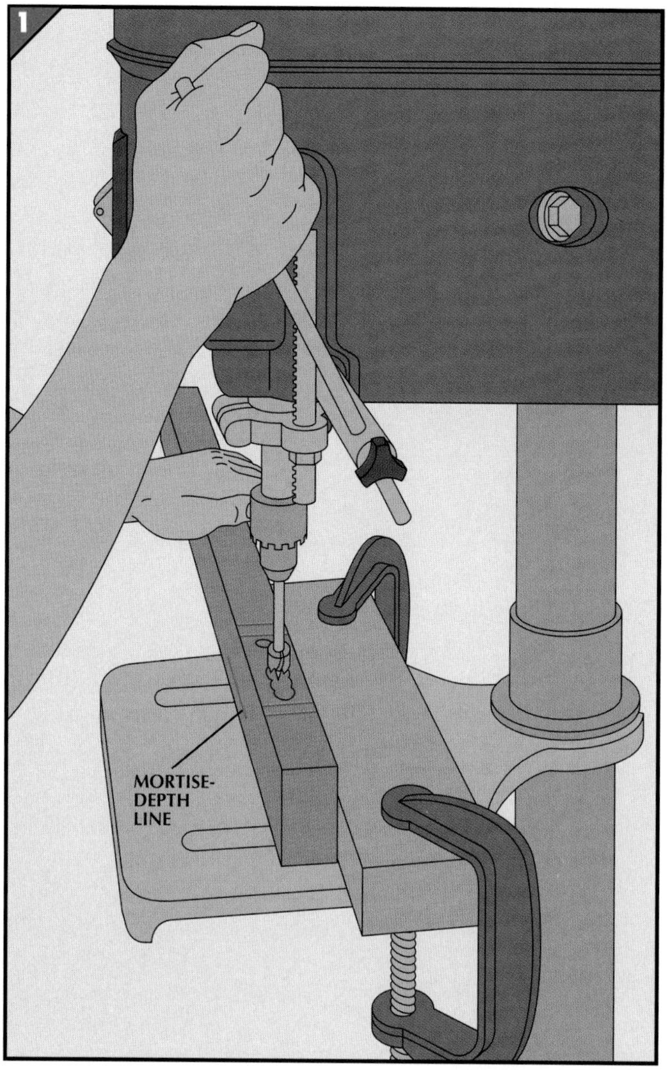

1. Drilling out the mortise.

◆ Install a Forstner bit the same width as the mortise in a drill press.
◆ Mark the depth of the mortise on the board face, place the board on the drill-press table, and lower the bit alongside the board until the tip of the bit reaches the marked line; lock the depth stop.
◆ Align the mortise centerline under the tip of the bit, set a wood block up against the board as a stop, and clamp the block to the drill-press table.
◆ Drill a hole at each end of the mortise line just inside the shoulder lines, then drill holes in between, overlapping adjacent holes *(left)*.

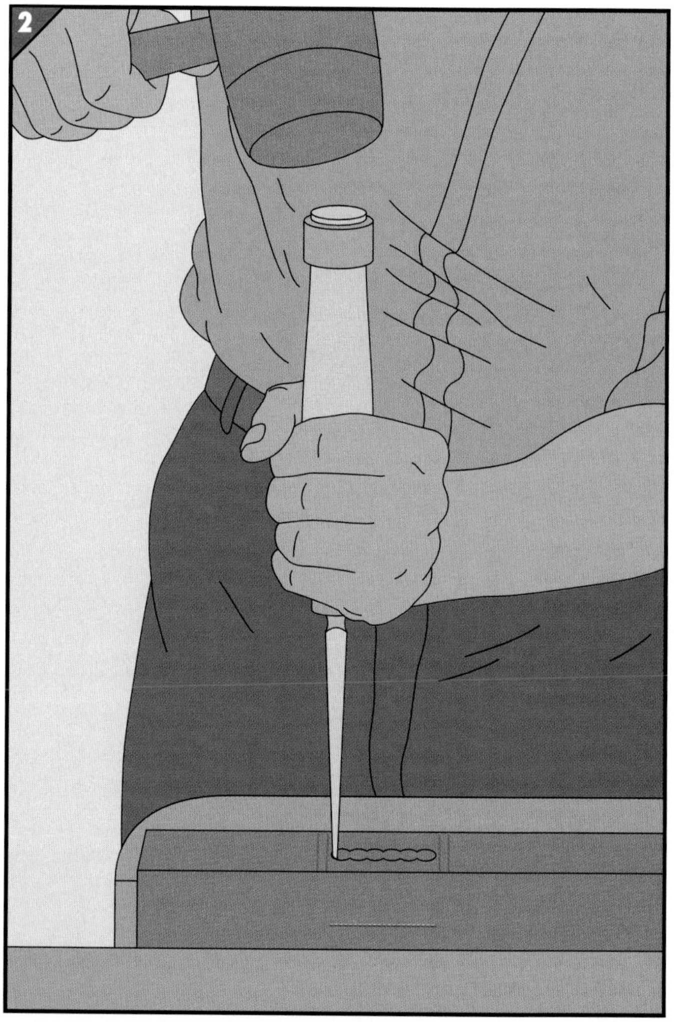

2. Squaring the mortise with a chisel.

◆ Clamp the board in a vise, and scribe a line along each side of the holes with a marking gauge.
◆ Holding a chisel the same width as the mortise vertically at one end, bevel facing the waste, tap the handle with a mallet to square the end *(above)*. Repeat the chiseling to square the opposite end of the mortise as well as the sides.

Drill-Press Safety

In addition to the safety rules for power tools listed on page 14, observe these precautions:

✓ Use bits specifically designed for drill presses—not auger bits, which are not made for high-speed drilling.
✓ Hold the stock firmly against the table as you drill; clamp small pieces to the table.
✓ When making a deep hole, raise the bit frequently to clean out fragments of waste wood, and keep the drill-press table clean as you work.
✓ Turn off the machine if the bit begins to bind.

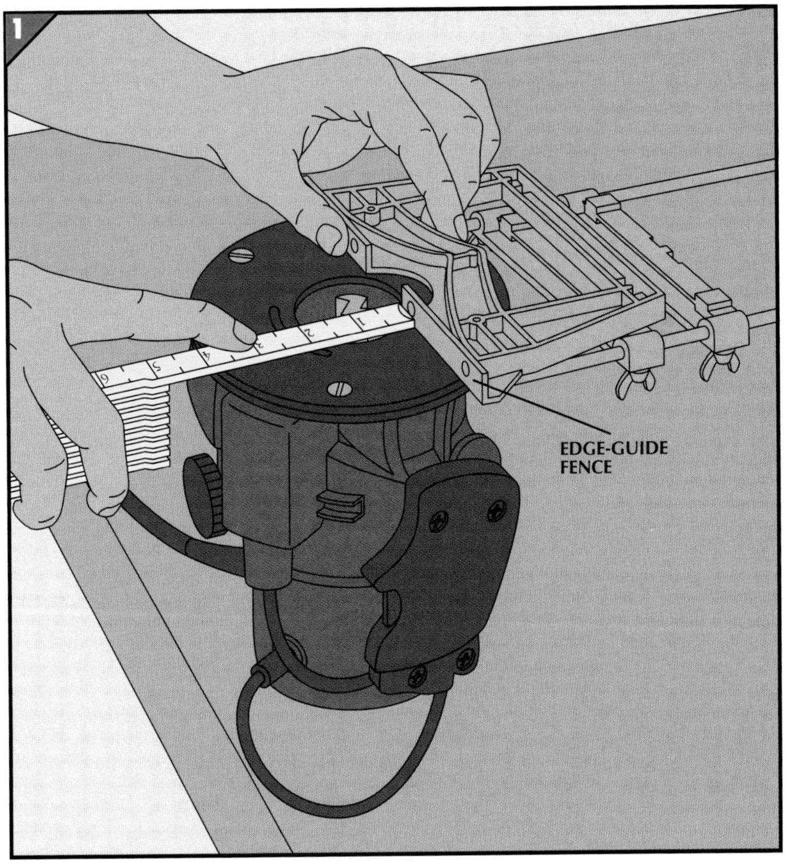

1. Setting up the cut.

◆ In your router, install a straight bit with a diameter at least half the mortise width, but no larger than the mortise.

◆ Fit a commercial edge guide on the router's base and position it so the distance between the bit and guide fence equals the width of the tenon shoulder you plan to cut *(right)*. Lock the guide in place.

◆ Adjust the bit depth no greater than $\frac{1}{2}$ inch. For a deeper mortise, make as many passes as necessary, increasing the cutting depth $\frac{1}{2}$ inch at a time.

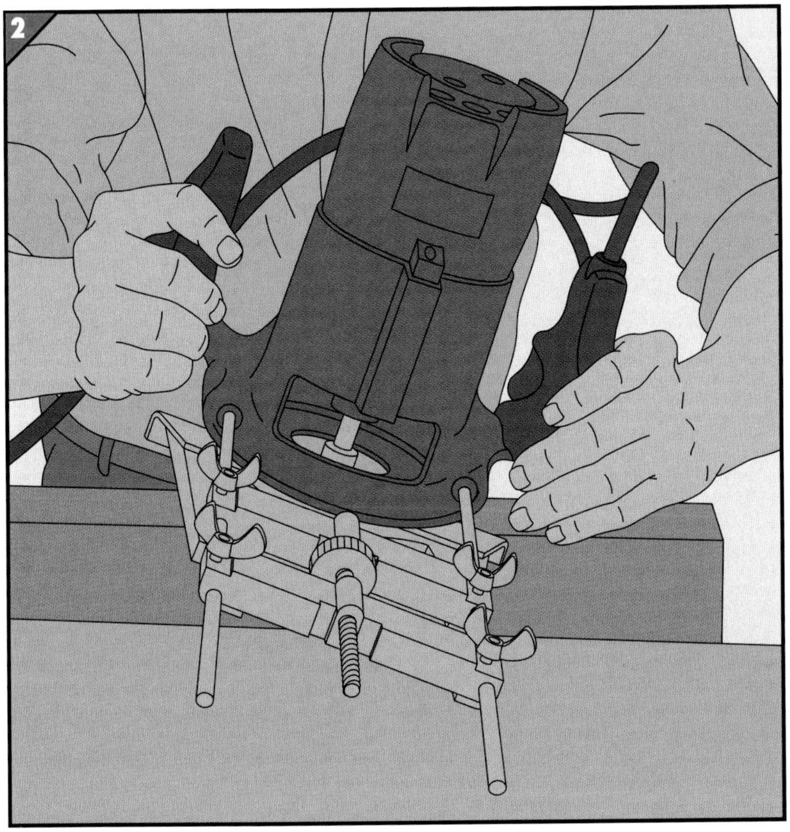

2. Plowing out the mortise.

◆ Clamp the board in a vise with the marked edge facing up.

◆ Holding the router over the board at an angle, align the bit just inside one of the marked shoulder lines.

◆ Pressing the edge-guide fence against the board face, turn on the router and slowly sink the bit into the wood *(left)*. Once the router is flat on the board, move the tool to the opposite shoulder-line mark, stopping just short of the line. Turn off the router and wait for the bit to stop.

◆ Turn the board around in the vise and rout the other side of the mortise.

◆ Square the ends of the mortise with a chisel *(opposite, Step 2)*.

SHAPING A TENON ON A TABLE SAW

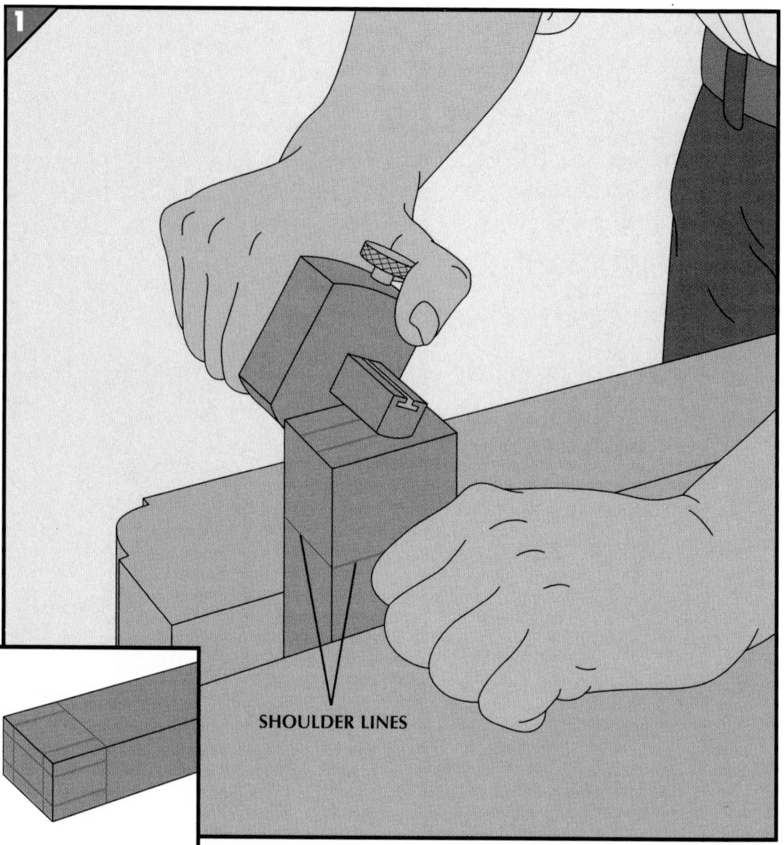

1. Outlining the tenon.

◆ Mark the length of the tenon—$\frac{1}{8}$ inch less than the depth of the mortise—on the board.

◆ With a try square, extend the mark around all four sides of the board, defining the tenon shoulders.

◆ Clamp the board in a vise, adjust a marking gauge to the width of the mortise shoulders, then scribe two lines across the end of the tenon piece, pressing the gauge fence first against one face, then the other *(right)*.

◆ Extend the lines down both edges to the shoulder lines *(inset, left)*. For a tenon with four shoulders, mark two more lines across the end, perpendicular to the first two, and extend them to the shoulder lines *(inset, right)*.

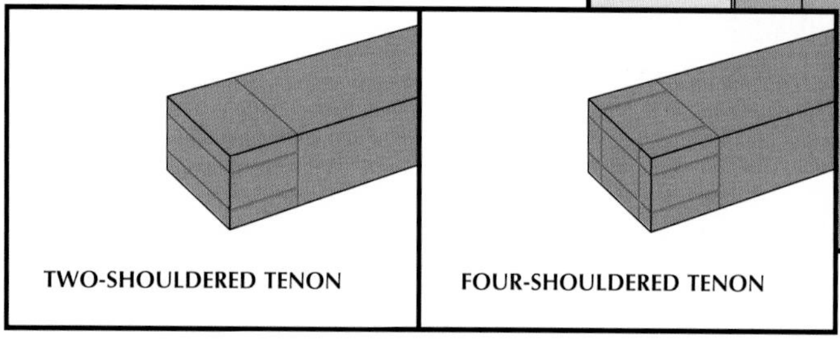

2. Adjusting the saw blade height.

◆ Install a dado head, set to make a $\frac{1}{2}$-inch-wide cut, on the table saw *(page 39)*. Lay the tenon board flat on the saw table and raise the head to a point just below the tenon outline.

◆ Feeding the board with the miter gauge, cut a $\frac{1}{2}$-inch rabbet in the bottom corner of the piece *(above)*.

◆ Turn the board over and make the same cut on the other side.

◆ Test the tenon against the mortise, then raise the dado head slightly, repeat the cuts, and retest, continuing the process, as necessary, until the tenon fits.

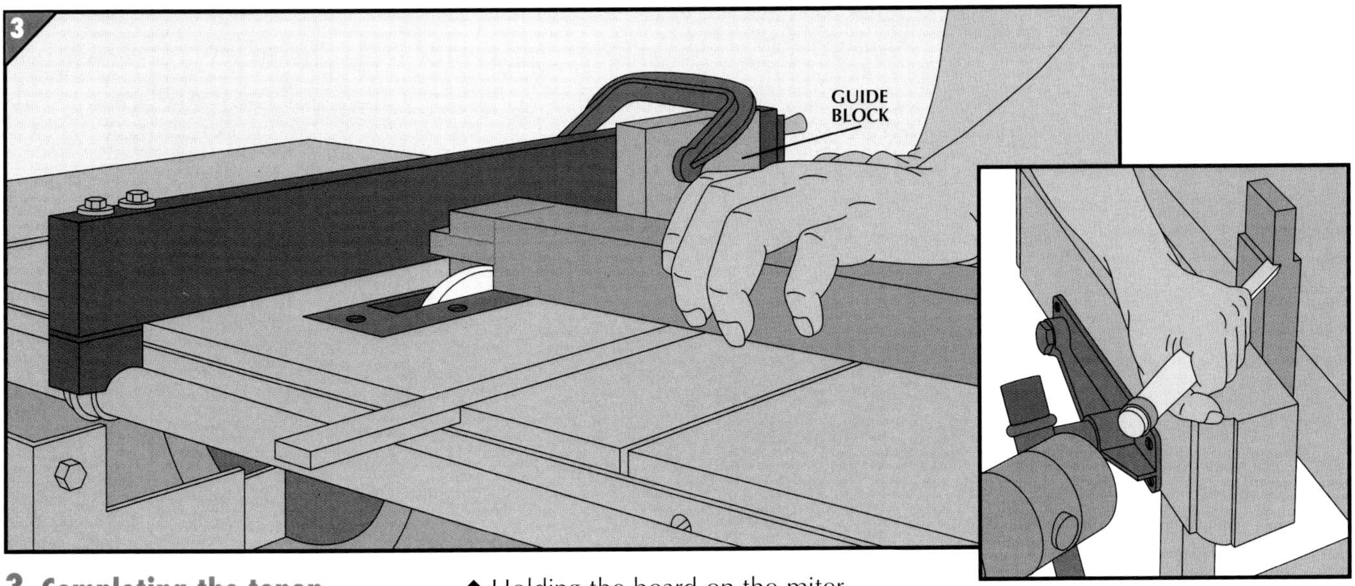

3. Completing the tenon.

◆ Clamp a guide block to the rip fence.

◆ Holding the tenon piece against the miter gauge, align the shoulder line with the left-hand edge of the dado head. Then, pull the miter gauge back until the board lines up with the guide block. Move the rip fence to butt the guide block against the board, then lock the fence in place.

◆ Holding the board on the miter gauge, its end against the guide block, feed the board forward to cut one tenon shoulder *(above)*. Moving the piece away from the block $\frac{1}{2}$ inch each time, make additional cuts to expose the side of the tenon. Then turn the board over, and cut the other side in the same way.

◆ For a four-shouldered tenon, use the same technique to cut waste from the board edges.

◆ If you have left the ends of a router-cut mortise rounded *(page 59)*, clamp the tenon board in a vise and round the corners of the tenon to fit with a chisel and mallet *(inset)*, then a rasp *(page 88)* and sandpaper.

PINNING A MORTISE AND TENON

Drilling the hole.

◆ Once the glue securing the joint is dry, remove the clamps. In a drill press, install a bit of the same diameter as the dowel pin you plan to use.

◆ Place a wood scrap on the drill-press table to prevent tearout, and clamp the boards on top so the midpoint of the tenon is directly under the bit. Drill the dowel hole through the stock *(right)*.

◆ Cut a dowel $\frac{1}{4}$ inch longer than the hole and bevel it around the end so it is easy to insert. Spread wood glue in the hole and around the bottom half of the dowel, and tap it into the hole.

◆ Let the glue dry, then trim the dowel flush with the surface using a chisel *(inset)*.

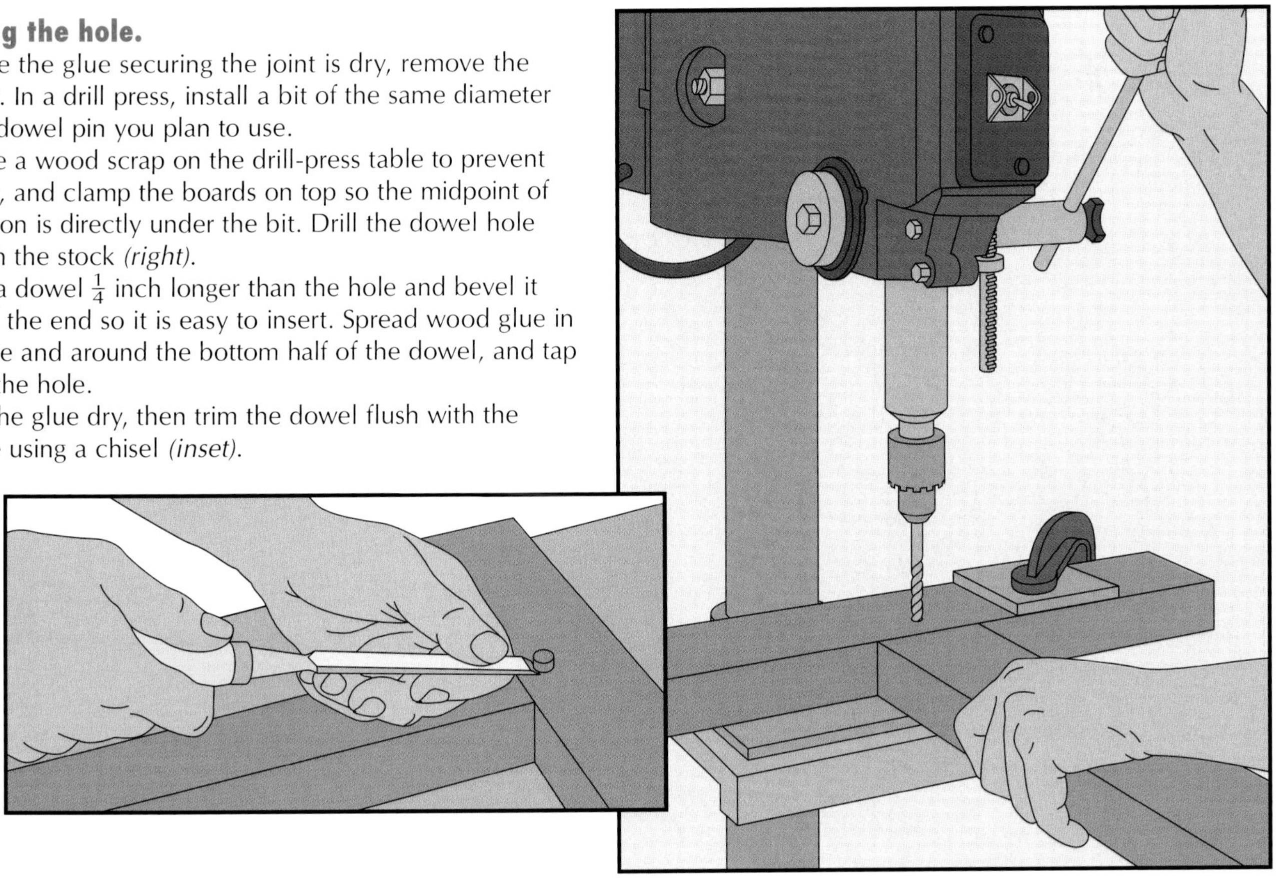

MAKING A SLIP JOINT

Slicing a slip joint.

◆ Outline the mortise *(page 57)* at the end of a scrap board. On a table saw, install a dado head adjusted about $\frac{1}{4}$ inch narrower than the mortise width *(page 39)*; set the blade height to the mortise depth.

◆ Clamp the scrap board to a tenoning jig—the model shown slides in the miter slot—and adjust the lateral position of the board to align the right-hand edges of the dado head and mortise outline.

◆ Push the jig and board forward across the table, cutting one side of the mortise. Then, turn the board around in the jig and make another pass to cut the other side of the mortise.

◆ Check the size of the mortise, and adjust the blade's height and the lateral position of the board in the jig, if necessary, and make additional passes. Once the mortise is the correct size, use the setup to cut the mortises in your stock *(right)*.

◆ Cut tenons *(pages 60-61, Steps 1-3)* to fit the mortises.

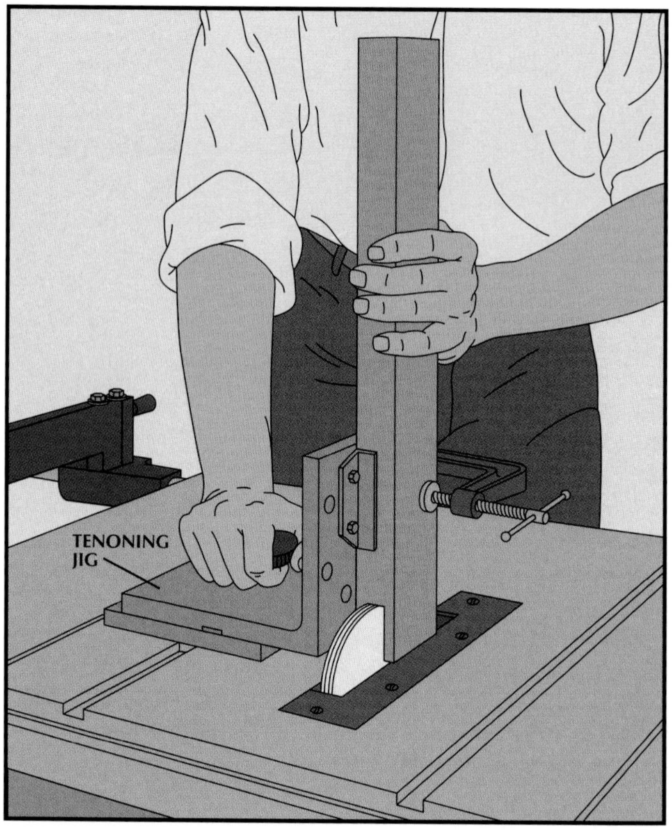

SPLICING ENDS WITH A LAP JOINT

Cutting overlapping tenons.

◆ Place one of the boards on the saw table and the other on top at a right angle, resting it level on a block. Mark the edge of each board on the face of the other *(above, left)*.

◆ With a try square, extend the lines around the boards, forming shoulder lines. On each piece, mark a line down the center of both edges from the shoulder line to the end.

◆ Install a dado head on the saw, raising it to just below the centerline on one of the boards.

◆ Make a test cut at the end of each piece, then fit the two ends together *(above, right)*. If the top faces of the boards are not flush, raise the dado head slightly and repeat the cuts until they are flush.

◆ Saw away the remaining waste wood on each board from the end to the shoulder lines *(page 61, Step 3)*.

Reinforcing Miters

Miter joints are formed by cutting 45-degree angles on two boards and joining the pieces to form a square corner. This attractive joint conceals the end grain of both boards, but it is weaker than most other corner joints. Reinforcing a miter joint with hidden wood biscuits or a plywood spline adds strength, and takes nothing away from the joint's visual appeal.

Two Types: Flat miters, cut across the face of the wood, are common on such items as picture frames. Edge miters, made by cutting bevels at the ends of the stock, connect boxlike structures such as cabinet carcasses. Flat miters can be strengthened with either splines or ready-made biscuits that are glued into slots cut into adjoining pieces. Edge miters are more easily strengthened with biscuits.

Cutting and Reinforcing Miters: With the help of jigs, you can cut multiple identical miters quickly and precisely on a table saw and produce the spline grooves for a flat miter joint *(pages 64-65)*. The splines are usually made from $\frac{1}{8}$-inch plywood, but for thick wood, $\frac{1}{4}$-inch plywood gives added strength. Depending on the thickness of the spline, the grooves can be sawn with a standard $\frac{1}{8}$-inch saw blade or a $\frac{1}{4}$-inch dado blade. To cut slots in edge miters for biscuits *(pages 66-67)*, you'll need a plate joiner.

TOOLS

- Handsaw
- Electric drill
- Countersink bit
- Screwdriver
- Table saw
- Tenoning jig
- Carpenter's square
- Protractor
- Corner clamp
- C-clamps
- Plate joiner
- Band clamps with corner brackets

MATERIALS

- Hardwood lumber
- 1 x 2s
- 2 x 4
- Plywood ($\frac{1}{8}$", $\frac{3}{4}$")
- Wood screws ($1\frac{1}{4}$" No. 6)
- Sandpaper (medium grade)
- Wood glue
- Plate-joiner biscuits

SAFETY TIPS

Put on goggles when using a power tool.

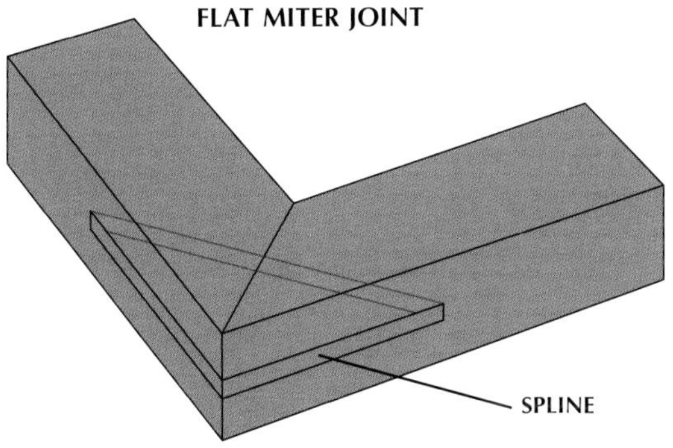

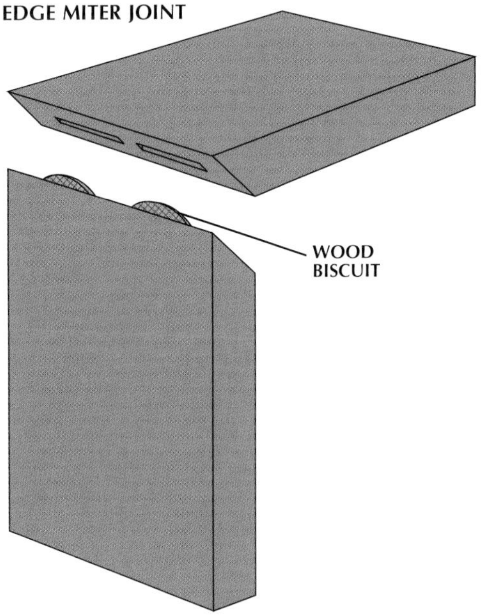

Two mighty miters.
These joints illustrate two methods of reinforcing miters. A triangular plywood spline set into the outside corner formed by two mating boards strengthens a flat miter joint. An edge miter is bolstered by wood biscuits set in glue-filled slots cut by a plate joiner. Made from compressed wood, the biscuits absorb glue and swell slightly once they are inserted in the slots, resulting in a very strong bond.

BRACING WITH A SPLINE

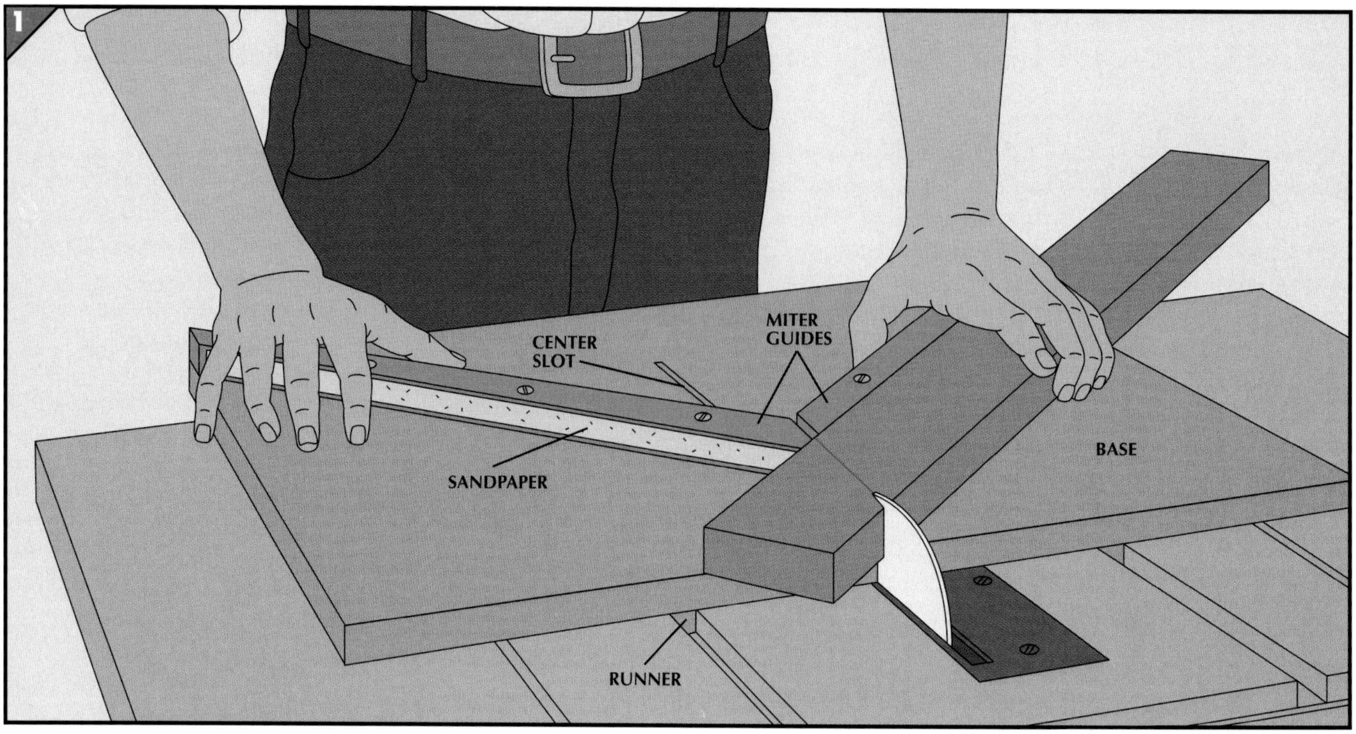

1. Cutting multiple miters with a jig.

◆ To make the jig, cut an 18- by 24-inch rectangle of $\frac{3}{4}$-inch plywood for a base. Also cut two hardwood runners to fit the saw table's miter slots and fasten the runners with No. 6 countersunk wood screws to the underside of the base. Lay the base on the table with the runners in the slots and saw a slot two-thirds of the way across the center. For the miter guides, trim two 1-by-2s with a 45-degree angle at one end and fasten them to the base with $1\frac{1}{4}$-inch screws so the mitered ends sit on either side of the center slot, about 6 inches from the edge of the base, and form a right angle. Trim the square ends of the guides even with the base and glue sandpaper strips to the outer edges of the guides.

◆ To use the jig, hold a board against either miter guide with the cutting mark lined up with the center slot and push the jig across the blade *(above)*. Cut the mating board in the same way, holding it against the opposite guide. Miter the ends of all the other boards you will be connecting.

◆ Spread glue on one end of each mating board and secure two opposite corners, each with a corner clamp *(page 68)*.

2. A jig for cutting the spline grooves.

◆ Cut a 2-by-4 about 18 inches long, then make a mark on one edge a few inches from one end and a second mark $5\frac{1}{2}$ inches further along.

◆ With a protractor, draw a 45-degree-angle line on the board face from one of the marks toward the other; repeat from the other mark so the two lines intersect at 90 degrees about $\frac{3}{4}$ inch from the opposite edge.

◆ Clamp the board in a vise, and cut out the triangle with a handsaw *(right)*.

◆ Trim both ends of the 2-by-4 to leave the jig 8 inches long with the triangle centered between the ends.

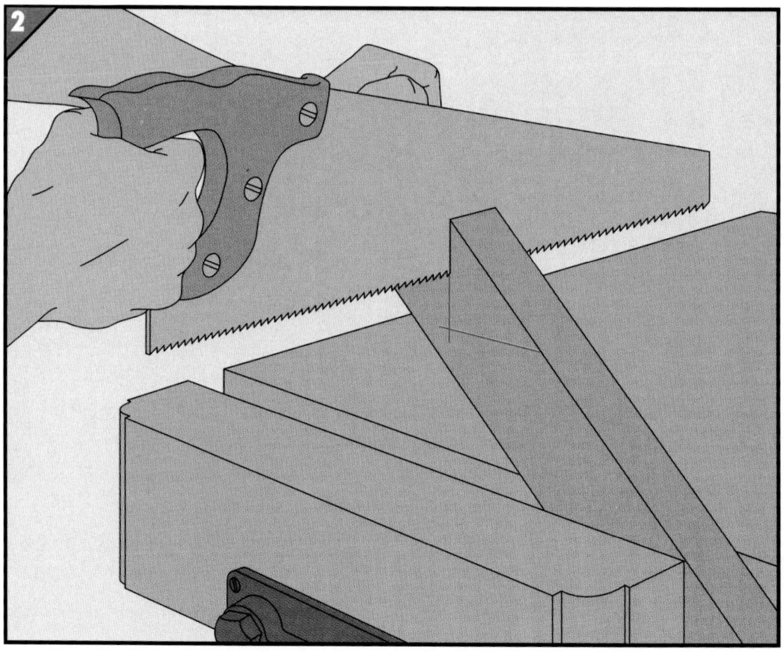

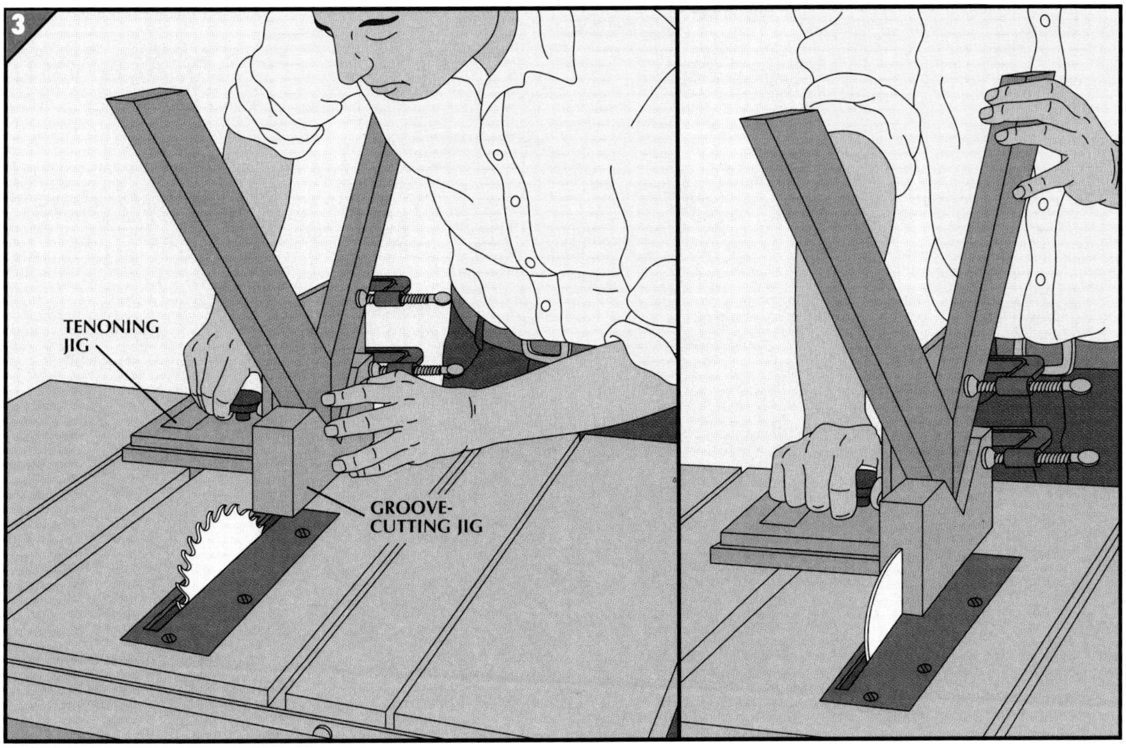

3. Cutting the spline groove.

◆ Set the corner of the miter joint in the groove-cutting jig and place the jig on the saw table.
◆ Clamp one of the boards to a commercial tenoning jig and adjust the jig so the miter joint is centered on the blade *(above, left)*.
◆ Raise the blade to a height slightly below the center of the miter joint.
◆ Clamp the groove-cutting jig to the tenoning jig, ensuring that the clamp is above the blade.
◆ Push the tenoning jig forward until the blade cuts through the groove-cutting jig and miter joint *(above, right)*.
◆ Turn off the saw and pull the jig back.

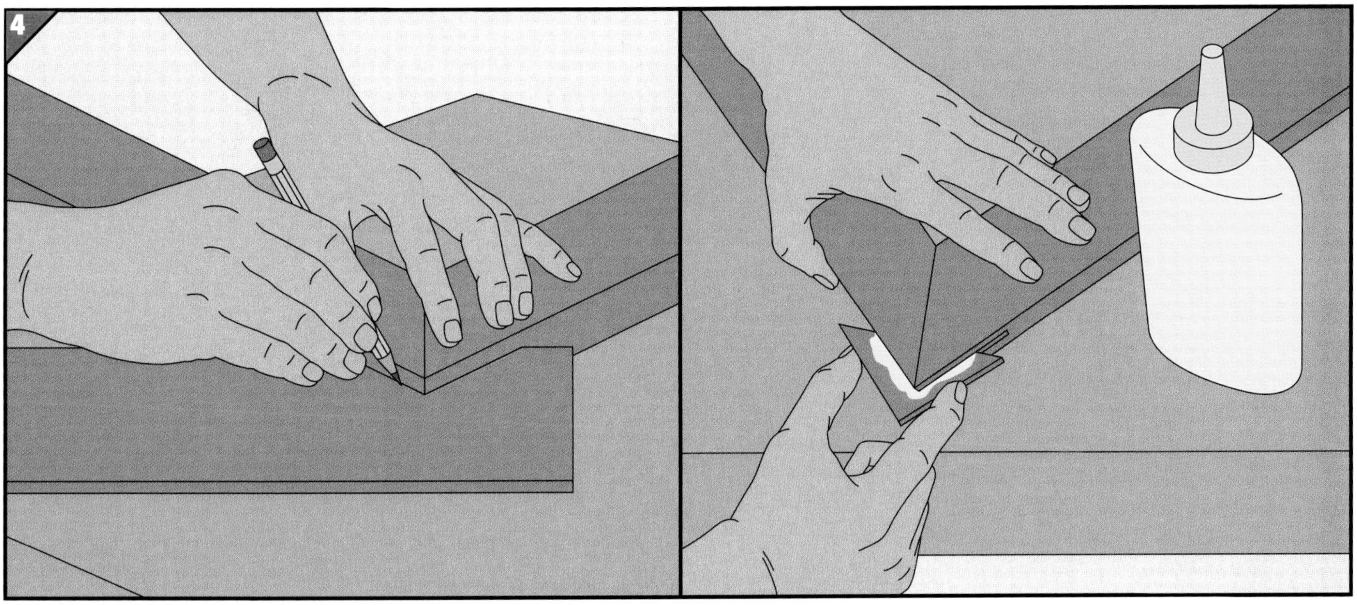

4. Making and inserting the spline.

◆ Slide a piece of $\frac{1}{8}$-inch plywood into the groove you cut in the frame corner.
◆ Outline the outside of the corner on the plywood *(above, left)*.
◆ Cut out the spline, spread wood glue on both sides, and fit it into the groove *(above, right)*.
◆ Install a clamp to apply pressure on both board faces. Once the glue is dry, sand the edges of the spline flush with the frame pieces.

A CARCASS HELD TOGETHER WITH BISCUITS

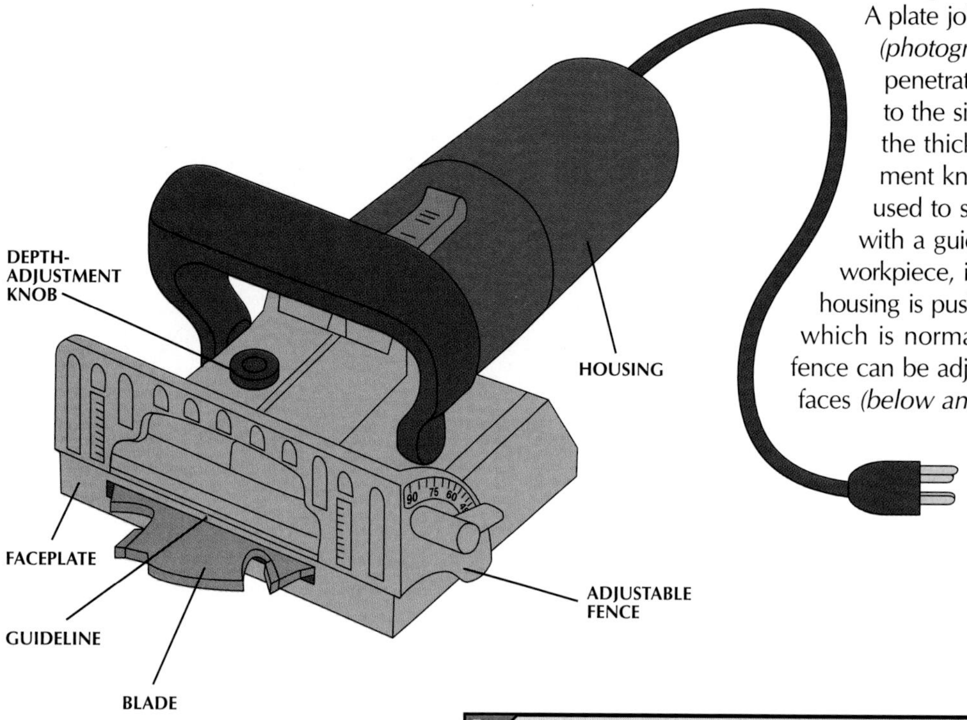

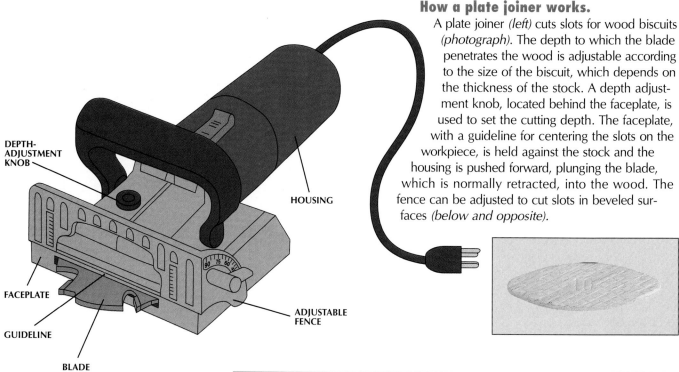

How a plate joiner works.

A plate joiner *(left)* cuts slots for wood biscuits *(photograph)*. The depth to which the blade penetrates the wood is adjustable according to the size of the biscuit, which depends on the thickness of the stock. A depth adjustment knob, located behind the faceplate, is used to set the cutting depth. The faceplate, with a guideline for centering the slots on the workpiece, is held against the stock and the housing is pushed forward, plunging the blade, which is normally retracted, into the wood. The fence can be adjusted to cut slots in beveled surfaces *(below and opposite)*.

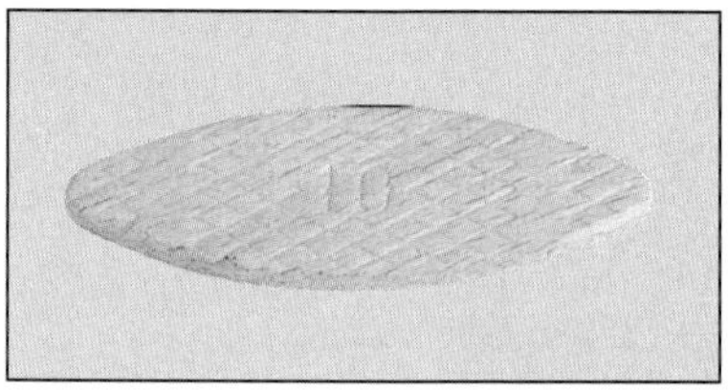

1. Setting up the fence angle.

◆ On a worktable, stack two panels whose edges will be joined by biscuits inside-face up, and mark slot locations at the mating edges on both pieces; locate the marks 2 inches from each end and every 4 to 8 inches in between. Label the edges with reference letters to help you assemble the carcass later.

◆ Mark slot locations and reference letters on the other three corners of the carcass in the same way.

◆ Protecting the surface with wood pads, clamp a panel to the table and, holding the faceplate of a plate joiner against the panel's edge, loosen the fence locking lever, tilt the fence against the top face of the panel, and lock the lever *(right)*.

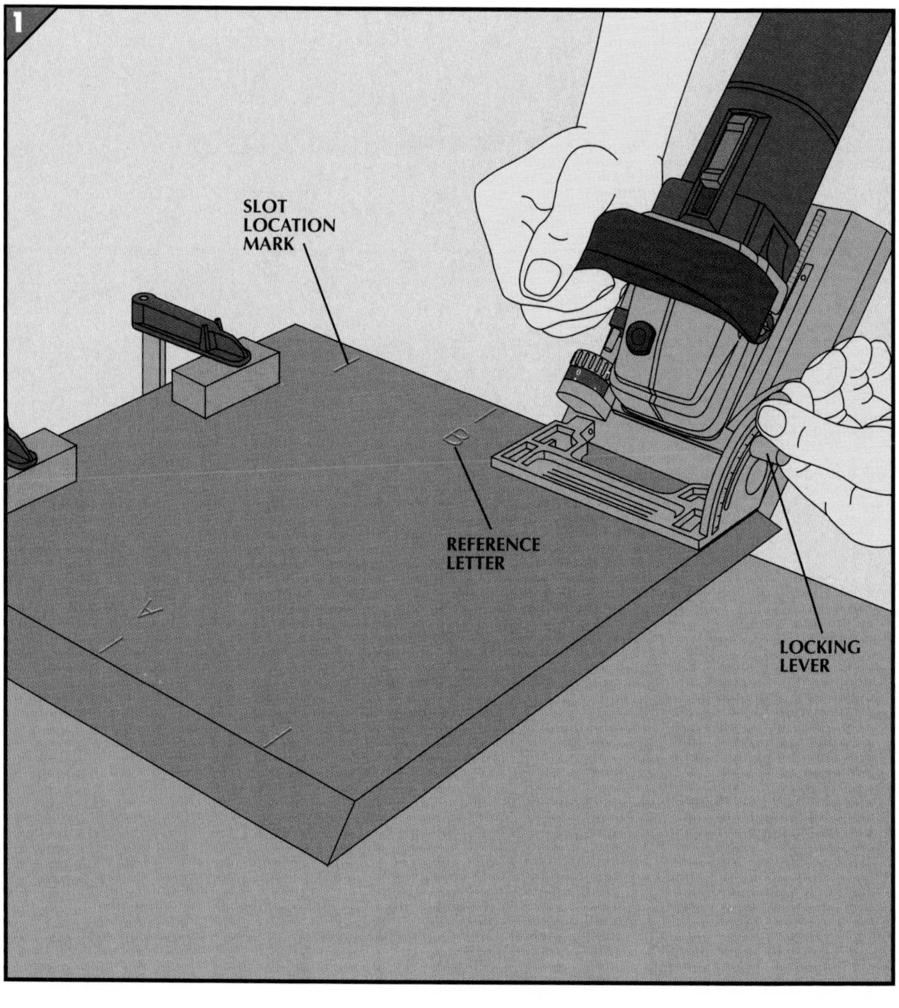

2. Cutting the slots.

◆ Holding the plate joiner firmly against the stock, align the guideline on the faceplate with a slot location mark.

◆ Switch on the tool and push on the housing, plunging the blade into the edge of the panel *(right)*.

◆ Cut the remaining slots on this and the other panels in the same way.

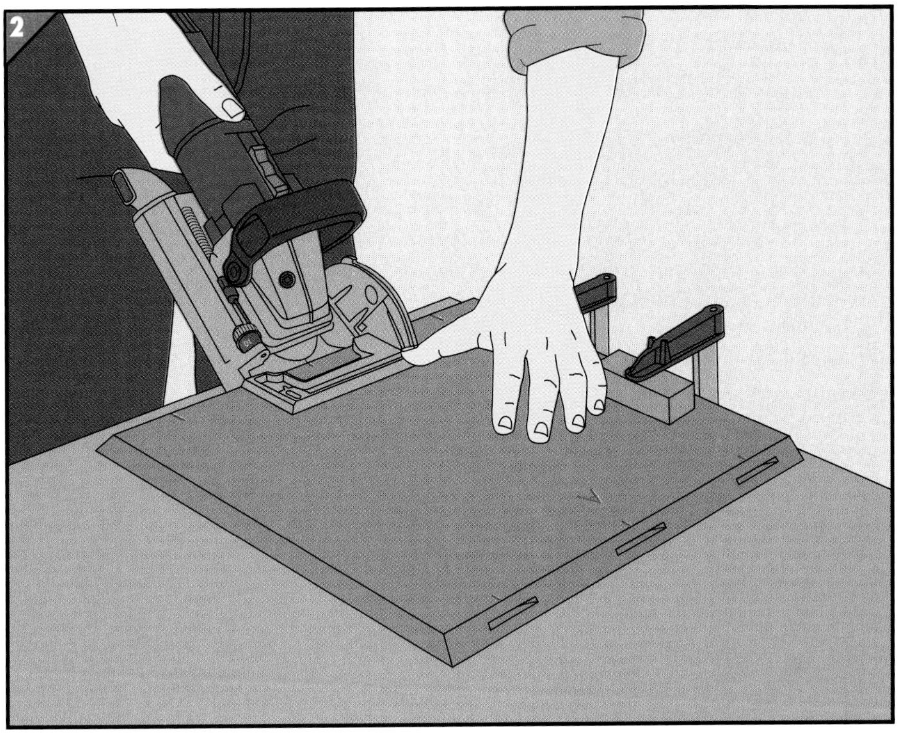

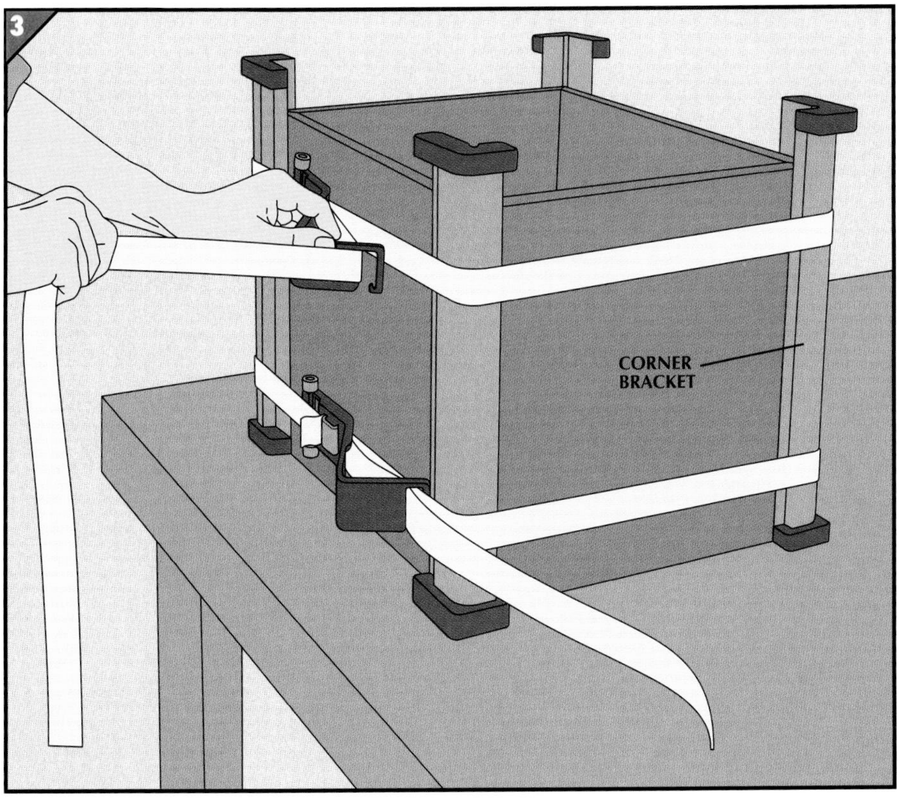

3. Gluing up the carcass.

◆ Set the panels on the table inside face up.

◆ Squeeze wood glue into the slots and along the edges of the panels, inserting biscuits as you go. Assemble the carcass quickly, before the biscuits swell.

◆ To secure the carcass with band clamps, first fit special corner brackets around each corner, then tighten the bands around the carcass, one near the top and one near the bottom *(above)*.

THE COMPACT BISCUIT JOINER

The smallest biscuit slot that a standard plate joiner can cut is $1\frac{13}{16}$ inches wide. If you plan to join narrow stock, such as a small picture frame, the tool will be awkward, if not impossible, to use. The solution is to work with a detail plate joiner *(below)*; it operates like its larger cousin, but can cut slots as narrow as $\frac{5}{8}$ inch.

Clamping Work of Varied Shapes and Sizes

While clamps will not make poorly cut joints fit together properly, well-cut ones owe much of their strength and holding power to clamping pressure. Correctly applied, clamps allow the glue to spread on contacting surfaces to penetrate the wood fibers.

Basic Techniques: For any clamping setup, first assemble the joint without glue to test and adjust the fit. Then, once the glue is added, install the clamps so they apply even pressure all along the joint. Raw force in selected spots is ineffective—it may even shift pieces out of alignment.

Gluing Edging and Panels: When gluing wood edging to a panel, you need to apply even pressure along the entire length of the edge. Rather than installing a bank of clamps arranged side by side, you can secure the edging with a curved caul held in place by only a couple of bar clamps *(opposite, top)*. When installing several clamps in a line, snug up the center clamp first, then work toward the ends. Tighten the clamps until a thin bead of glue begins to squeeze out of the joint. For panels glued up from individual boards, or for square-cut frames, shop-made jigs *(opposite, bottom)* provide an inexpensive and effective alternative to commercial bar clamps.

Dealing with Miters: Frames and carcasses with mitered corners can be tricky to clamp. The jigs on pages 70 and 71 enable you to apply even pressure on all four corners without pushing the assembly out of square.

TOOLS
- Handsaw
- Circular saw
- Band saw
- Table saw
- Dado head
- Screwdriver
- C-clamps
- Bar clamps
- Hand-screw clamps
- Electric drill
- Hole saw

MATERIALS
- Hardwood lumber
- Scrap wood
- Plywood ($\frac{3}{4}$")
- Wood screws
- Machine bolts ($\frac{5}{16}$" x 2"), washers, and wing nuts
- Cord
- Dowel
- Rope ($\frac{3}{8}$")

SAFETY TIPS

Goggles will prevent injury to your eyes when you are using a power tool.

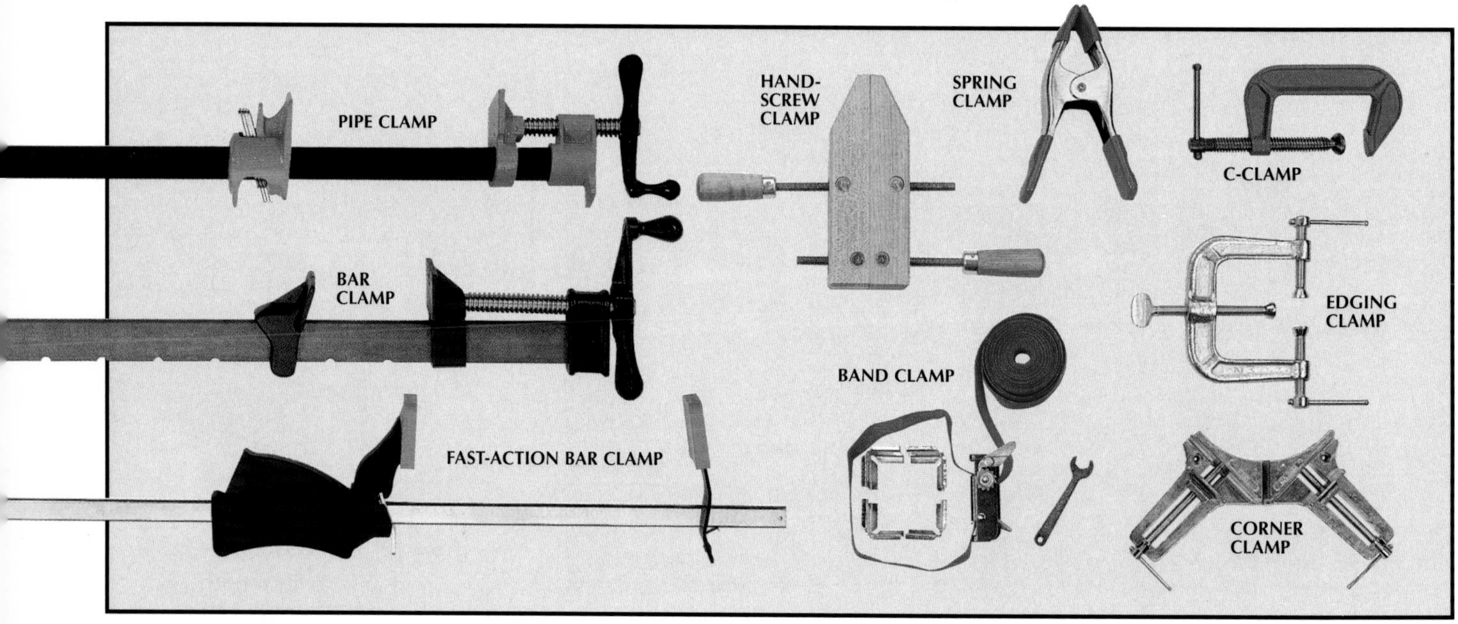

A catalog of clamps.
A wide range of commercial clamps is available to fulfill a variety of applications. Pipe and bar clamps can span large assemblies such as panels and frames. Consisting of two fittings that slip over ordinary steel plumbing pipe, pipe clamps are cheap and versatile, but bar clamps are easier to handle. Fast-action bar clamps come in different lengths and can be set up quickly. The wooden jaws of a hand-screw clamp can be adjusted to fit nonparallel surfaces. A band clamp, with its long flexible tape, can be wrapped around a carcass or a set of chair legs. Quick and easy to use, the spring clamp is ideal for securing thin, delicate pieces of wood, but C-clamps apply much greater pressure for all-purpose use. The E-shaped edging clamp holds trim against panels. Designed to secure two boards at a 90-degree angle to each other, corner clamps are ideal for holding frame corners.

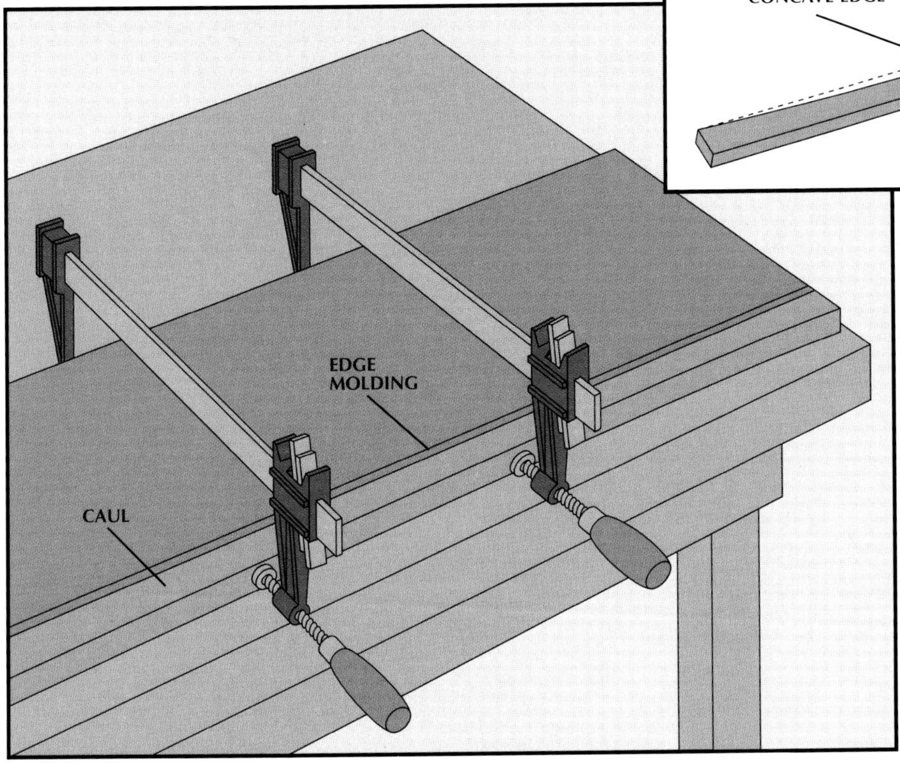

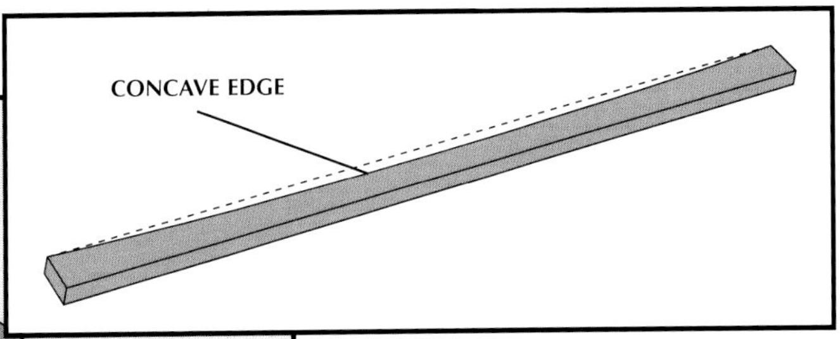

Securing edging with a caul.

◆ Make an edging caul from a hardwood board the same thickness as the panel, cut 2 inches wide and as long as the panel. Mark a gentle arc on the face so the curve is $\frac{1}{4}$ inch deeper at its midpoint than at the ends, and cut the curve on a band saw to obtain the shape shown in the inset.

◆ Place the concave edge of the caul against the edging and apply a bar clamp about 6 inches to each side of the caul's midpoint. If the caul is shorter than 2 feet, apply only one clamp. Pressing in the concave center will distribute even clamping pressure out to the ends.

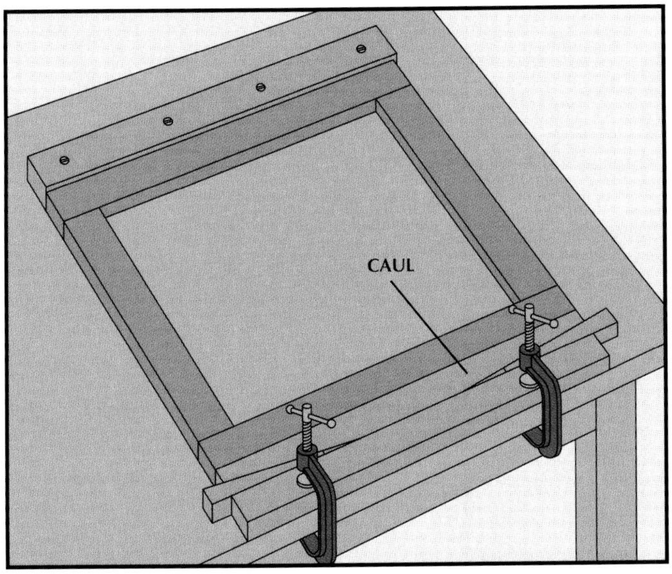

Wedging a square-cut frame.

◆ Cut three hardwood strips the same length as the frame, as well as two wedges that narrow from $\frac{3}{4}$ inch at the wide end to $\frac{1}{4}$ inch at the other.

◆ Screw one of the strips to a work surface, far enough from the near edge to accommodate the frame and the other two strips of wood.

◆ Taper the ends of the second strip to make a caul.

◆ Butt the caul against the frame, clamp the third wood strip against the caul, then drive a wedge between the caul and the strip at each end, pressing the frame together *(above)*.

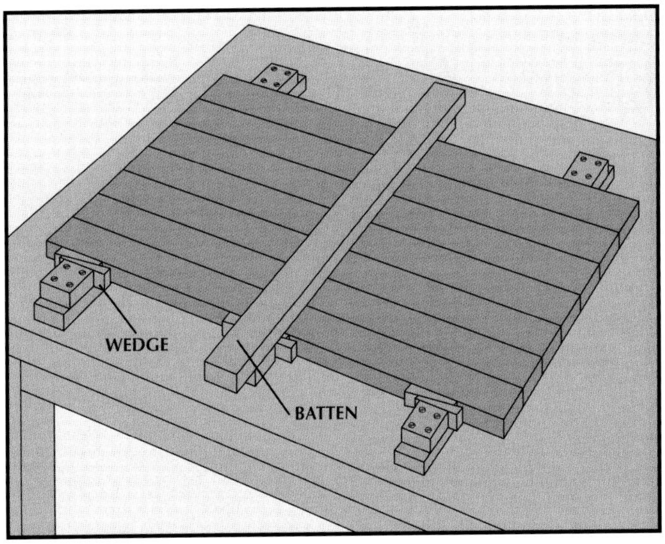

Clamping a panel.

◆ From hardwood make three battens—more, in multiples of two, if the panel exceeds 3 feet in length—by screwing a square block to each end of a wood strip; space the blocks to accept the width of the panel—plus 1 inch.

◆ Lay two battens on a worktable and place the panel boards on them, applying glue as described on page 32. Drive two wedges *(above)* between the outside boards and each block to press the pieces together.

◆ Install a third batten across the top, centered between the others.

JIGS FOR MITERED FRAMES

Pulling corners together.

◆ To make a jig, cut arms and square corner blocks from hardwood stock that is $\frac{3}{4}$ inch thick and 2 inches wide.
◆ Drill a centered row of holes for $\frac{5}{16}$-inch machine bolts through each arm at 1-inch intervals.
◆ For the corner blocks, first drill two holes through each block, one near a corner for a bolt and one in the center; then, cut each block into an L shape, sawing through the center hole.
◆ Connect each pair of arms in a V shape with hardwood connectors, bolts, washers, and wing nuts *(inset).*
◆ To use the jig, set it on a worktable and fasten the corner blocks to the arms so the corners of the frame will sit in them snugly with the connector strips about 1 inch apart. Then, with a hand-screw clamp, pull the strips toward each other, tightening the clamp until all the corner joints on the frame are closed *(right).*

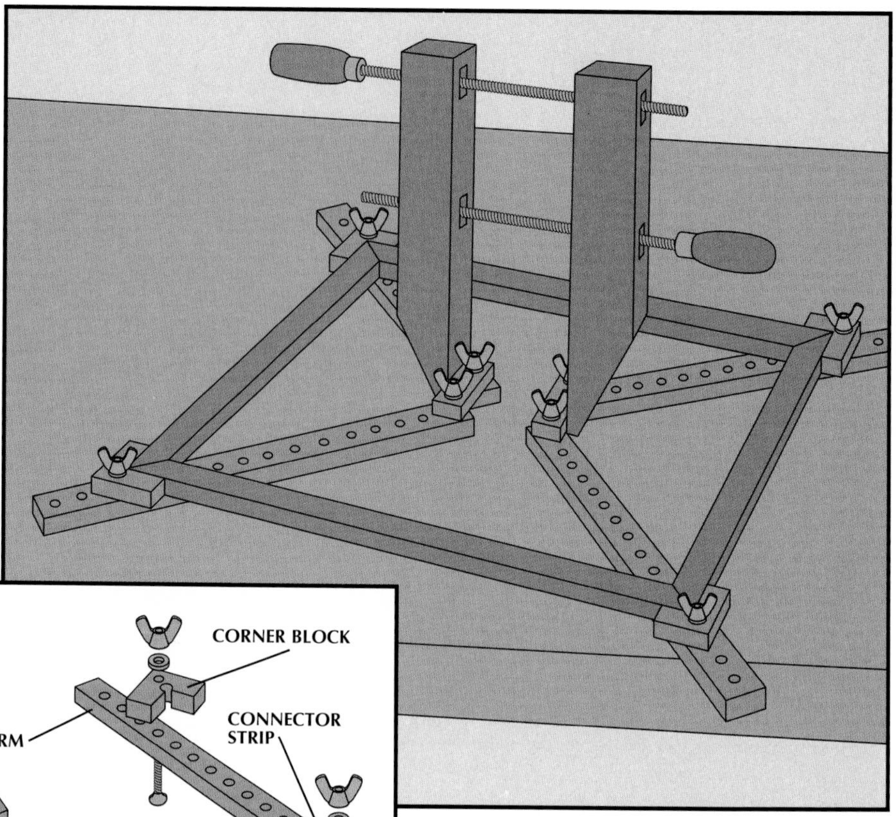

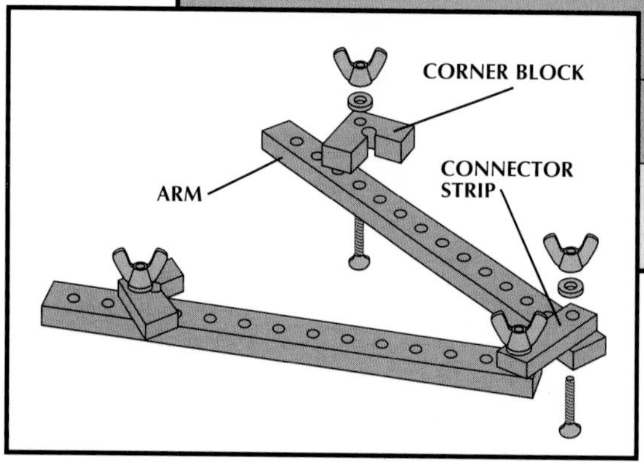

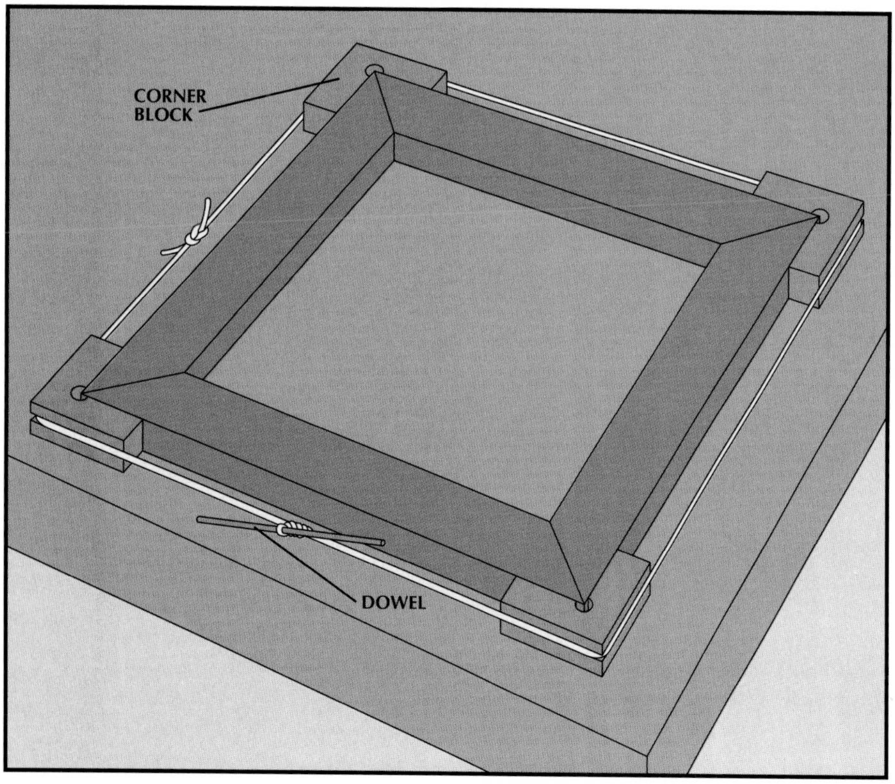

Using a Spanish windlass.

◆ Cut four corner blocks as you would for the jig described above, but drill only one hole in the center, and cut a shallow groove around the outside edges.
◆ To use the jig, lay the frame on a worktable, fit a block at each corner, and tie a length of cord around the assembly, leaving some slack.
◆ Twist the cord tight with a dowel, then fix the dowel in place by bracing it between the frame and the table top *(left).*

AIDS FOR GLUING UP CARCASSES

Gluing up small carcasses.
The technique shown at right uses $\frac{3}{8}$-inch rope with two C-clamps and scrap wood to fashion a shop-made web clamp.

◆ Cut two lengths of rope that, when knotted, are slightly shorter than the perimeter of the carcass.

◆ Cut two wood blocks slightly longer than the width of the carcass sides and drill two $\frac{3}{8}$-inch holes through each one.

◆ Protecting the corners of the carcass with cardboard pads, wrap the ropes around it and knot them to the blocks so the blocks are parallel and about 2 inches apart.

◆ With two C-clamps, pull the blocks together to tighten the ropes.

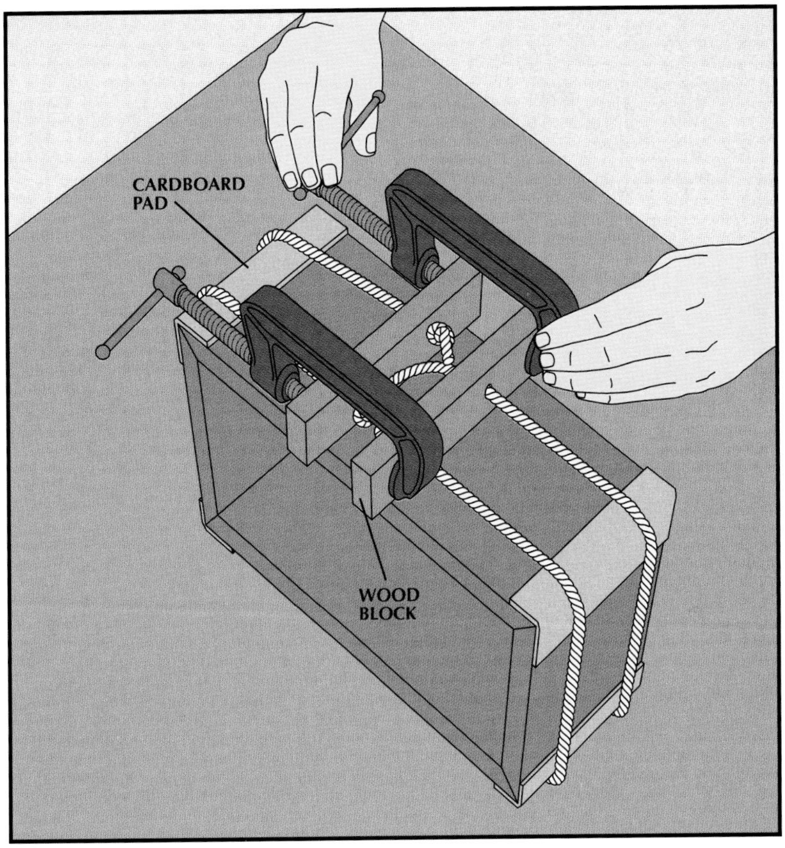

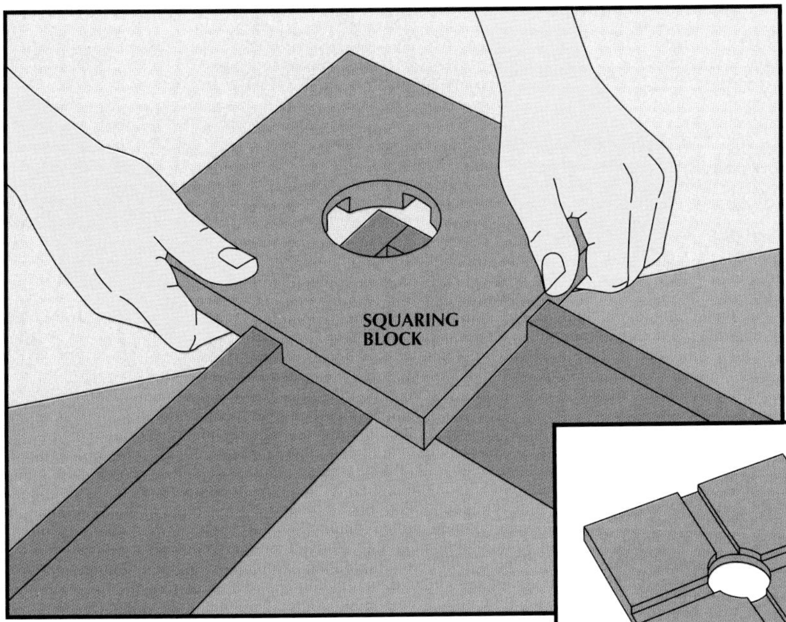

Keeping a carcass square during glue-up.

◆ Make a squaring block for each corner of the carcass: Cut $\frac{3}{4}$-inch plywood into 8-inch squares and, with a hole saw, drill a 2-inch hole through the center of the blocks. Install a dado head the same width as the carcass stock in a table saw, set the cutting height at $\frac{3}{8}$ inch, and make two cuts that intersect at the center of the blocks as shown in the inset.

◆ Assemble the carcass with glue and fit a block over each corner *(left)*.

◆ Clamp the corner joints closed.

3 Shaping by Hand and Machine

Many woodworking projects require a combination of power and hand tools to achieve the desired shapes. With machines such as the band saw, lathe, and belt-disk sander, you can cut, turn, and smooth wood into curves and cylinders. For shaping fine details, hand tools are needed, including spokeshaves, drawknives, rasps, and rifflers.

Scraping a blank on a lathe →

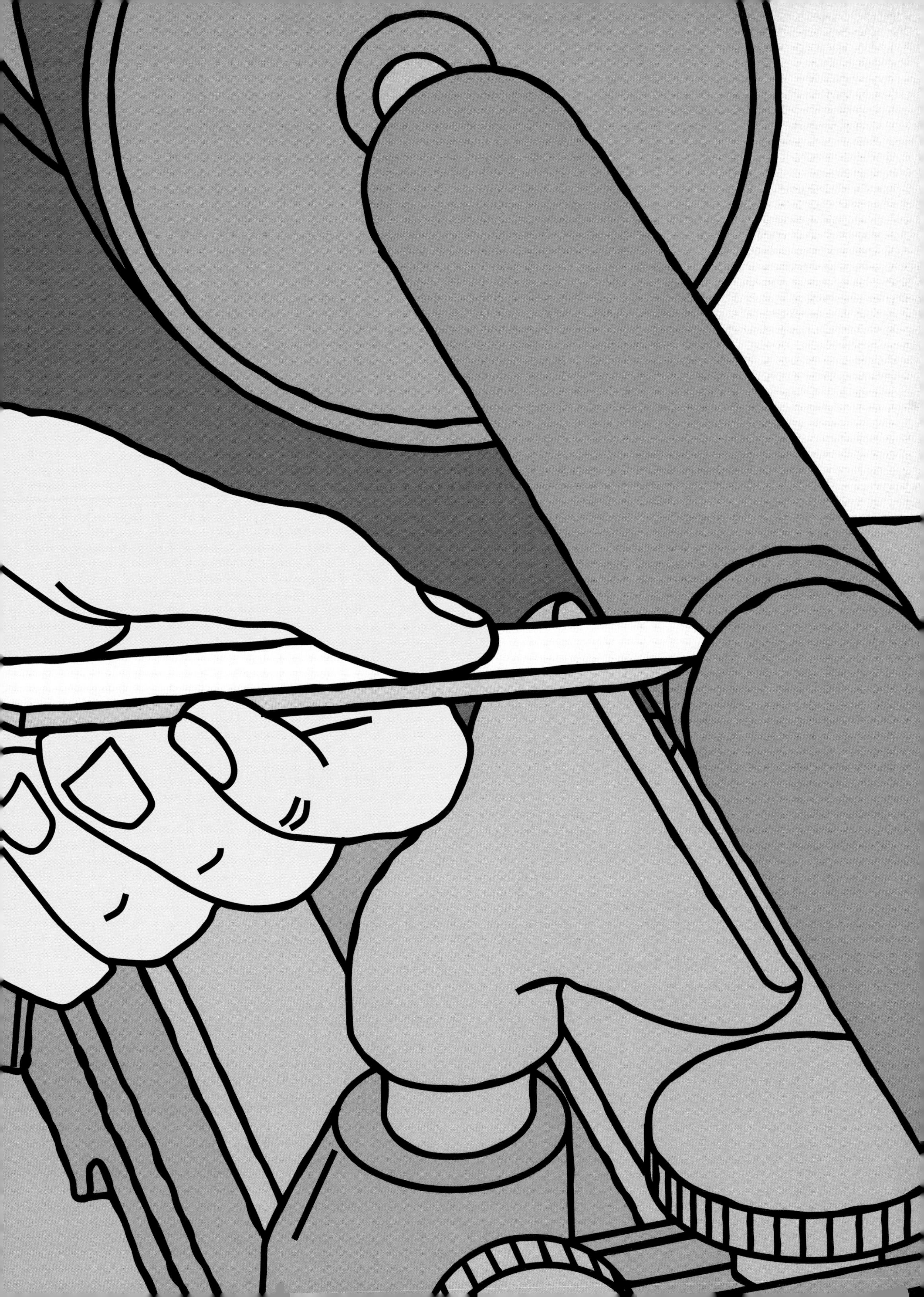

Sawing Curves

Shaping a rough curve with a hand tool, even one designed expressly for the purpose, is tedious work at best. Much quicker alternatives are the two power saws shown here and on the following pages.

The Band Saw: The most versatile blade for a band saw is $\frac{1}{4}$ inch wide. It will cut a curve with a radius as small as $\frac{5}{8}$ inch in wood up to $1\frac{1}{2}$ inches thick. Narrower blades can cut tighter corners, but only in thinner wood; wider blades will cut thicker wood, but as the width increases, the ability to negotiate curves decreases. The saw can make simple cuts *(below and pages 75-77)* or compound curves *(pages 80-82)* and, with the addition of a shop-made jig, large circles *(pages 77-80)*.

On home-shop saws, the distance between the blade and the saw's arm is only 10 to 14 inches, so the wood that can pass through it is limited to this width. In some instances, you may be able to cut wider stock by stopping in the middle of a cut, turning off the saw, backing out of the cut, and then beginning again in another direction.

The Scroll Saw: This smaller cousin to the band saw can be fitted with a variety of delicate blades to make fine cuts. Unlike a band saw, however, the end of the blade can be detached, making it ideal for cutting sections inside a pattern where no waste area leads to the cut *(page 83)*.

CAUTION *When cutting with a band or scroll saw, observe the safety precautions on page 18.*

TOOLS

- Band saw
- Compass
- Electric drill
- Countersink bit
- Screwdriver
- Carpenter's square
- C-clamps
- Center punch
- Mallet
- Try square
- Straightedge
- French curve
- Bar clamp
- Spokeshave
- Rasp
- Scroll saw
- Hex wrench

MATERIALS

- 2 x 4s
- Plywood ($\frac{1}{2}$")
- Wood screws (1" No. 6, 2" No. 8)
- Double-sided tape
- Cardboard
- Sandpaper (range of grades)

SAFETY TIPS

Goggles protect your eyes when operating a power tool.

SIMPLE CUTS ON A BAND SAW

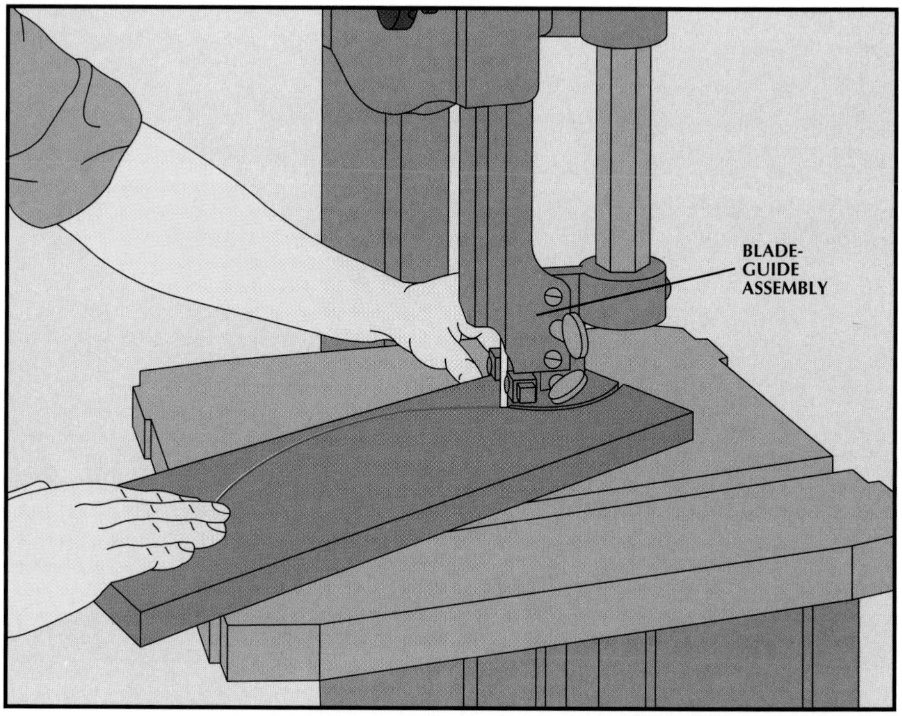

Cutting a curve.

- Mark the curve and place the board on the saw table.
- Adjust the blade guide to clear the wood *(page 19)*, and turn on the saw.
- Guiding the board with your left hand, push it forward, steering it with your right so the blade cuts just to the waste side of the cutting line *(right)*. Feed the board at a moderate rate—too slowly may burn the wood; too quickly may stall the blade or produce an inaccurate cut.

Cutting parallel curves.

◆ Mark one edge of the curve on the board, then set and lock the legs of a carpenter's compass to the planned width of the piece.

◆ Move the point along the first mark so the pencil leaves a line on the face, keeping both points equidistant from the ends at all times *(right)*.

◆ Saw the curves along the marked cutting lines *(opposite, bottom)*.

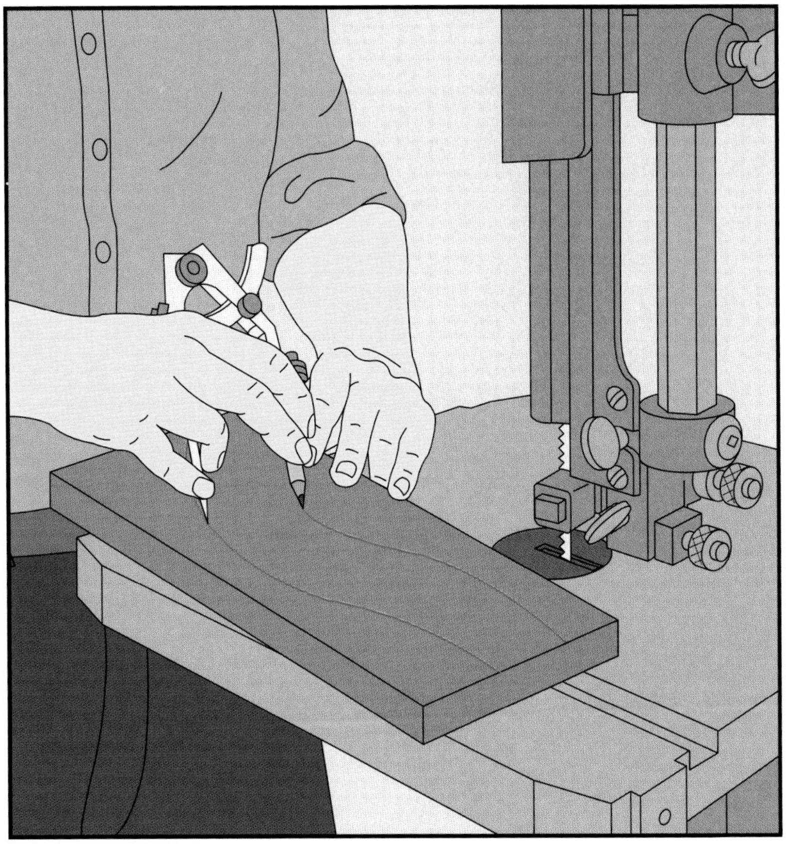

STACKING BOARDS FOR IDENTICAL SHAPES

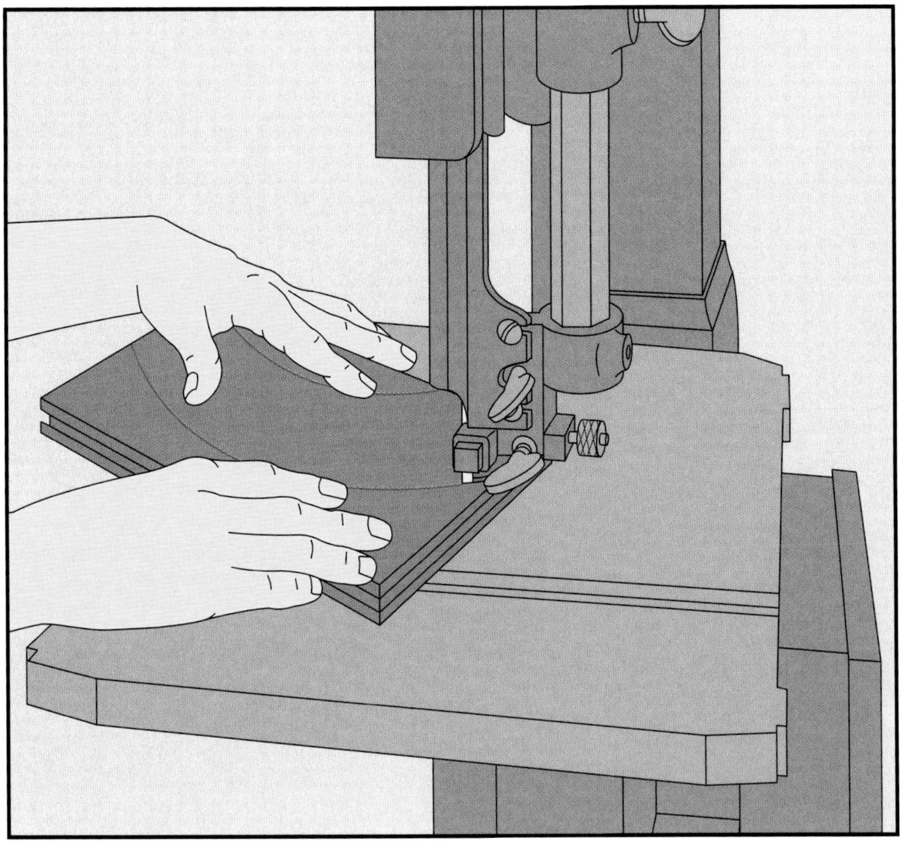

Sawing several pieces at once.

◆ Mark the cutting lines on one of the pieces, then stack the remaining boards under it, forming a pile no higher than 6 inches.

◆ Secure the boards together with strips of double-sided tape.

◆ Saw through the stack as you would a single board *(left)*.

FORMING SCROLLWORK AND CIRCLES

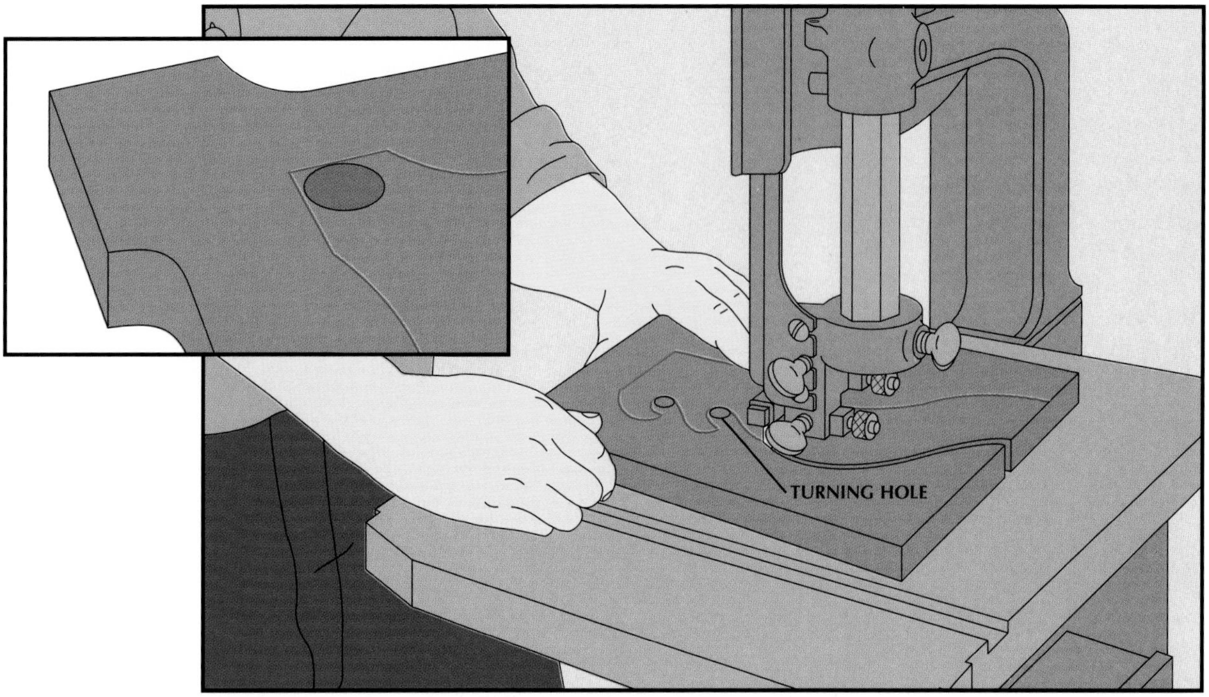

Turning holes for tight inside corners.
◆ With an electric drill or a drill press, cut a hole slightly larger than the band-saw blade's width at each tight curve along the cutting line, locating each hole so a portion of its circumference touches the line.
◆ Cut the curve *(page 74)*, letting the blade enter the first turning hole, then pivot the stock on the saw table and continue to the end of the cutting line *(above)*.

To cut a 90-degree corner, first drill a turning hole in the corner as shown in the inset. Then, cut into the circle and pivot the board as necessary to make a series of cuts squaring off the corner.

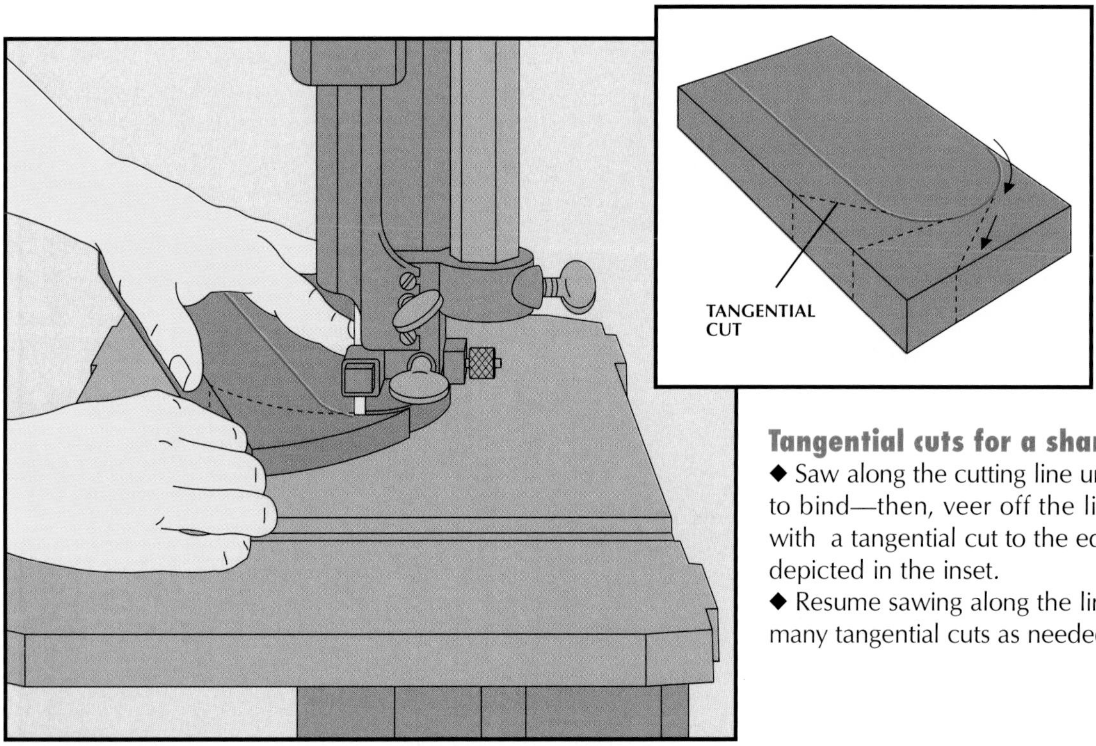

Tangential cuts for a sharp outside curve.
◆ Saw along the cutting line until the blade begins to bind—then, veer off the line into the waste with a tangential cut to the edge of the board as depicted in the inset.
◆ Resume sawing along the line *(left)*, making as many tangential cuts as needed to clear the curve.

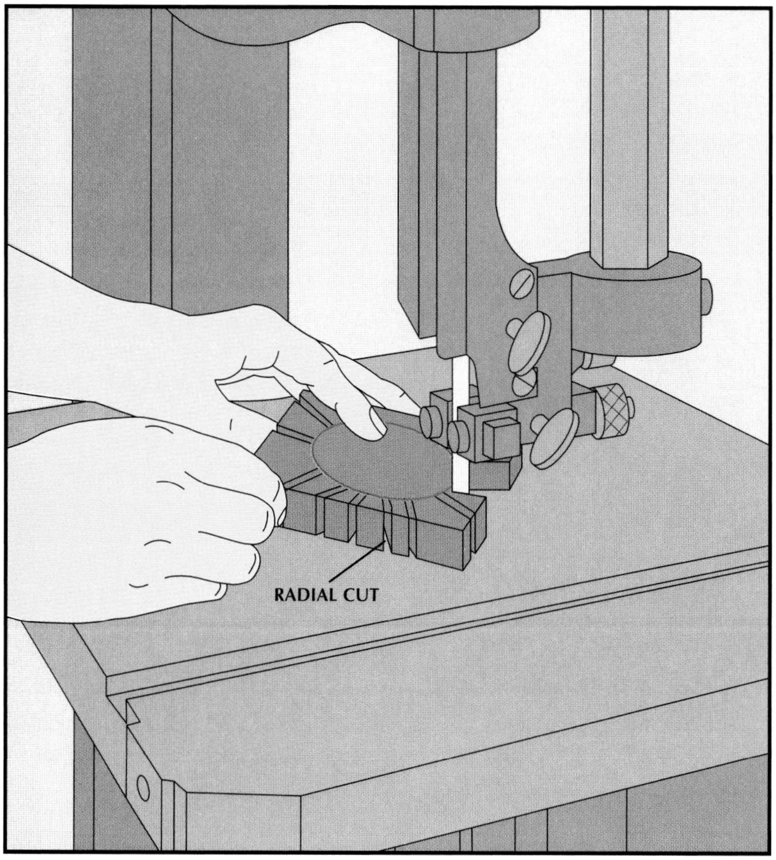

Radial cuts for tight interior curves. To ease the saw blade around a tight, continuous curve, first make a series of radial cuts, spaced 1 inch apart, from the edges of the board through the waste to the rim of the curve. As you saw along the cutting line *(left)*, pieces of waste will be detached from the stock as you reach the radial cuts.

A CIRCLE-CUTTING JIG

1. Making an auxiliary saw table.

◆ Cut two 2-by-4s equal to the length of the saw table plus the radius of the planned circle.

◆ Tilt the table so the edge nearest the throat is up. Fasten the 2-by-4s to the table's sides so the top edge of each board is flush with the table top and one end is flush with the edge of the table nearest the saw's throat, driving screws through the predrilled holes in the table.

◆ From $\frac{1}{2}$-inch plywood, cut a rectangle 2 inches wider than the distance between the outsides of the 2-by-4s and 12 inches longer than the radius of the planned circle.

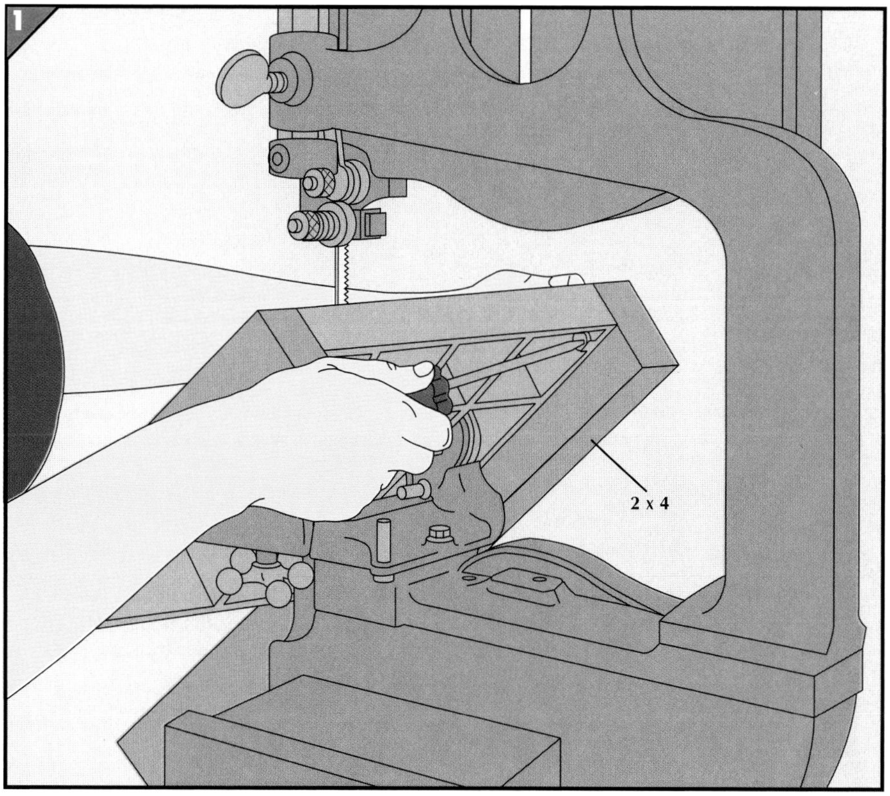

2. Sizing the table.

◆ Place the plywood piece on the saw table so about 6 inches of the rectangle is to the left of the blade.

◆ Turn on the saw and cut a slot into the plywood until the leading edge projects beyond the 2-by-4 on the table's back edge by 1 inch *(right)*.

◆ Stop the saw and clamp the plywood in place.

◆ Drill two countersunk pilot holes for 1-inch No. 6 wood screws through the plywood into each 2-by-4.

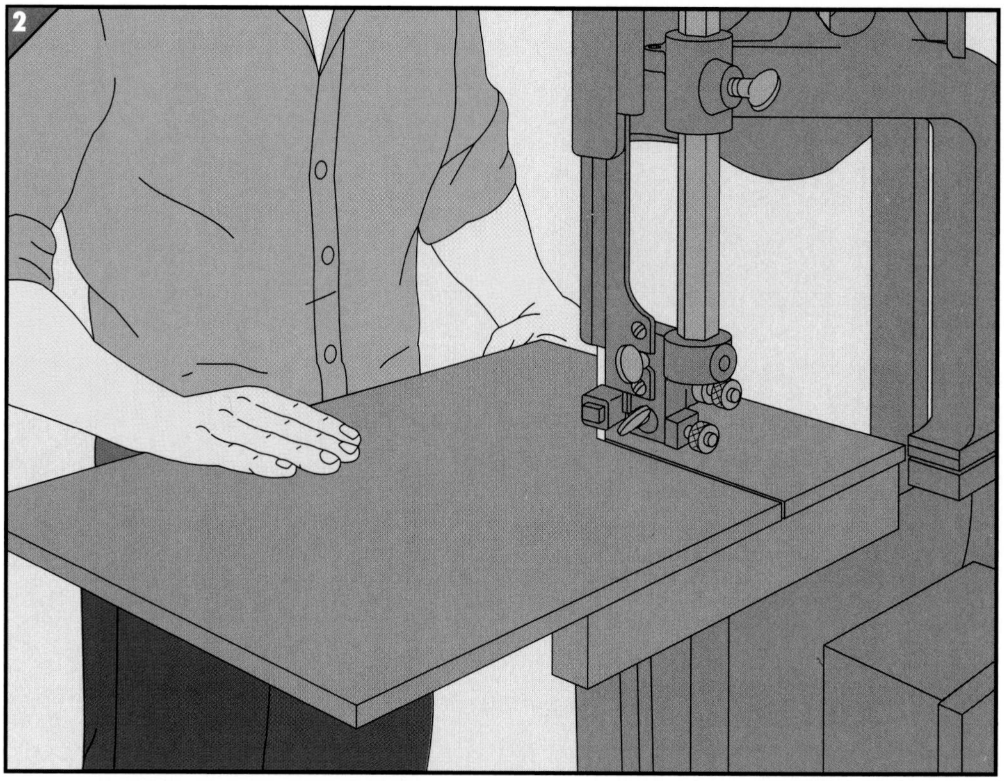

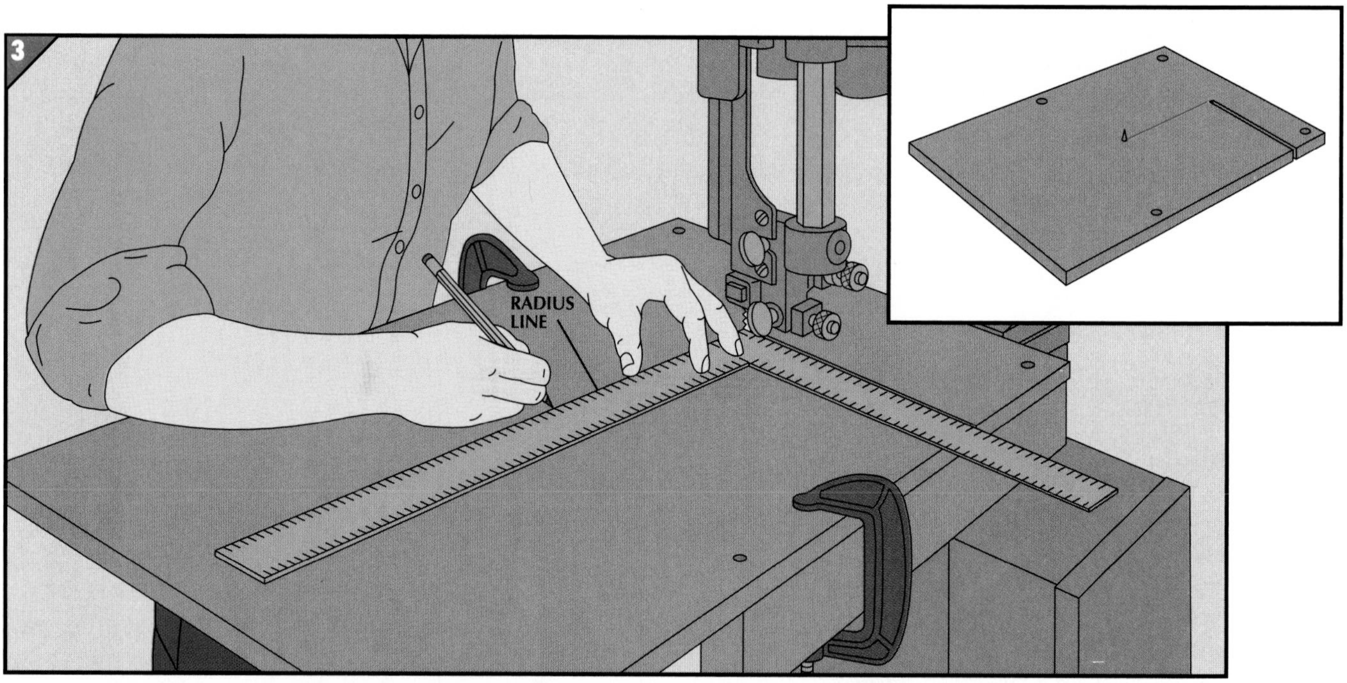

3. Readying the auxiliary table for circle-cutting.

◆ Place a carpenter's square on the plywood with its corner just touching the blade and the short arm lined up with the slot in the plywood.

◆ Measuring along the long arm from the blade, mark a line equal in length to the radius of the planned circle *(above)*.

◆ Unclamp the plywood from the table.

◆ Drill a pilot hole through the plywood at the end of the marked line—the circle's center—for a 2-inch No. 8 screw. From the underside of the board, drive the screw into the hole so the tip protrudes by $\frac{1}{4}$ inch *(inset)*. The screw tip will anchor the workpiece and allow it to pivot as you cut the circle.

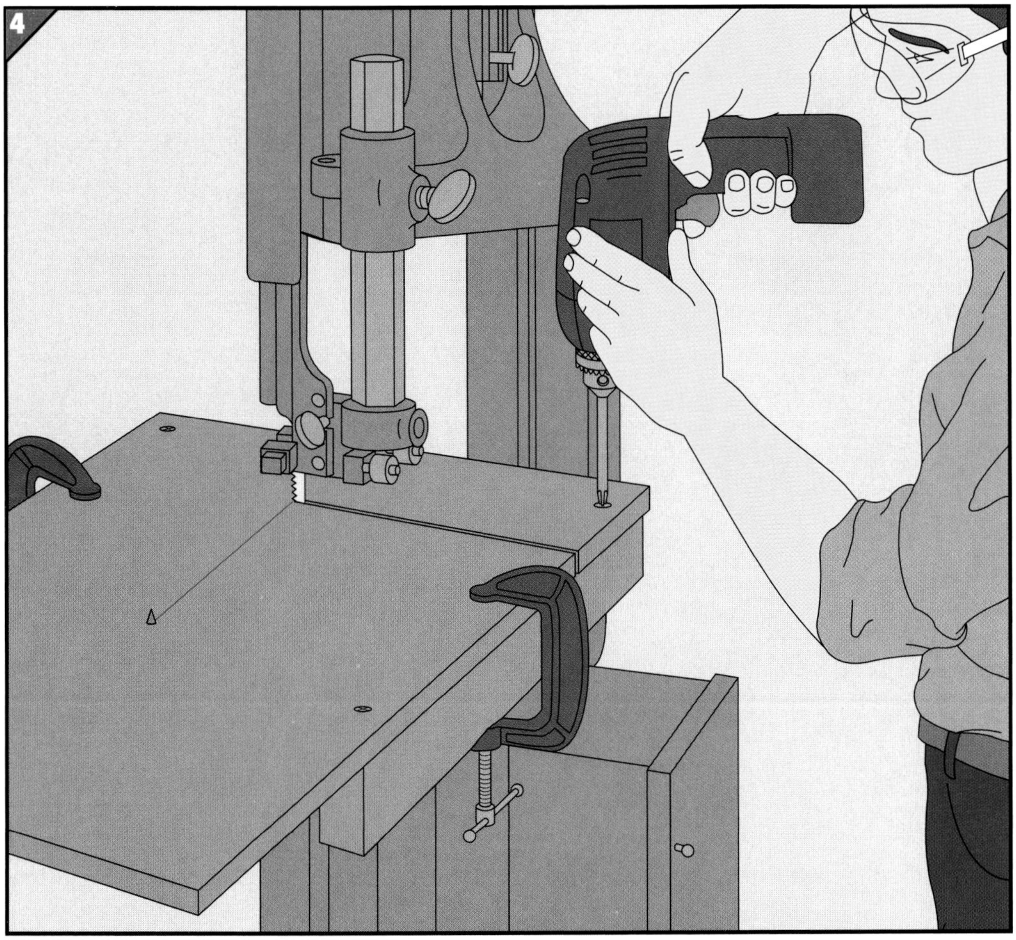

4. Fastening the auxiliary table in place.

◆ Reposition the plywood rectangle on the table as at the end of Step 2 and clamp it in place.

◆ Secure the plywood to the boards by driving in the screws *(left)*.

5. Marking the stock for cutting.

◆ Cut your circle stock into a square, then mark two corner-to-corner diagonal lines on the underside; the intersection of the lines is the center of the circle. Make a $\frac{1}{8}$-inch-deep indentation at the center with a center punch or nail set and a mallet.

◆ With a carpenter's square held against an edge of the board, mark a line from the center equal to the length of the circle's radius. Then, from the end of the radius line, mark a perpendicular line to an edge of the board *(right)*, providing the band saw with an entrance route to the circle's rim.

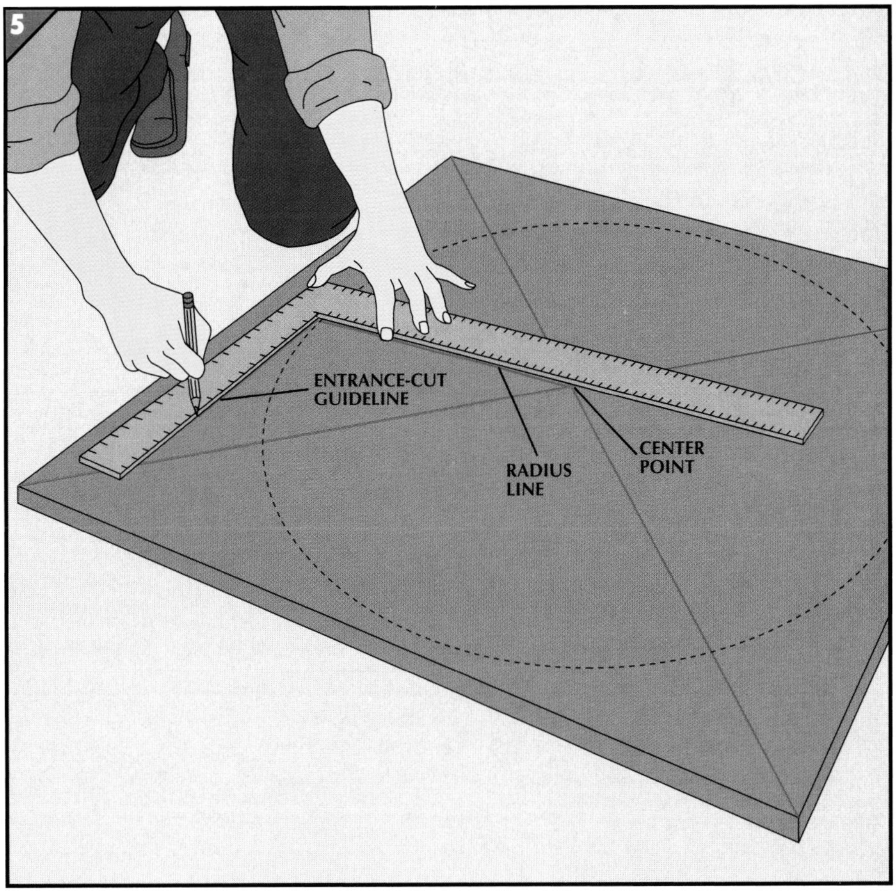

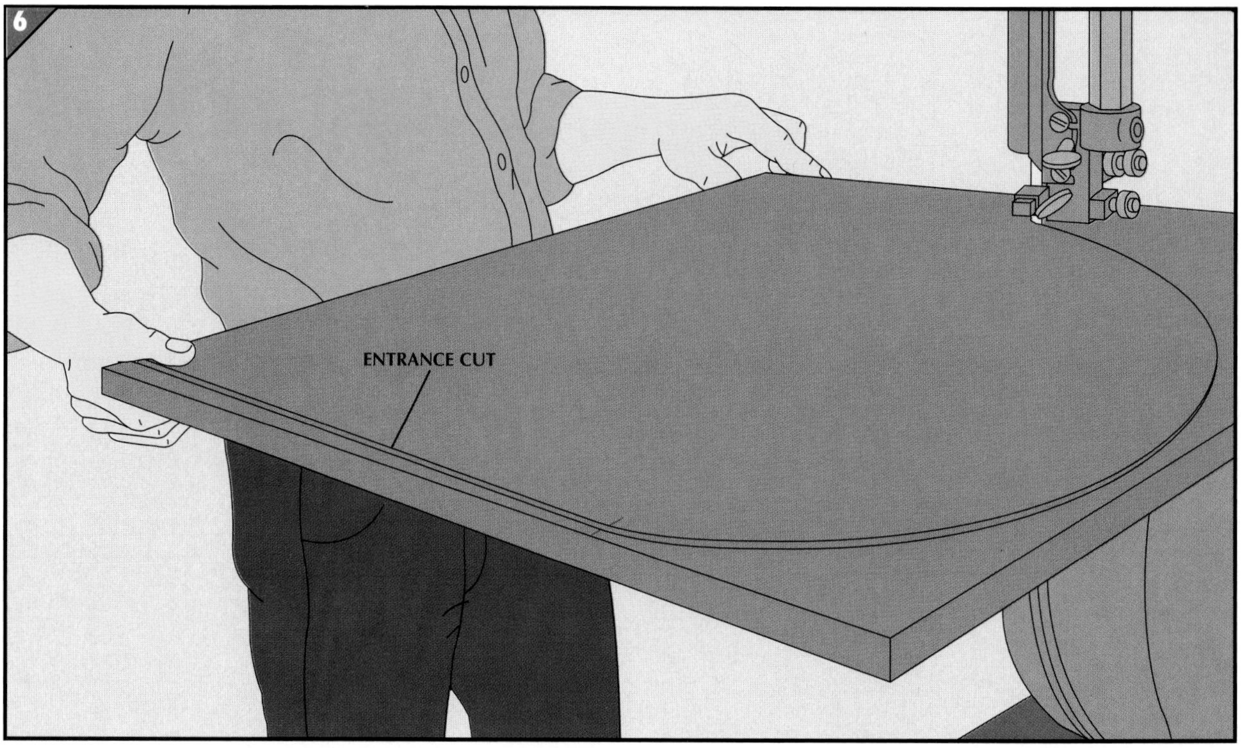

6. Cutting the disk.

◆ Retract the pivot screw at the center of the auxiliary table so its tip is below the surface. Place the stock wrong side up on the table and cut from the edge of the square along the entrance-cut line to the rim of the circle, then stop the saw and turn the board over.

◆ Reach under the table, raise the pivot screw back to $\frac{1}{4}$ inch above the surface, and position the stock so the pivot screw sits in the indentation in the table's underside. Press down on the stock so it lies flat on the table.

◆ Turn the saw on and pivot the stock into the blade, rotating the wood on the pivot screw *(above)* until the circle is cut.

BAND-SAWING A COMPOUND CURVE

1. Designing the shape.

◆ First, make a template for outlining the object—in this case a cabriole leg—on the stock by cutting a piece of cardboard to the length and width of the item.

◆ Mark the straight sections first with a square and a straightedge, then draw the curved sections with a French curve *(right)*. Cut out the template *(inset)*.

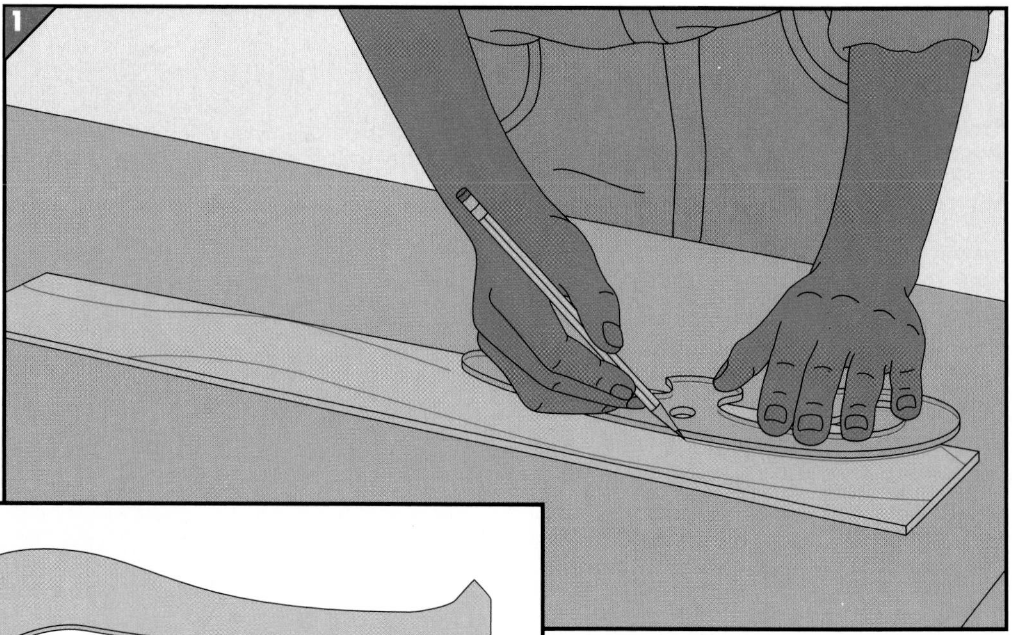

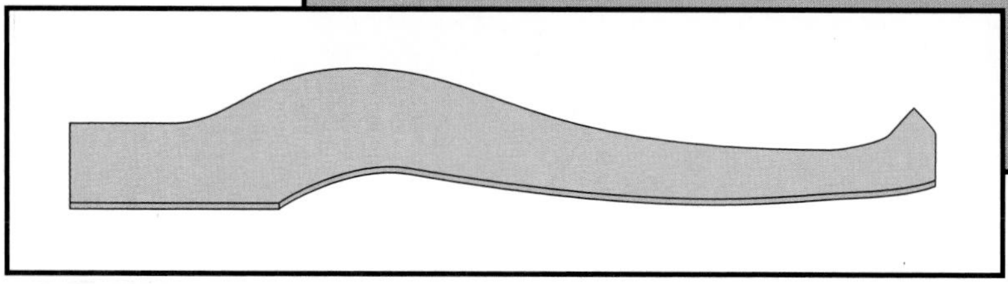

2. Marking the curves on the stock.

◆ Cut a wood block to the same length and width as the template.
◆ Trace the design on one side of the block with the top end and back edge of the template aligned with a corner of the block.
◆ Transfer the design onto an adjacent side of the block so identical parts meet at the same points along one edge of the stock *(right)*.

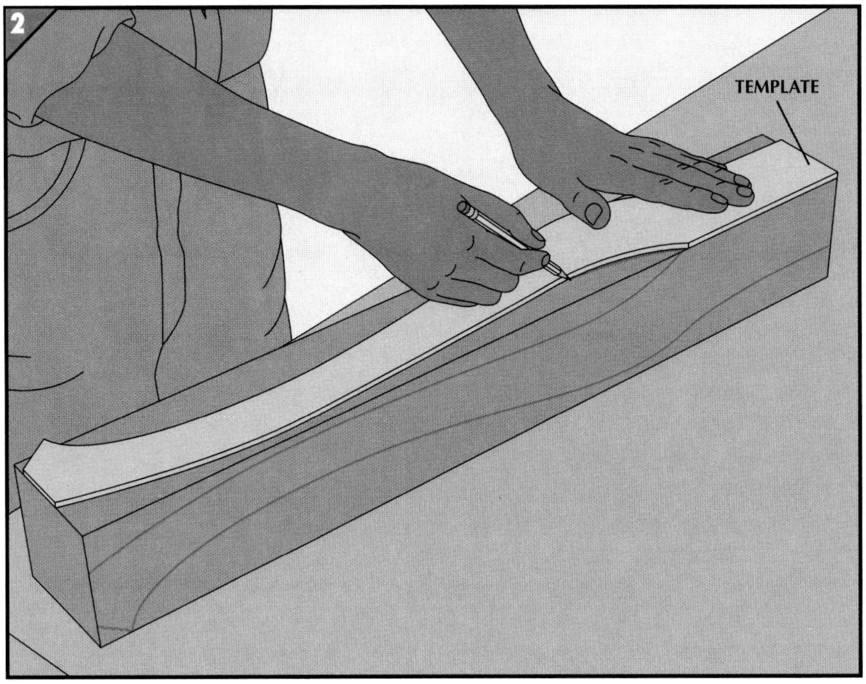

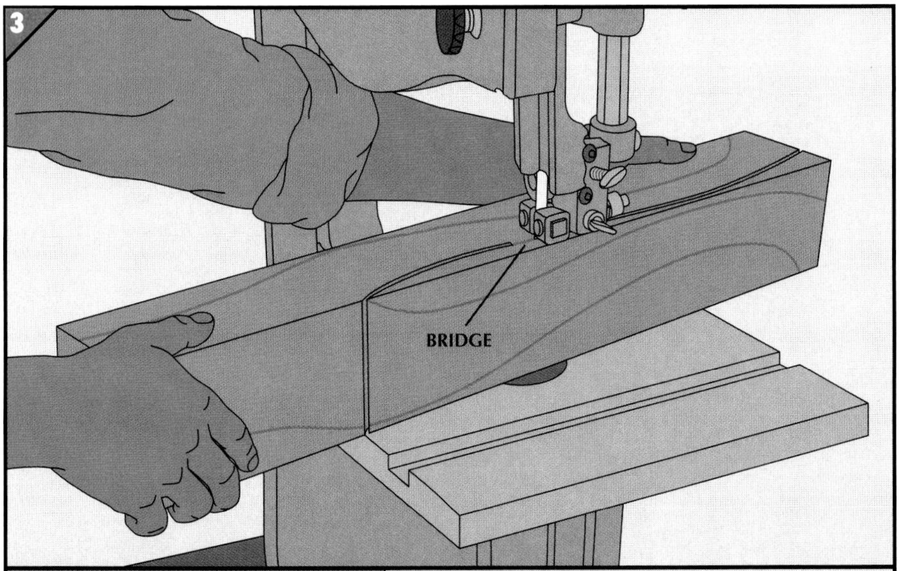

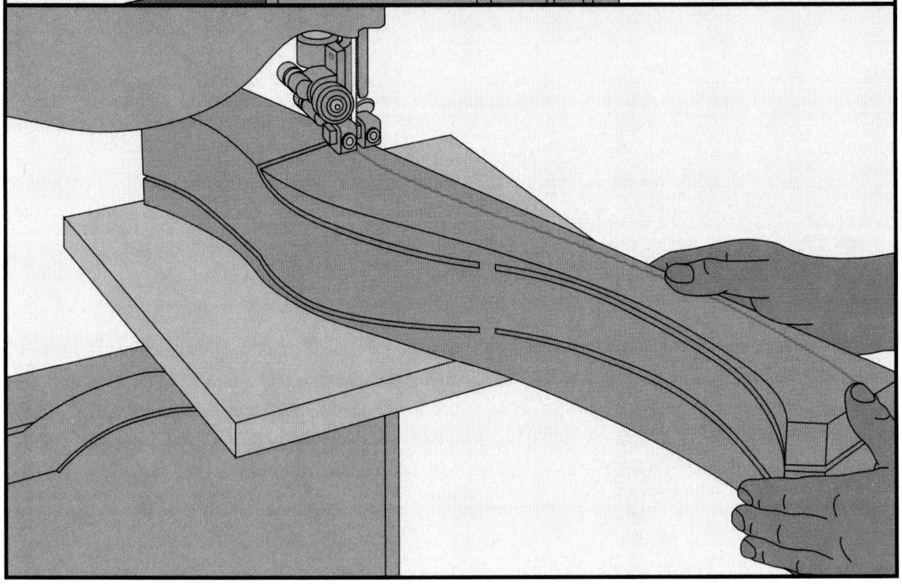

3. Sawing the outline.

◆ Set the stock on a band-saw table with one of the outlined profiles facing up. Start cutting along one of the lines, then stop and turn off the saw half-way through the cut.
◆ Turn the stock around and cut along the same line from its other end, stopping $\frac{1}{2}$ inch from the first kerf and leaving a short bridge between the two cuts *(left, top)*.
◆ Cut the other line on the same side of the block in the same way; by preventing the waste wood from detaching from the stock, the bridges keep the outline on the adjacent side intact.
◆ Reposition the block so the adjacent outline faces up and saw along the two lines on this side straight through without leaving bridges *(left, bottom)*, then turn off the saw.

4. Severing the bridges.

◆ Reposition the stock so the bridges are facing up.
◆ Slip the blade into one of the kerfs, turn on the saw, and cut through the bridge.
◆ Sever the other bridge in the same way *(right)*.

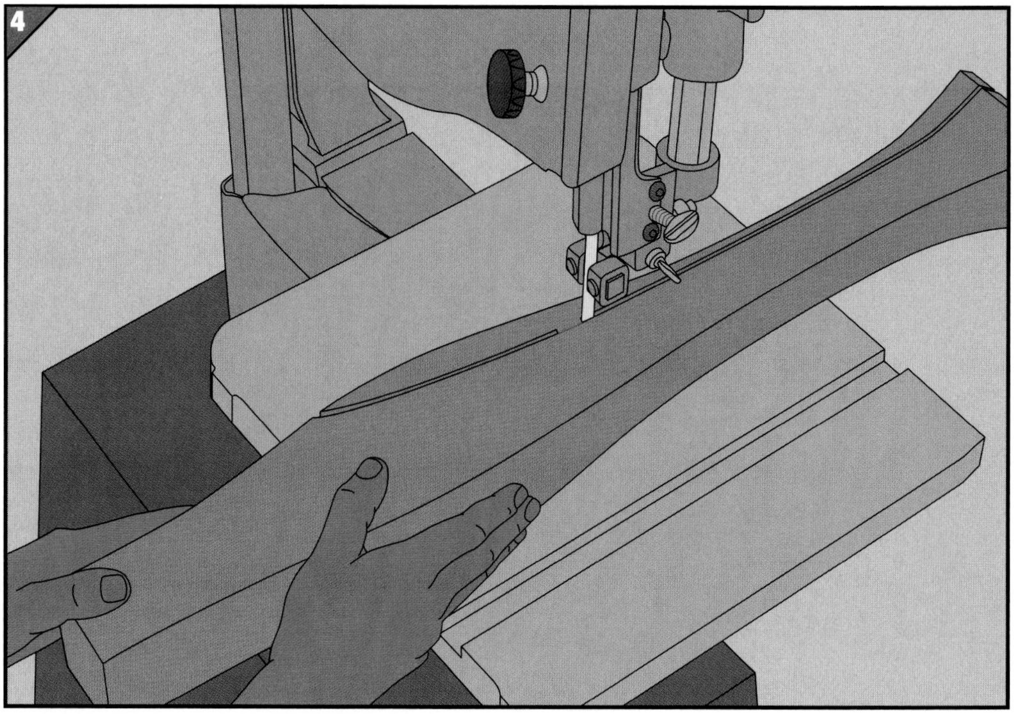

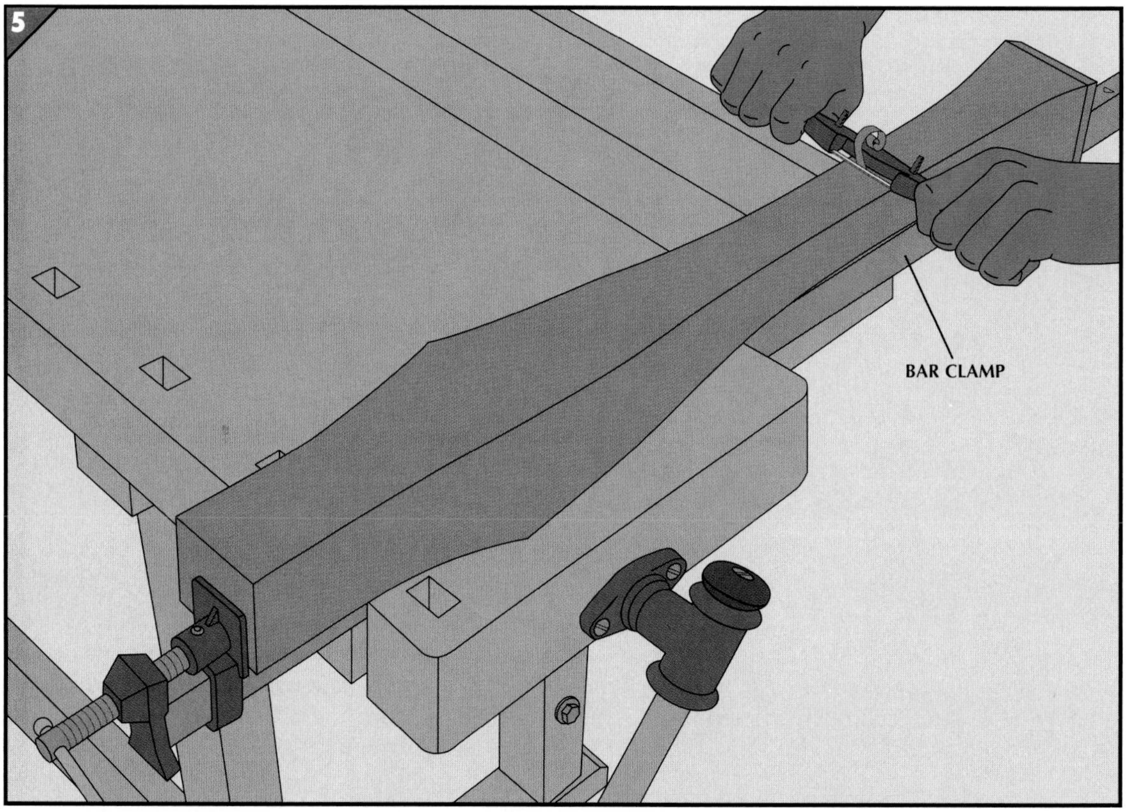

5. Smoothing the contour.

◆ Secure the piece in a bar clamp, then fix the clamp in a vise.
◆ With a spokeshave *(page 86)*, shape the surface that is facing up, pulling the tool toward you in the direction of the grain until all the band-saw marks are gone *(above)*.
◆ Reposition the workpiece in the clamp and smooth the other surfaces in the same way.
◆ Shape any areas the spokeshave cannot reach with rasps or rifflers *(pages 88-89)*.
◆ Finish the job with sandpaper, using progressively finer grits until the surface is smooth.

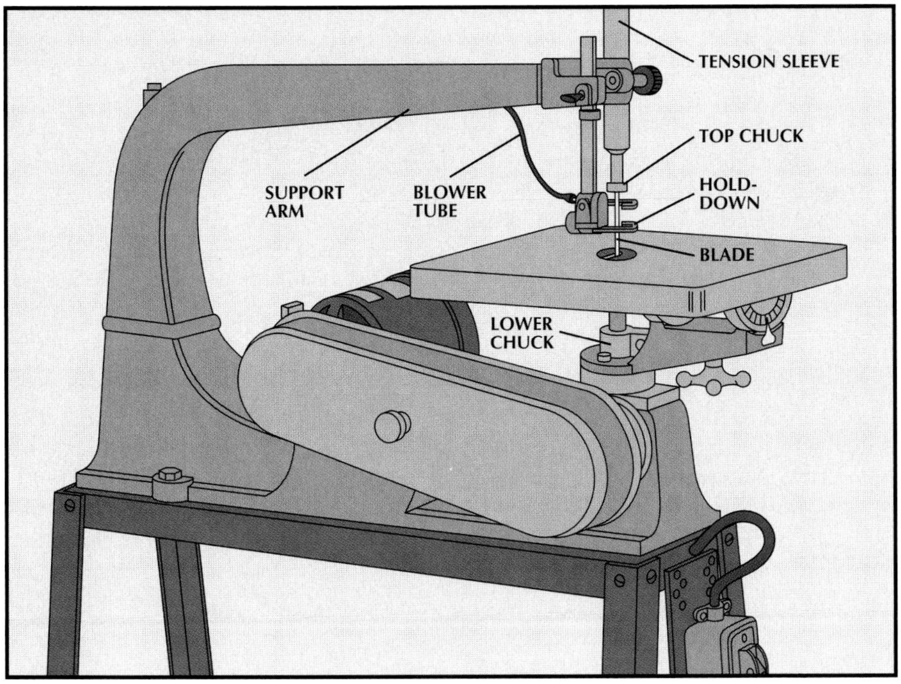

Anatomy of a scroll saw.
With its thin detachable blade, the scroll saw can make fine inside cuts without having to start at an edge of the stock; the blade can be removed from the top chuck and bent to the side, then slipped through a hole in the workpiece, and then reattached to the chuck. Loosen the lower chuck only to remove the blade for replacement. The blade moves in a rapid up-and-down motion and, because the teeth point down, it cuts only on the downstroke. A hold-down prevents the workpiece from jumping on the upstroke, and a tiny pump sends air through a tube to blow sawdust away from the cutting line. In addition to blades that cut hard and soft woods, the saw can be equipped with types that can cut ceramics or nonferrous metals.

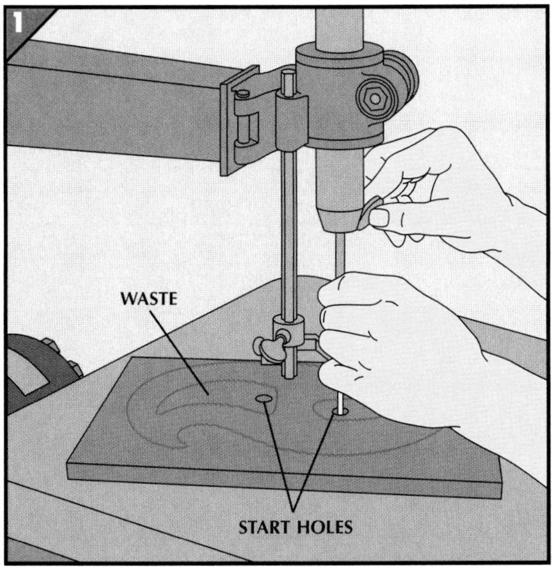

1. Adjusting the blade for an inside cut.
◆ Drill a start hole larger than the blade width through each enclosed waste section of the board.
◆ With a hex wrench, loosen the top chuck to detach the blade, flex the blade to the side, then feed the blade through the start hole and place the stock on the saw table.
◆ Insert the end of the blade in the top chuck and tighten the chuck *(above)*.
◆ Adjust the hold-down to press the workpiece firmly against the table.
◆ Push the workpiece up against the blade to check the tension; if the blade doesn't deflect about $\frac{1}{8}$ inch, adjust the tension sleeve.

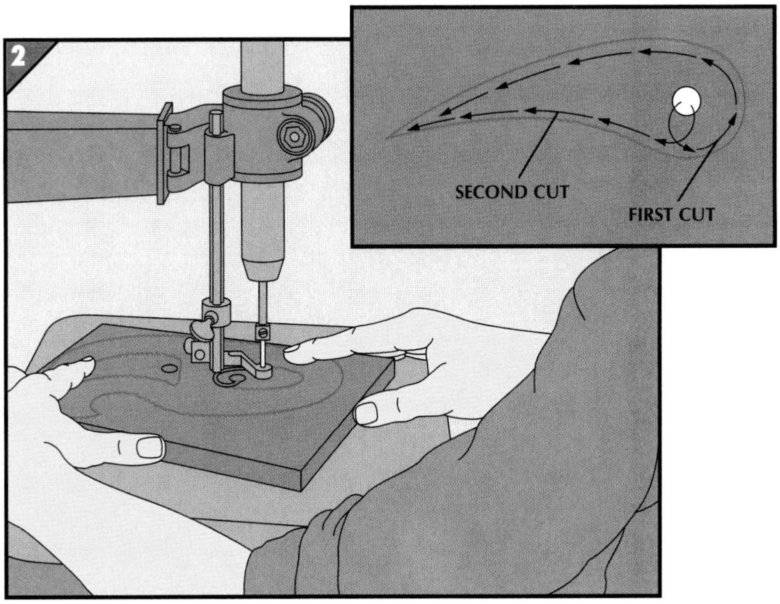

2. Making the cuts.
◆ Turn on the saw and guide the workpiece into the blade so it meets the cutting line at a shallow angle. Continue the cut until you reach your starting point *(above)*. If there is a sharp turn in the design, make two cuts from the hole to the turn, one clockwise and the other counterclockwise *(inset)*.
◆ Turn off the saw, detach the blade from the top chuck, and reposition the workpiece and reattach the blade to make other interior cuts.
◆ Saw standard curved cuts as you would with a band saw *(page 74)*.

Contouring Wood with Hand Tools

Despite the versatility of power tools, hand-shaping tools are indispensable for the finishing touches that give contoured wood its unique beauty. Each of these tools has its special uses and techniques.

Tools That Shape by Cutting: Drawknives, forming tools, spokeshaves, and planes cut cleanly through wood, leaving a smooth surface and discernible grain. Drawknives shape curves roughly *(below and opposite, top)*; remove the rest of the wood with a spokeshave, file, or rasp. The forming tool, with its cutting face covered by hundreds of tiny blades, excels at rounding off square corners *(opposite, bottom)*. Spokeshaves can cut precise, paper-thin shavings to refine curved surfaces *(page 86)*. The diminutive thumb plane shaves away wood in areas where larger planes cannot fit *(page 87)*.

All these tools work best when cutting in the direction of the wood grain. Keep their blades razor-sharp, honing them with a whetstone when necessary.

Scrapers: Scraping tools do a better job in very tight spots, or in cases when you need to finish intricately carved surfaces or shape pieces in which the grain runs in more than one direction. Files, rasps, and rifflers *(pages 88-89)* have tiny teeth that tear wood rather than cut it, and allow them to work well in any direction, regardless of grain. Since scrapers leave tiny scratches that can obscure grain patterns and dull surfaces, use tools with the finest teeth possible.

TOOLS

Drawknife	Files
Forming tool	Rasps
Spokeshave	Rifflers
Thumb plane	

SAFETY TIPS

Don goggles when using a drawknife to protect your eyes from flying wood chips.

ROUGH-SHAPING WITH A DRAWKNIFE

Cutting a concave curve.

◆ Mark the curve on the edges of the piece, cut away most of the waste with a band saw *(page 74)*, then clamp the stock in a vise.

◆ Place the drawknife, with the blade bevel facing down, at the far end of the curve. Tilt the blade down slightly and pull it toward you, lifting the handles to cut to the bottom of the curve. As you lift the tool, it will pry off wood in thin chips. Repeat the cut, continuing until the wood chips do not break off easily.

◆ Reverse the piece in the vise and shave the other side of the curve, pulling the drawknife from the end to the curve's bottom *(right)*. As you near the bottom, make shallow, slicing cuts to avoid breaking the grain on the side of the cut you cut first.

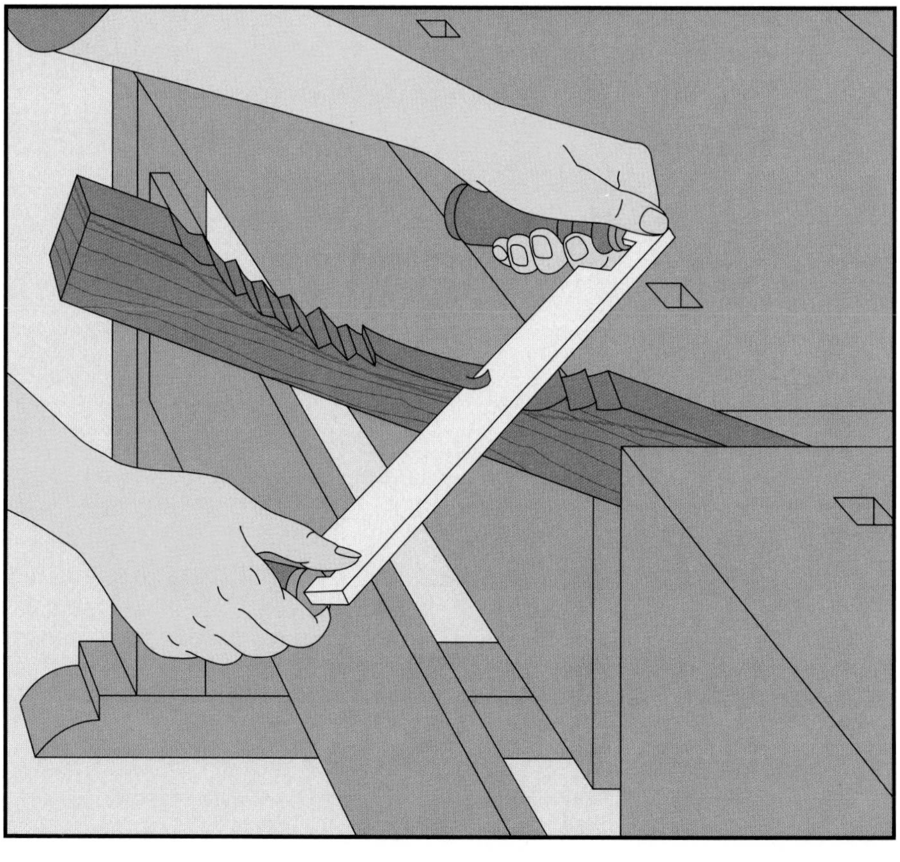

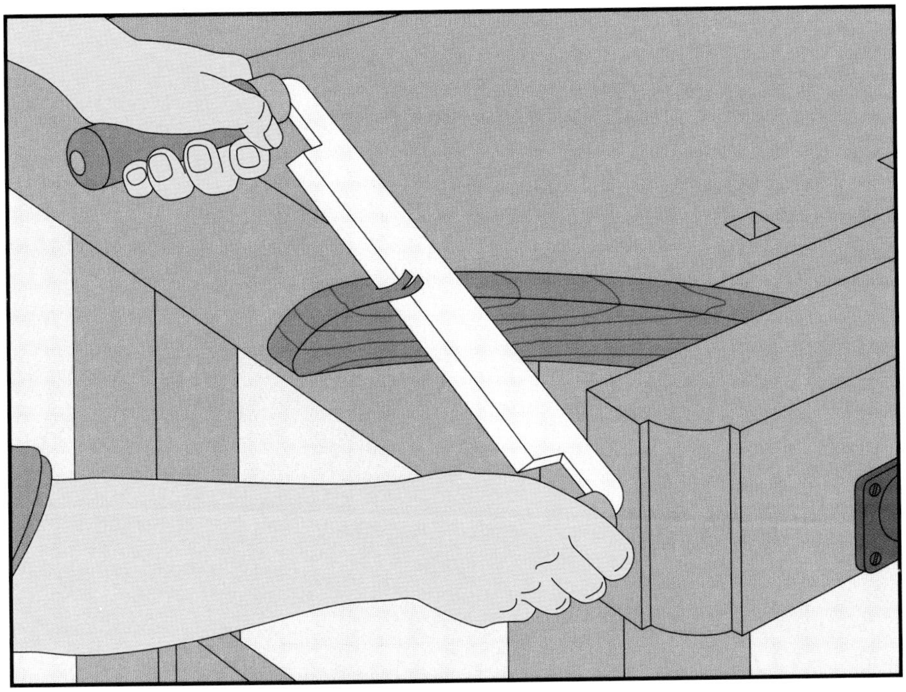

Making a convex cut.

◆ Cut any sharp curves before working on gradual ones. Holding a drawknife blade at the high point of the curve, bevel up and at a 30-degree angle to the surface, pull the blade toward you in shallow, shearing cuts that produce thin shavings.

◆ Shape gradual curves in the same way, holding the tool at a shallower angle *(left)*.

ROUNDING A CORNER WITH A FORMING TOOL

Rounding a square corner.

◆ Clamp the piece in a vise with the corner facing up.

◆ Hold the forming tool by both handles so the cutting face sits on the surface but slightly skewed in relation to the edges. Push the tool with gentle but steady pressure, stopping the cut when the teeth are halfway over the corner with the tool in a horizontal position *(right)*.

◆ Make as many cuts as necessary to round the near half of the corner, then reverse the joint in the vise and repeat the process to shape the other side.

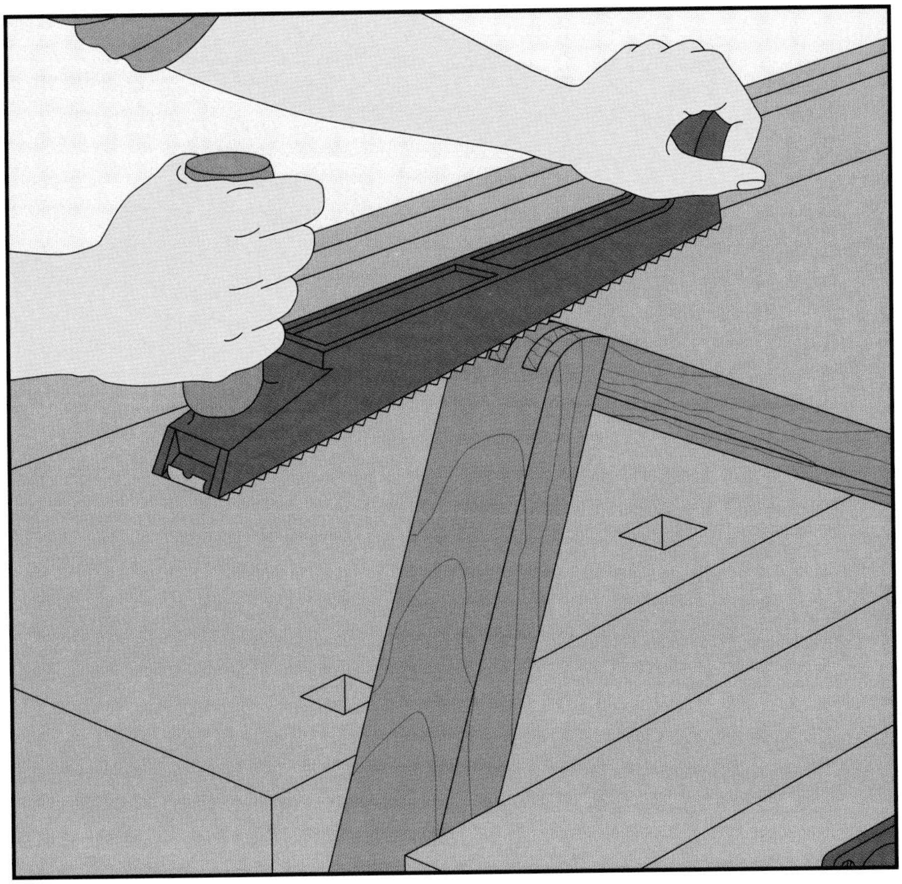

SPOKESHAVES FOR SMOOTHING CURVES

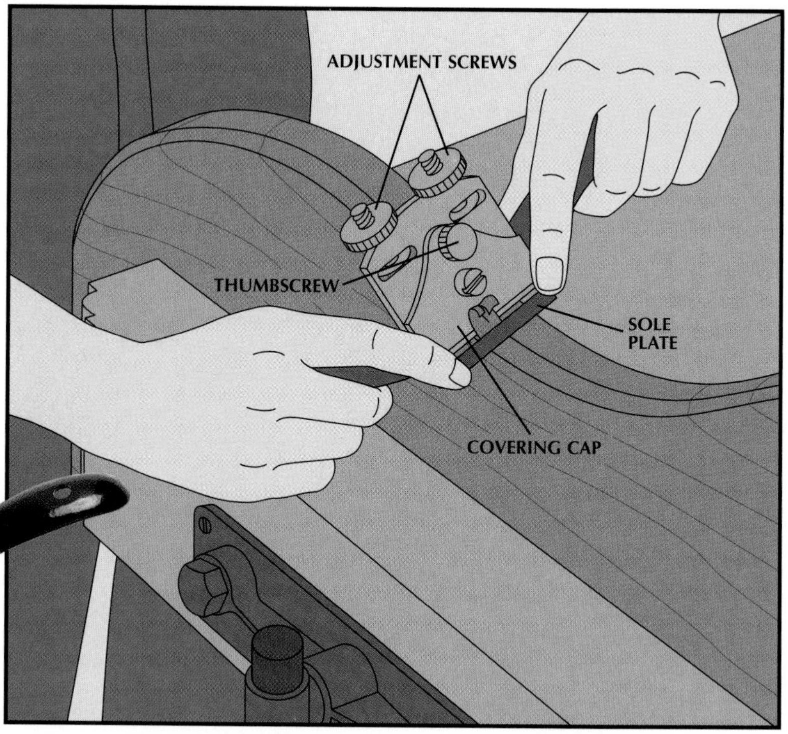

Making a rounded bevel on a curved edge.

◆ Adjust a straight-blade spokeshave *(photograph)* by loosening the thumbscrew on the covering cap and turning the adjustment screws so the blade just projects from the slot in the sole plate. Tighten the thumbscrew.

◆ Place your thumbs in the indented thumb rests on top of the handles and your index fingers on either side of the front of the tool.

◆ For a concave curve, start at the end of the curve and work down to the bottom, using gentle pressure and repeated strokes to push the spokeshave along the edge of the curve, lifting thin shavings *(right)*. Change the tilt of the tool with each stroke to round the edge completely. On a convex curve, work from the high point of the curve down toward the ends.

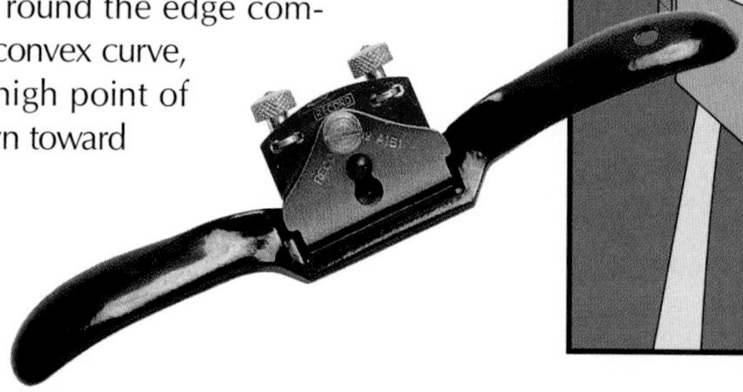

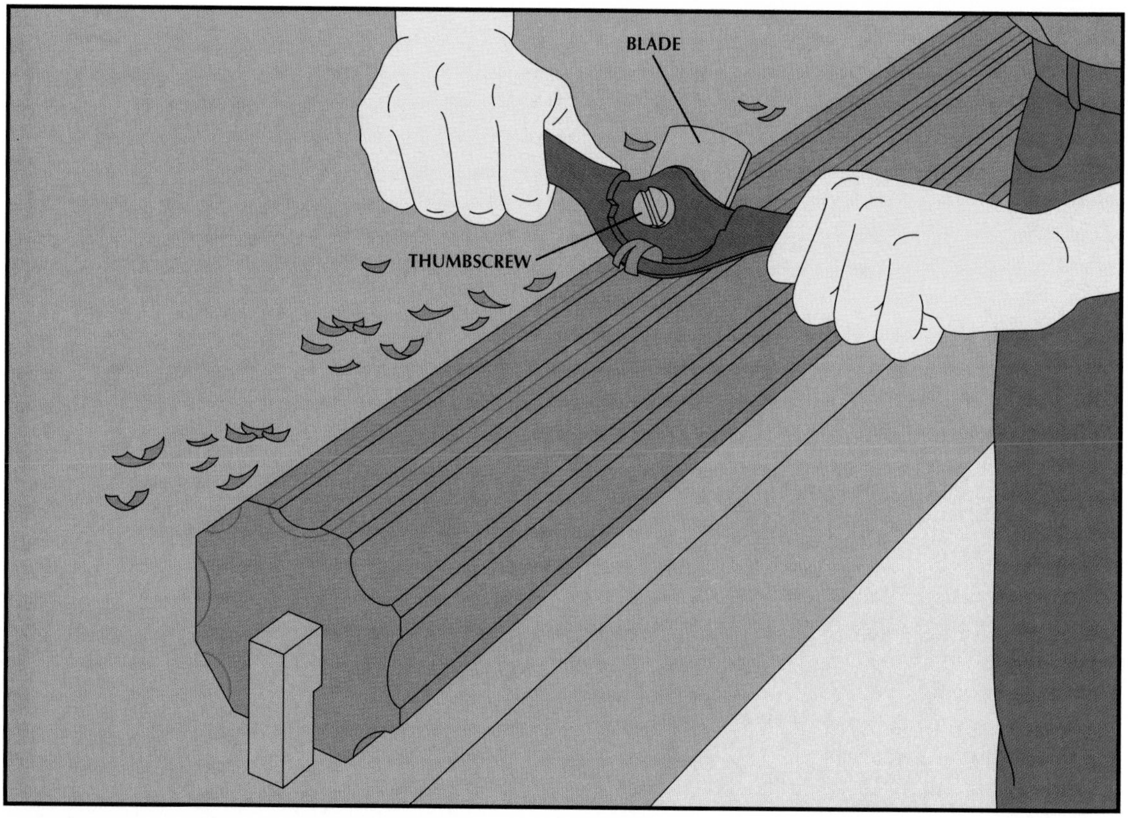

Smoothing a wide, shallow channel.

◆ Adjust a half-round spokeshave with a curved blade as described above.

◆ Grasp the handles by pressing your thumbs against the back and wrapping your fingers around the front.

◆ Tilt the spokeshave slightly, set the edge of the blade in the channel, and push the tool away from you with gentle, steady strokes *(above)*, shaving wood in thin strips. If the grain direction changes, reverse the tool, tilt the top away from you, and pull it toward you.

A TINY PLANE FOR TIGHT PLACES

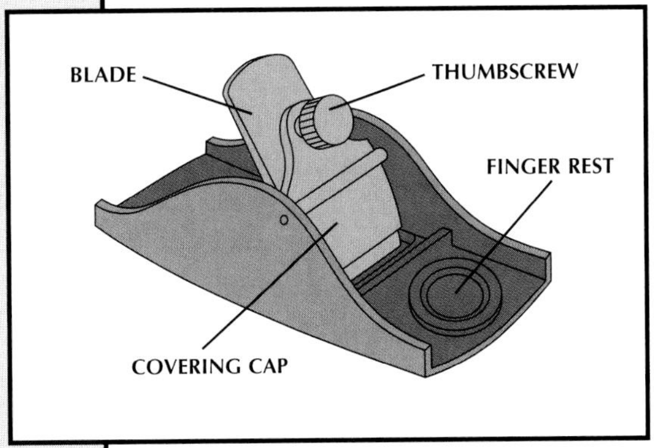

Operating a thumb plane.

◆ For a shallow cut, adjust the blade of the plane by loosening the thumbscrew on the covering cap and setting the blade to barely project beyond the opening in the sole; then tighten the thumbscrew *(inset)*.

◆ Hold the plane with your index finger on the finger rest and your thumb and remaining fingers on either side of the sole.

◆ Push down and forward with short, light strokes, guiding the tool parallel with the wood grain *(left)*.

TRICKS OF THE TRADE

A Flexible Plane That Follows a Curve

With its adjustable, flexible sole, the circle plane *(inset)* can follow a concave or convex surface. Mark the desired curve on the workpiece, cut to within $\frac{1}{8}$ inch of the mark with a band saw *(page 74)*, then set the sole of the plane to cut the same curve by turning the adjustment nut. Clamp the piece in a vise and plane down to the mark with long, smooth strokes, working parallel with the direction of the grain. For a concave cut, plane from the ends of the curve to the bottom *(below)*. For a convex curve, work from the high point of the curve to each end.

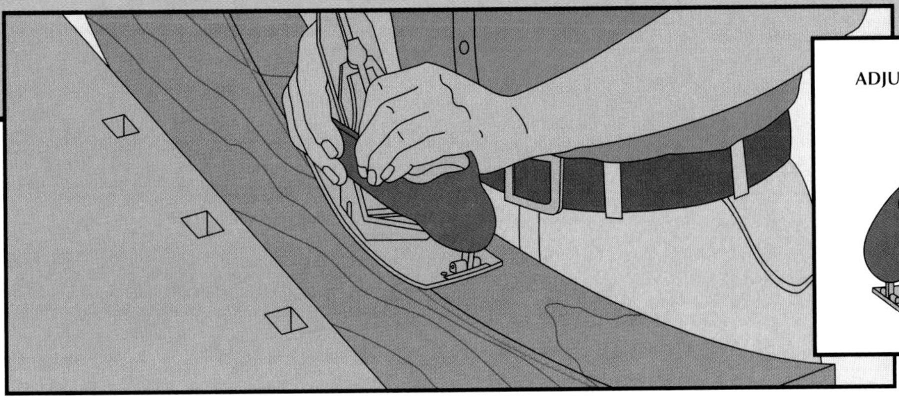

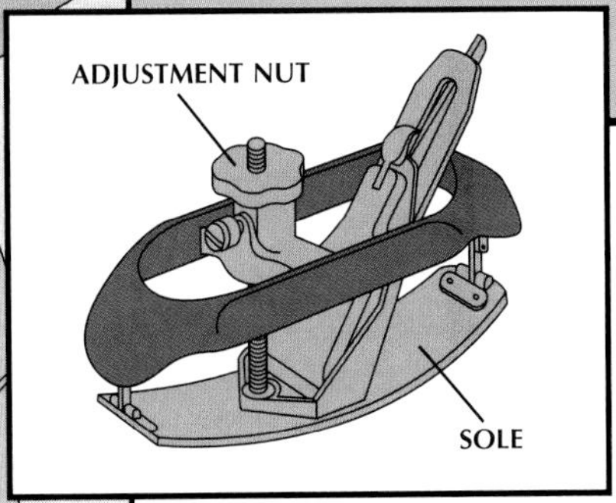

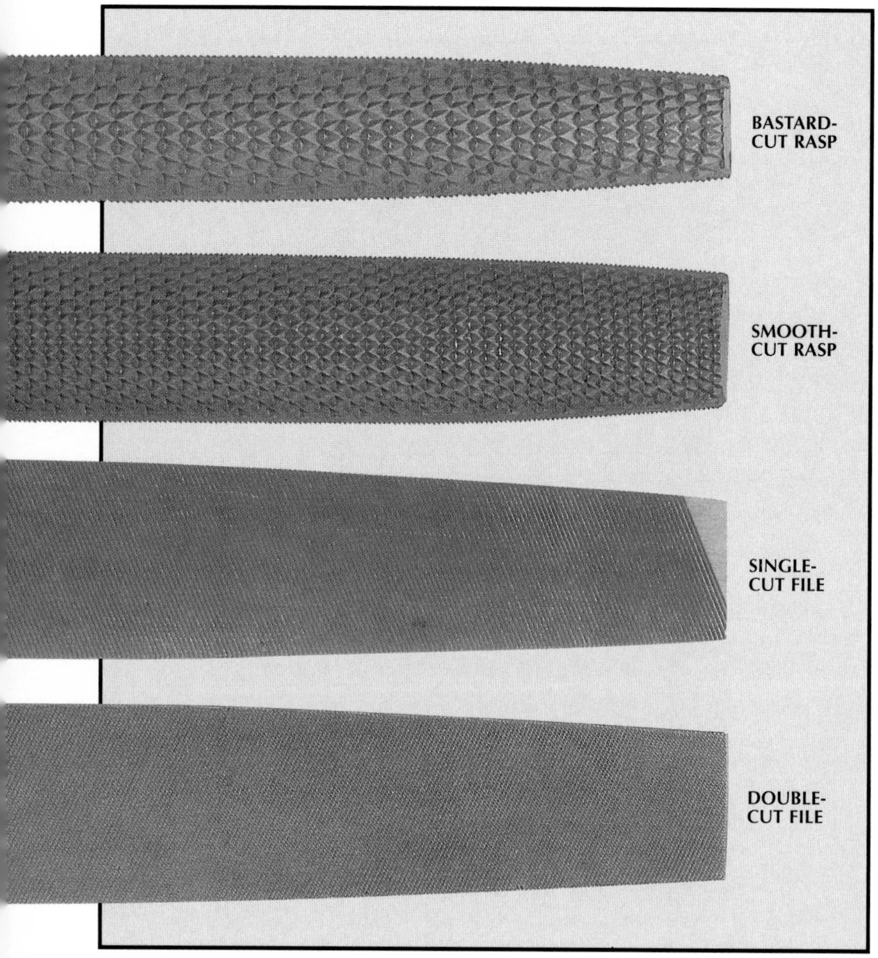

A phalanx of files and rasps.
Rasps and files have toothed scraping surfaces that may be flat on both sides, round on one face and flat on the other, or completely round *(left)*. With their teeth arranged in staggered rows, rasps are generally used for rougher work than files, whose teeth are formed by long grooves cut at an angle across the tool face. Rasps and files both come in varying degrees of coarseness, determined by the number of teeth per inch on the scraping surface. The bastard-cut rasp has approximately 26 teeth per inch and is used to rough shape hard woods. For rough shaping of softer woods, a medium-cut rasp, which has about 36 teeth per inch, works best. With approximately 60 teeth per inch set in a random pattern, a smooth-cut rasp leaves wood with a more finished surface. The single-cut file has grooves running in only one direction, and the more abrasive double-cut file has crisscrossing grooves. All files and rasps are made with a tang—a projection at one end that fits into a wooden handle.

Shaping with a rasp or file.
Rasps and files can be pushed in any direction along or across the wood grain. For the smoothest cut, start at the top of a curve and work down. Move the tool forward gently with one hand on the handle, guiding the front of the blade with the heel of your other hand to scrape the wood *(right)*. Lift the tool and move it backward—to avoid dulling the teeth—then repeat the stroke. To round over a sharp edge, use an up-and-over rocking motion diagonally across the grain of the wood.

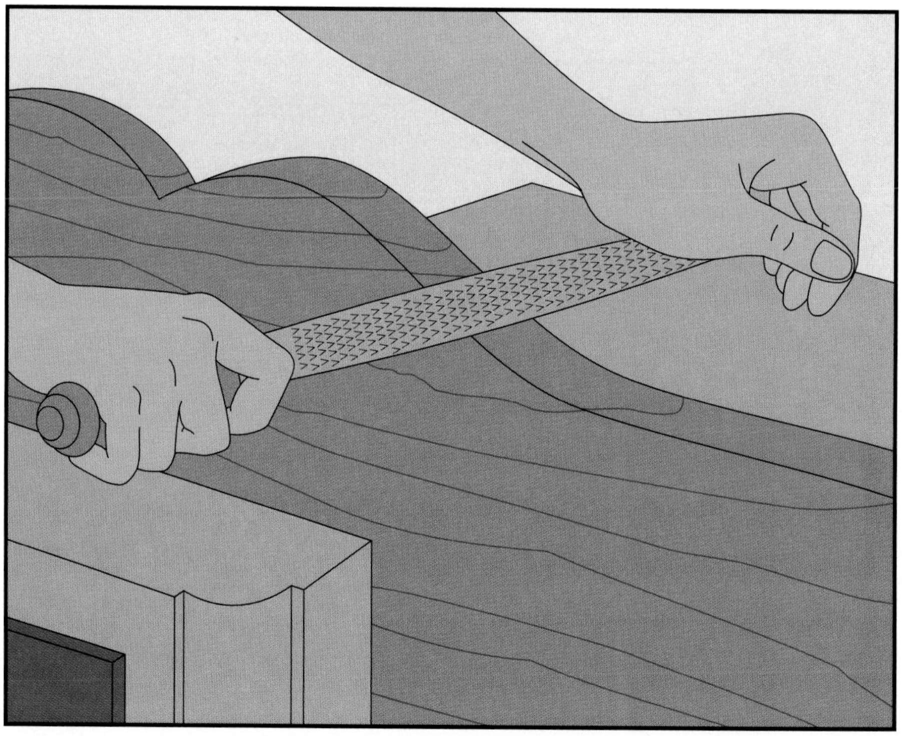

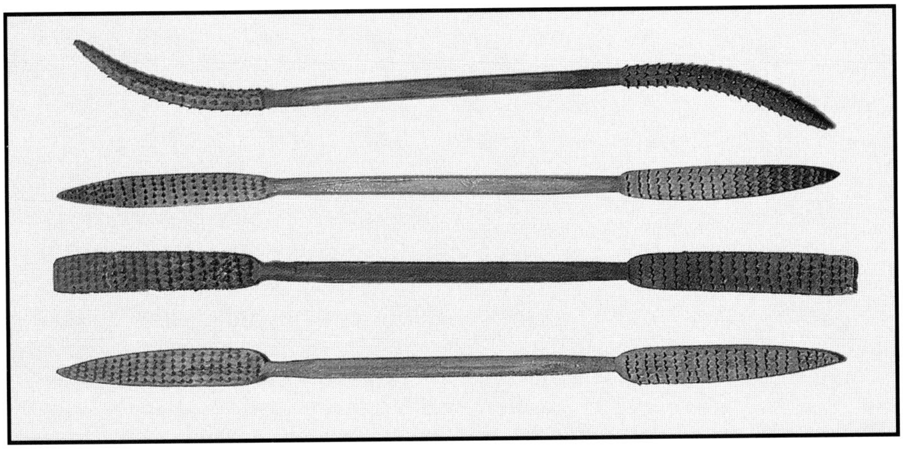

Rifflers for fine work.
Rifflers are double-ended tools available with a variety of spatulate, curved, or pointed heads *(left)*. Useful for cleaning intricately carved details and shaping hard-to-reach spots, their scraping surfaces are miniature versions of rasps and files. They come in the same range of coarseness as rasps and files.

Getting into tight confines.
Choose a riffler that matches the shape you want to smooth, then push the tool with the index finger of one hand while the thumb of the other hand guides the tool *(right)*. After the stroke, do not pull the riffler back along its path; instead, lift it clear of the wood and make another forward cut.

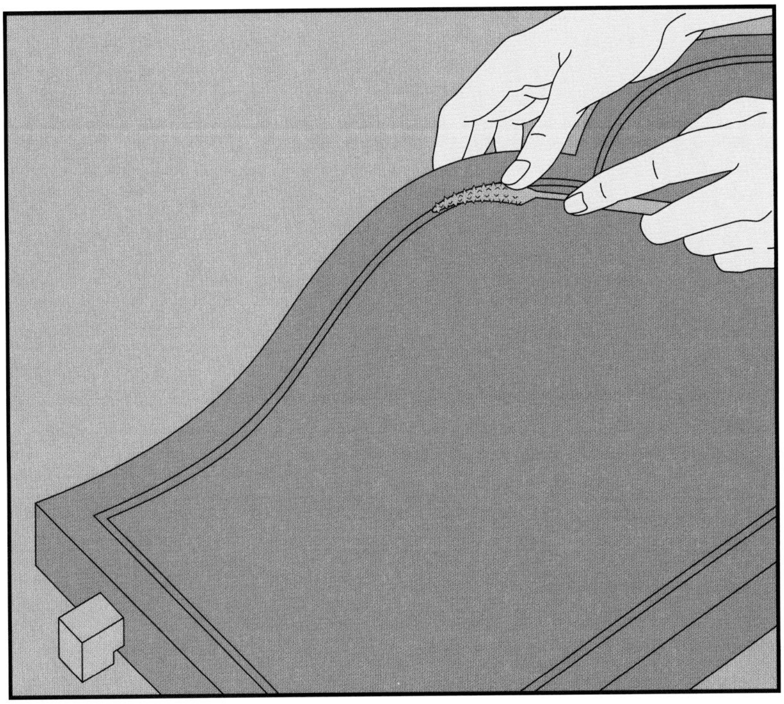

TRICKS OF THE TRADE

Cleaning Scraping Tools

The fine wood shavings produced by a file, rasp, or riffler tend to stick to the tool and clog its teeth, reducing the blade's cutting efficiency and scoring the work unevenly. Clean dust and shavings from the tool with a file card—a special brush with short wire bristles. First, lightly tap the tool on your bench to release some of the sawdust. Then, draw the file card's bristles across the blade, scrubbing parallel to the rows of teeth. Pick out stubborn particles with a nail.

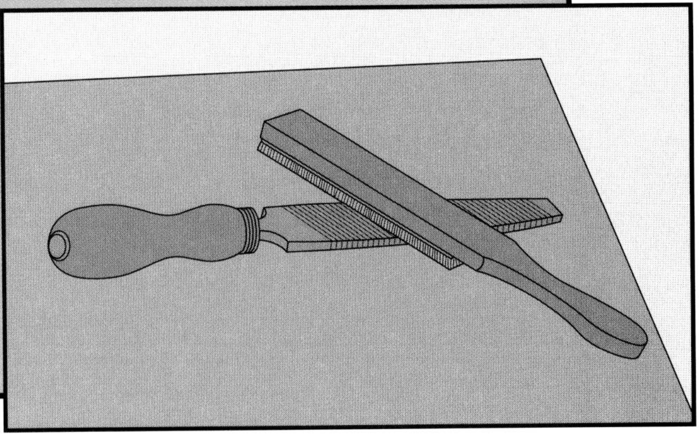

Working with a Lathe

The lathe *(below)* allows you to transform wood blocks, called blanks, into shaped cylinders for use as chair rungs, stair balusters, and table legs. Obtaining the shape you want is a matter of choosing the right tools and wood and mastering some basic techniques.

Wood for Turning: The best woods for lathe work are close-grained hardwoods such as maple and birch. Open-grained hardwoods like oak tend to splinter. Softwoods such as pine do not turn cleanly, but are inexpensive choices for practicing. Avoid blanks with splits or knots—these defects can catch the edge of a tool and ruin a workpiece.

Turning Techniques: There are essentially two types of turning tools and two ways of shaping wood on a lathe: cutting and scraping *(page 92)*. Cutting tools are held so that the blank spins into the cutting edge, shaving away wood in a very thin layer. Scraping tools, on the other hand, are pushed straight into the wood as it spins, so that the cutting edge scrapes away small wood particles.

Tool Maintenance: Oil the lathe's moving parts according to the manufacturer's instructions, and clean waste wood from it to prevent clogging.

Keep the cutting edges of the turning tools sharp by honing them on a fine oilstone: Set the bevel on the blade's underside flat on the stone and, with gentle pressure, guide the blade across the surface in a figure-8 pattern. To hone the curved bevel on a gouge, rock the bevel from side to side as you make the figure-8 pattern, then hone the inside of the gouge's curved cutting edge with a slipstone.

TOOLS

- Lathe
- Spur center
- Cup center
- Table saw
- Try square
- Ruler
- Mallet
- Roughing gouge
- Skew chisel

SAFETY TIPS

Protect your eyes with goggles when working on a lathe.

Anatomy of a wood lathe. Wood spun on a lathe is supported between a headstock, fixed in place on the bed, and a tailstock that slides along the bed to accommodate blanks of different lengths. Driven by a system of belts and pulleys connected to a motor, the headstock spindle holds a part called a center, which is equipped with spurs or screws to penetrate the wood. A cup center secures the other end of the blank; it fits into the tailstock spindle and is forced into the wood by turning the tailstock handwheel. The lathe is also fitted with a tool rest. Adjustable for height, angle, and position along the bed, it supports a tool as it cuts into the blank.

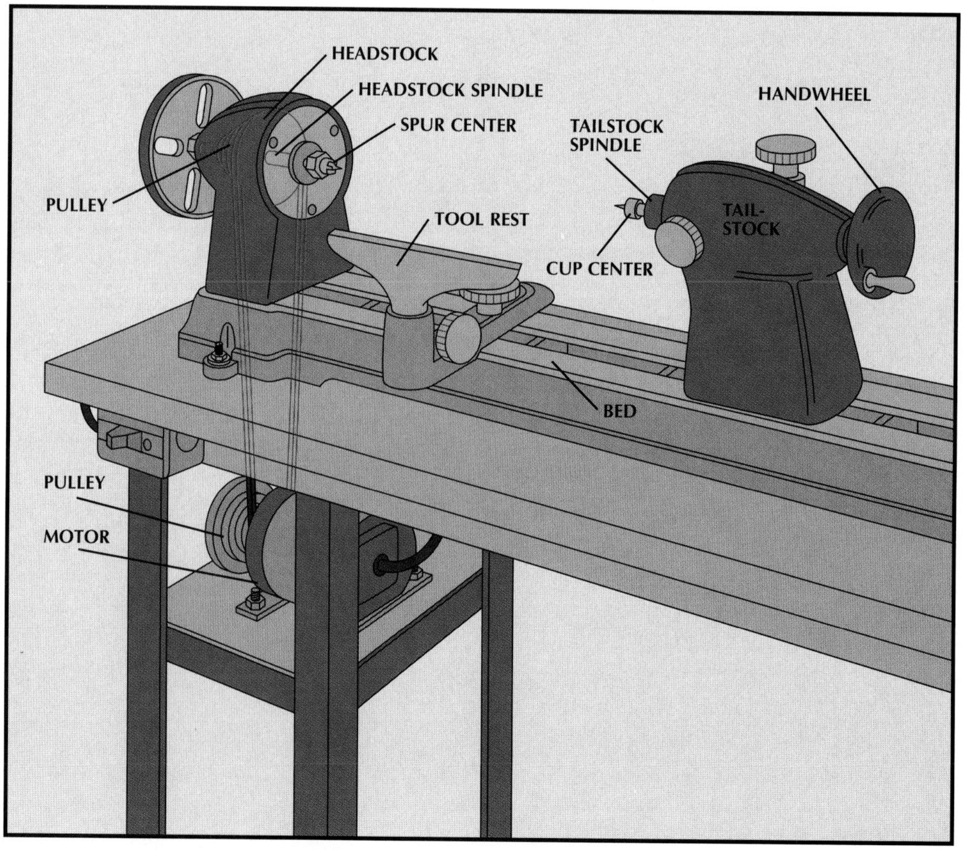

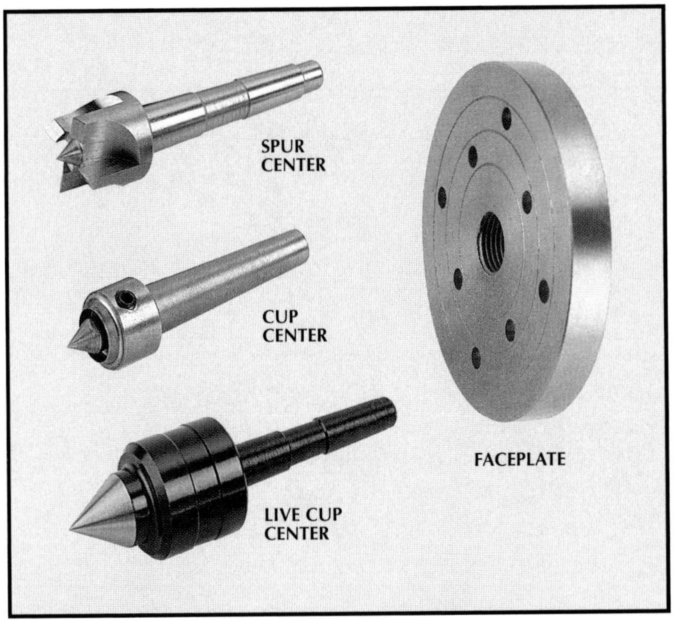

Mounting wood in a lathe.
Blanks are anchored to a lathe with centers or with a faceplate *(above)*, depending on the work being done. Spur centers in the headstock have two or four sharp spurs, while cup centers in the tailstock spindle have a concave end so only the thin rim and the point penetrate the blank. An alternative to the cup center is the live center; its ball bearings let it spin freely as the wood turns, reducing friction.

In some lathe work such as shaping bowls, the wood is attached only to the headstock with a faceplate—a metal disk screwed onto the headstock spindle. Ranging in diameter from 3 to 10 inches, faceplates grip a blank with screws.

Lathe Safety

In addition to the safety measures for power tools listed on page 14, observe these precautions:

✔ Before starting the lathe, ensure that the blank is anchored between the centers.

✔ Position the tool rest $\frac{1}{4}$ inch from the blank, and rotate the blank by hand to check that it will not strike the tool rest.

✔ As you turn the blank and its size is reduced, stop the lathe periodically and reposition the tool rest.

✔ Set the lathe at a safe speed for the size of the blank you are turning *(chart, page 92)*. Do not use a higher speed. If you are having difficulty controlling a turning tool, reduce the speed.

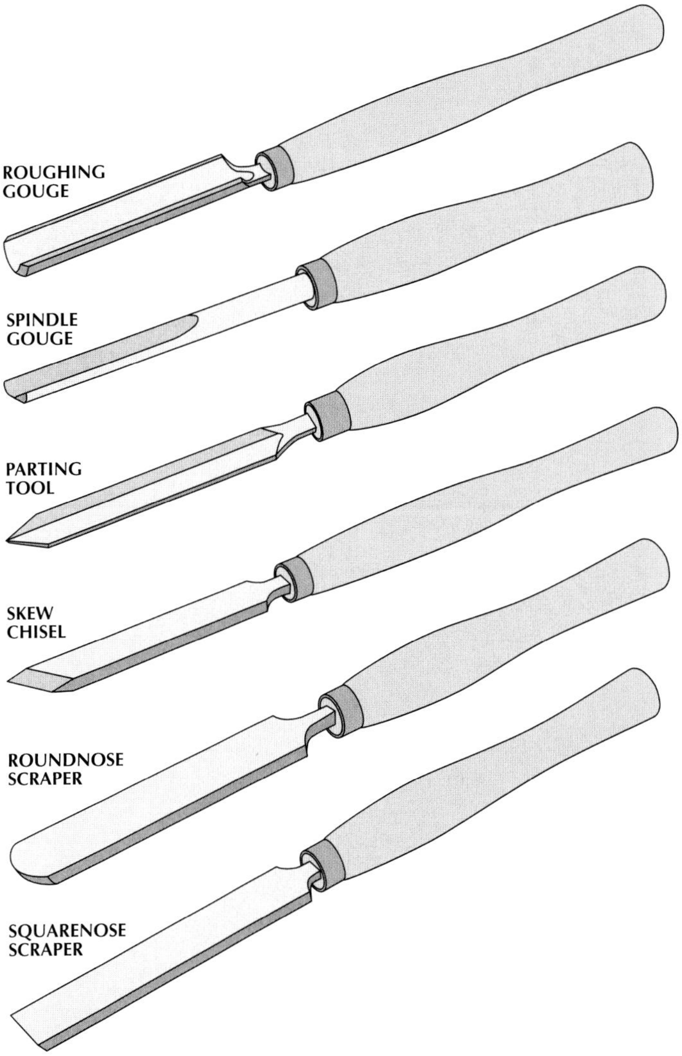

Cutting and scraping tools.
The two most common types of hand tools required in lathe work are cutting and scraping tools *(above)*. For most spindle-turning projects *(pages 95-101)*, cutting tools are employed. Gouges have a curved blade with a rounded cutting edge that is beveled on the convex side. The parting tool has two flat sides; its two bevels are angled toward each other to form a narrow cutting edge. A skew chisel has a cutting edge that is ground at an angle to the side of the blade; it is beveled on both sides of the cutting edge.

Roundnose and squarenose scrapers—used mostly for faceplate turning *(pages 102-103)*—have flat blades of various shapes and are beveled on one side.

GETTING A GOOD GRIP ON TOOLS

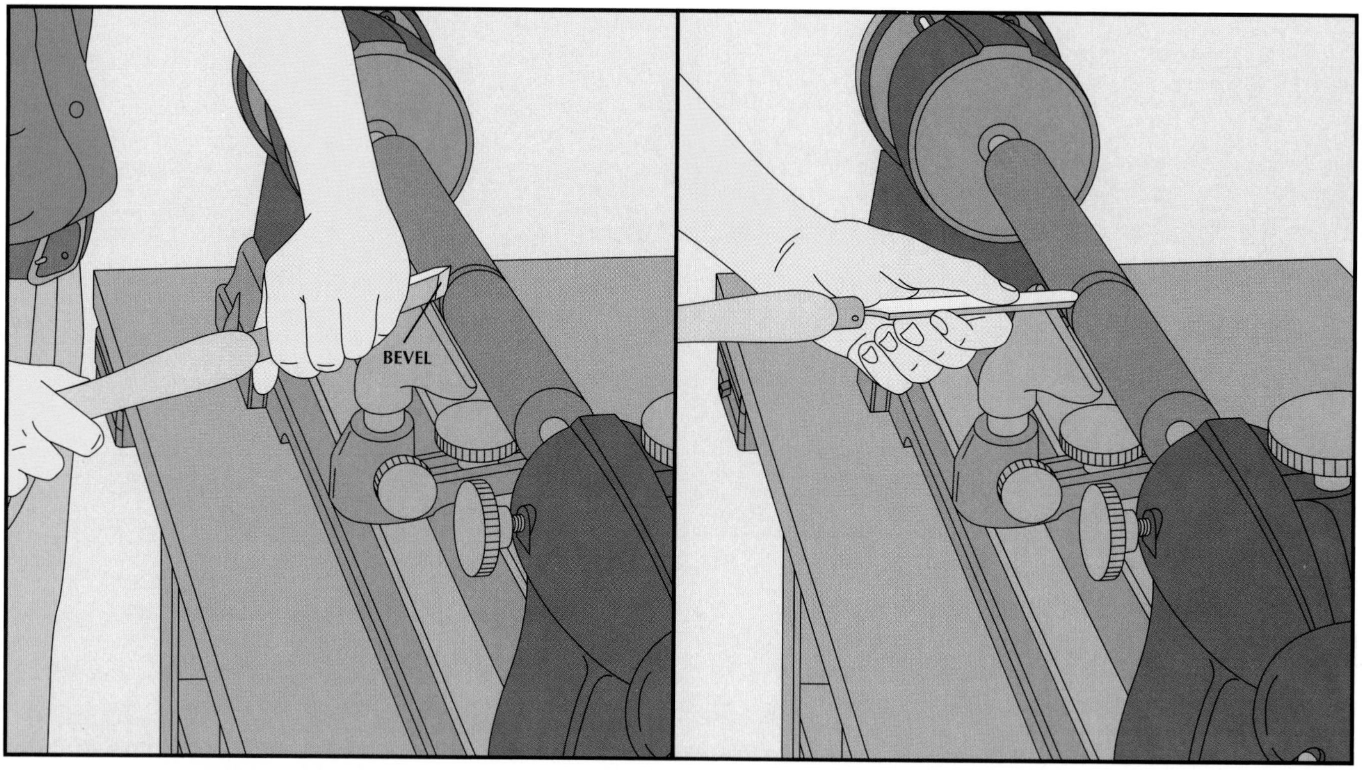

Cutting and scraping a blank. With both cutting and scraping tools, grasp the end of the handle firmly with one hand, keeping your forearm close to your body—this arm guides the tool. Hold the tool blade lightly against the tool rest with the other hand in either an overhand or an underhand grip. With a cutting tool, such as a skew chisel, hold the blade so only the bevel rubs against the stock and gently raise the handle until the cutting edge engages the wood *(above, left)*. Raise or lower the handle to control the cut, being careful to keep the point of the blade from catching on the wood. With a scraping tool, such as a roundnose chisel, hold the blade horizontally across the tool rest, with the bevel down, and feed the cutting edge straight into the wood *(above, right)*.

SETTING LATHE SPEED

Choosing the best speed. The chart at right listing lathe velocity in revolutions per minute (rpm) will help you set the appropriate speed for the size of the blank and task at hand. The larger the blank, the slower the turn. As a rule, use slow speeds for roughing cuts, which include faceplate turning and shaping rough blanks into cylinders. Moderate speeds are used for shaping, while the fastest speeds are reserved for final smoothing and sanding. If your lathe does not have a setting that corresponds to the recommended velocity, use the closest slower speed.

A RANGE OF TURNING SPEEDS TO SUIT THE JOB

Blank diameter	Roughing	Shaping	Finishing and sanding
Less than 2"	900-1,400	2,200-2,800	3,000-4,200
2"-4"	600-1,000	1,800-2,400	2,400-3,400
4"-6"	600-1,000	1,200-1,800	1,800-2,400
6"-8"	400-800	800-1,200	1,200-1,800
8"-10"	300-700	700-1,000	1,000-1,200
More than 10"	300-600	600-900	600-900

MOUNTING A BLANK

1. Finding the centers.
◆ Cut the blank to length on a table saw. If your design incorporates a square, unturned section, make the sides of the blank square, checking with a try square.
◆ With a ruler, draw diagonal lines from corner to corner on each end of the blank to locate the centers *(right).*

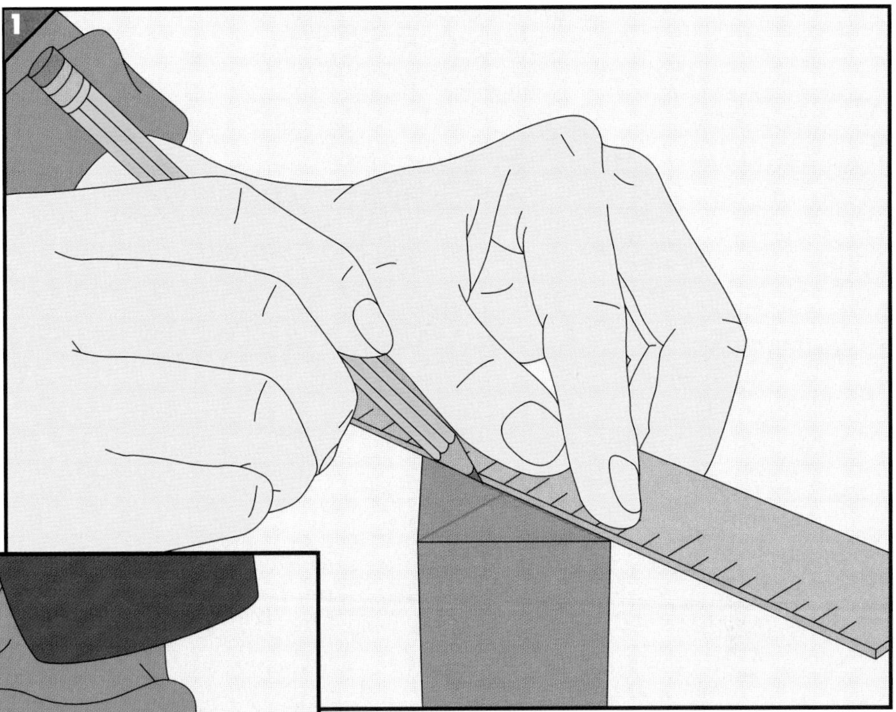

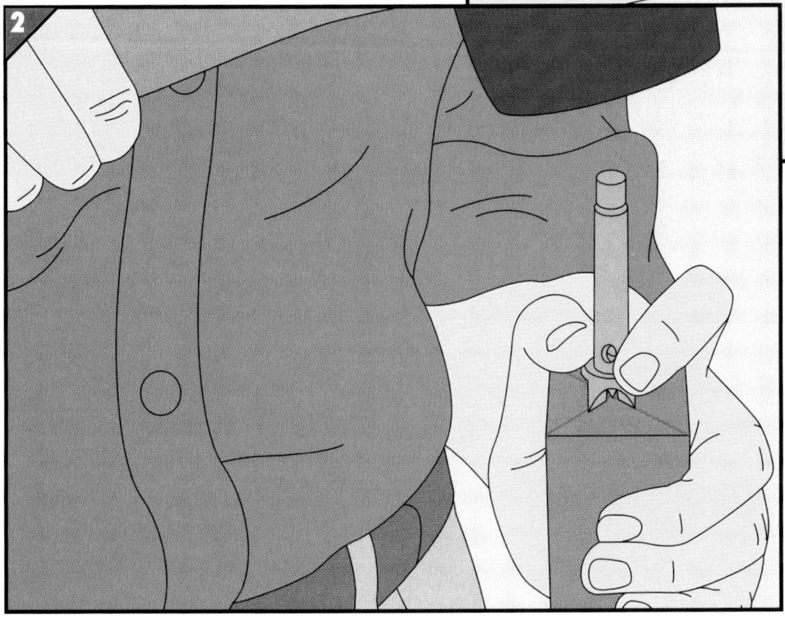

2. Positioning the spur center.
◆ Remove the spur center from the lathe's headstock spindle and place its point at the center of one end of the blank. With a mallet, tap the shank of the spur center lightly, embedding the spurs in the wood *(left).*
◆ Push the cup center's shank onto the tailstock spindle, then lubricate the point of the center with soap or wax. (A live center requires no lubrication.) Turn the tailstock handwheel to retract the spindle into the tailstock.

3. Mounting the blank.
◆ Loosen the tailstock lock. Push the spur-center shank into the headstock spindle and, supporting the blank with one hand, push the tailstock toward the headstock until the point of the cup center touches the wood at the center mark.
◆ Tighten the tailstock lock.
◆ Turn the tailstock handwheel to drive the cup-center point into the wood so the rim of the center penetrates the wood *(right).*
◆ Secure the tailstock-spindle lock.

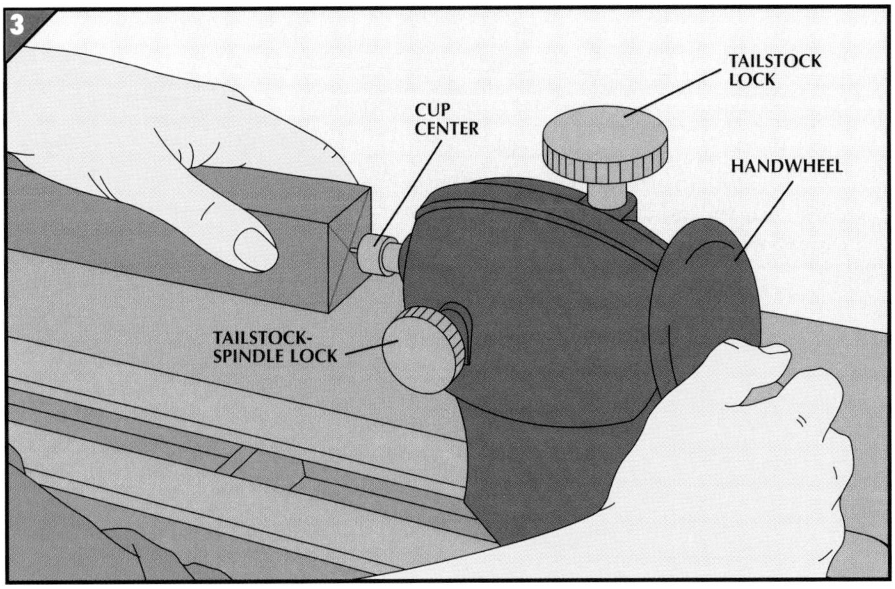

ROUGHING SQUARE STOCK INTO A CYLINDER

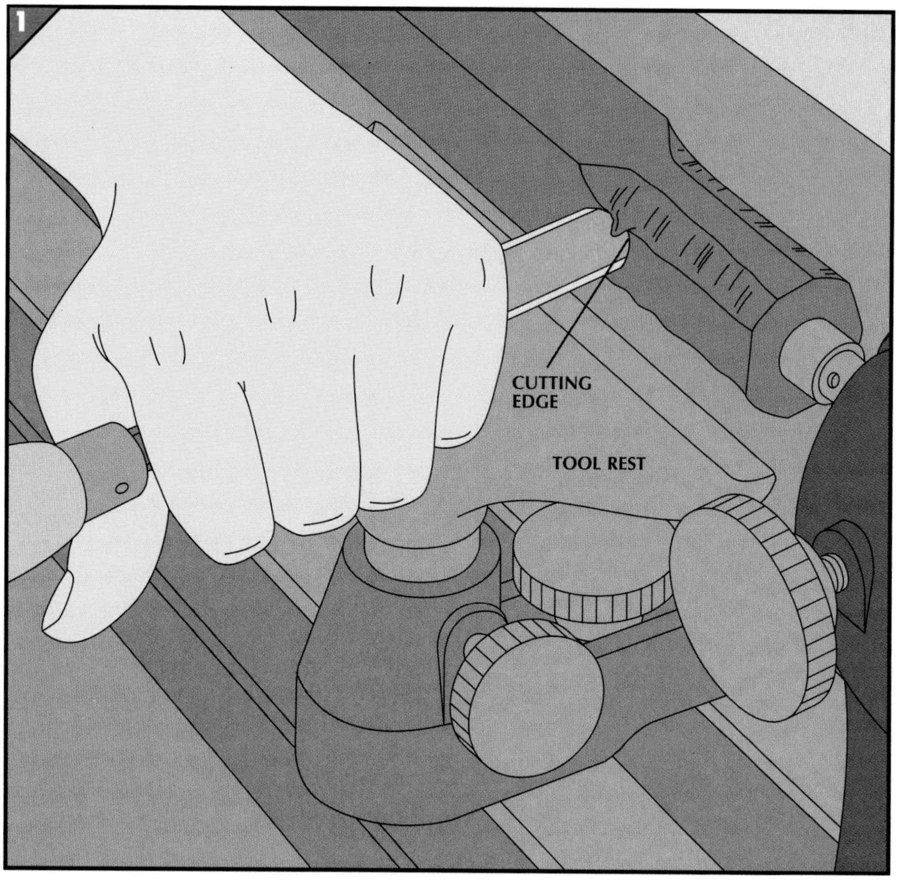

1. Using a roughing gouge.

◆ Slide the tool rest as far as possible toward the tailstock and set it level with the midpoint of the wood, $\frac{1}{4}$ inch away from it. Turn on the lathe and place a roughing gouge on the tool rest, its blade pointing slightly downward and its concave face turned to the right.

◆ Hold the gouge so the bevel touches the corners of the blank, then raise the handle to start cutting. Move the gouge steadily along the length of the tool rest from left to right, making a light cut *(left)*. Repeat the shearing motion until you have rounded the section, stopping the lathe periodically to move the tool rest closer to the wood blank as necessary.

◆ Round the rest of the stock, progressing from right to left along the stock but always cutting from left to right, repositioning the tool rest as needed. Leave a 2-inch section at the left end uncut.

◆ To round the last section, turn the gouge over so the concave side of the blade faces left. Round off the cylinder as before, but work from right to left.

2. Planing with a skew chisel.

◆ Position the tool rest as for the gouge in Step 1.

◆ Place a skew chisel on the tool rest so the point is above the wood and the bevel is inclined in the direction of the cut, typically at an angle of about 65 degrees to the axis of the wood.

◆ Let the bevel rub against the blank, keeping the point of the skew clear of the wood, then raise the handle slightly so the cutting edge contacts the wood. Move the blade along the tool rest, letting the bevel rub, keeping the point of the chisel from catching the wood *(right)*. The tool is positioned correctly when the cutting edge produces a series of thin, tubular shavings and leaves behind a glass-smooth finish.

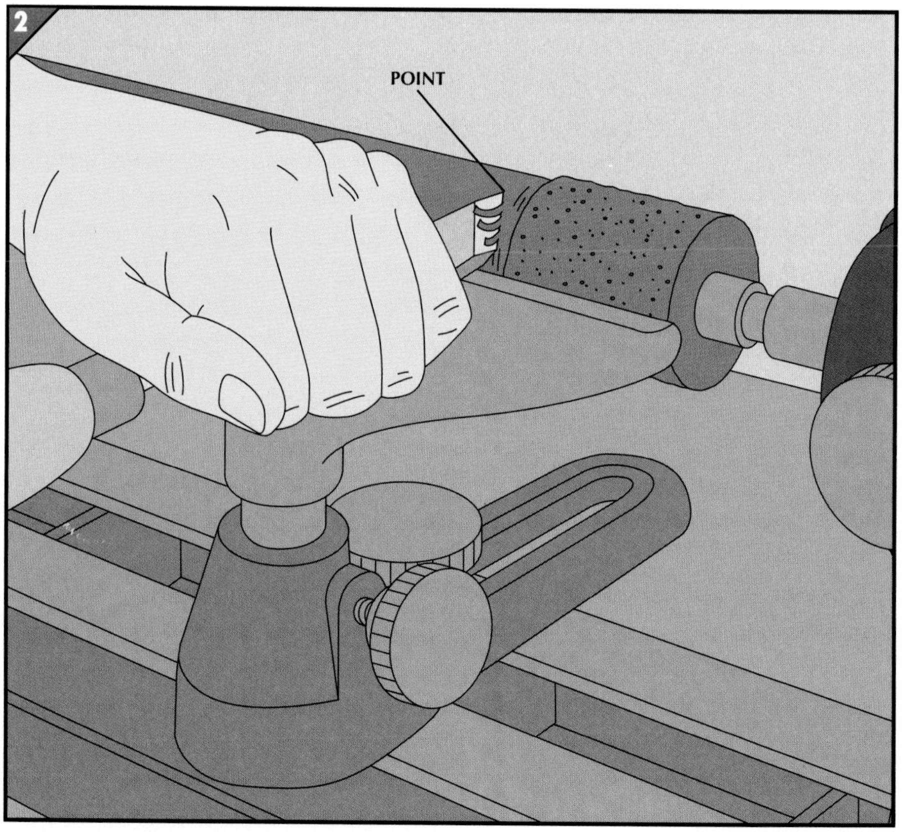

Spindle Turning to Produce Classic Shapes

Even the most elaborately turned table leg is, in essence, nothing more than a row of simple shapes cut side by side along a wood blank. The design possibilities of combining these basic elements in different ways are almost unlimited. Five classic shapes *(below)* are the foundation of most spindle turning. The size, placement, and frequency of these elements can be varied in virtually any fashion to suit your design. Learning these shapes will help you identify the turned elements of any piece you wish to duplicate.

Mastering the Techniques: Instructions for making each shape appear here and on the following pages—which chisels to use, in what sequence, as well as how to hold the chisel for each cut. To produce a number of identical turnings, make a template showing the location and diameter of each element *(pages 99-100)*. When the turning process is concluded, leave the piece on the lathe for sanding and finishing *(page 101)*.

TOOLS

Skew chisel
Roughing gouge
Spindle gouge
Parting tool
Calipers
Table saw
Combination square
Ruler
Plane
Band saw
File

MATERIALS

Hardboard ($\frac{1}{8}$")
Wood glue
Sandpaper (variety of grits)
Dowel or wedge
Cotton cloth
Linseed or tung oil
Turner's wax stick

SAFETY TIPS

Wear goggles when operating a lathe.

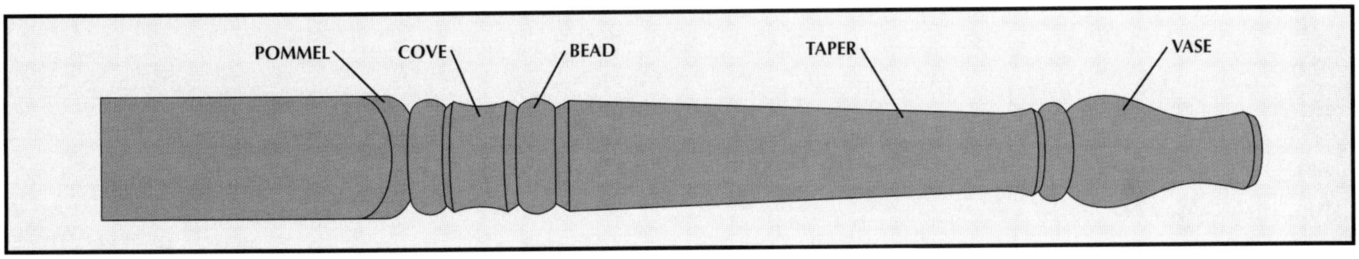

The five basic elements.
The table leg above includes the five basic wood turning shapes. A pommel is often used to create a transition between round and rectangular sections of a turning. A bead is a rounded segment made with a skew chisel. A cove is a concave section cut with a spindle gouge. Wider at one end than the other, with its diameter decreasing in a straight line, a taper is created with a parting tool. A vase starts as a bead, then turns into a taper with a more sweeping form. The top of a vase can be cut with a skew chisel; the rest of it can be shaped with a spindle gouge. Both the taper and the vase are planed smooth with a skew chisel.

RAISING A BEAD

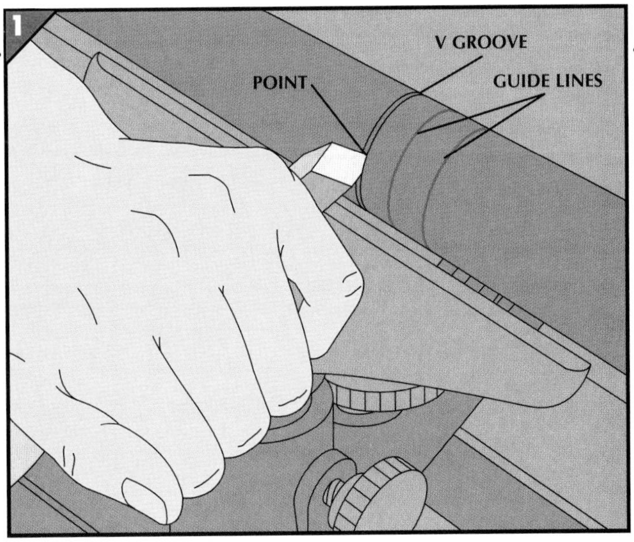

1. Making end grooves with a skew chisel.

◆ Turn the blank into a cylinder *(page 94)*, then set the tool rest near the proposed bead, slightly above the center of the blank and about $\frac{1}{4}$ inch from the wood.

◆ Turn on the lathe and mark each side of the bead with a pencil. If the bead is to be wider than $\frac{1}{2}$ inch, add a third guideline midway between the first two lines.

◆ Place a skew chisel on the tool rest, with the blade on edge and the point near the wood.

◆ Tilt the tool handle very slightly downward. Push the skew point straight into the stock at one of the outside marks, cutting a V-shaped groove $\frac{1}{8}$ inch deep *(right)*.

◆ Cut a groove at the other outside mark in the same way, but do not cut into the center mark.

2. Shaping the bead.

◆ With the stock spinning, place the blade of the skew chisel almost flat on the tool rest at the center of the bead. Position the heel of the cutting edge to the right of and lower than the center point, with the tool handle angled slightly downward. Push the blade forward until the chisel's heel, but not its cutting edge, rubs the wood at the center mark *(right, top)*.

◆ Raise the handle slightly until the cutting edge begins to shear the wood; then, with one continuous motion, roll the heel of the blade toward the right groove, raising the handle and pushing the blade forward into the wood as the chisel turns. End with the blade's cutting edge vertical in the groove, heel down *(right, bottom)*. To deepen the groove for a rounder bead, push the heel of the cutting edge farther into the groove before withdrawing the blade.

◆ Cut the other side of the bead in the same way, but start with the heel of the cutting edge pointing to the left. Alternate right and left cuts until the bead is the desired shape.

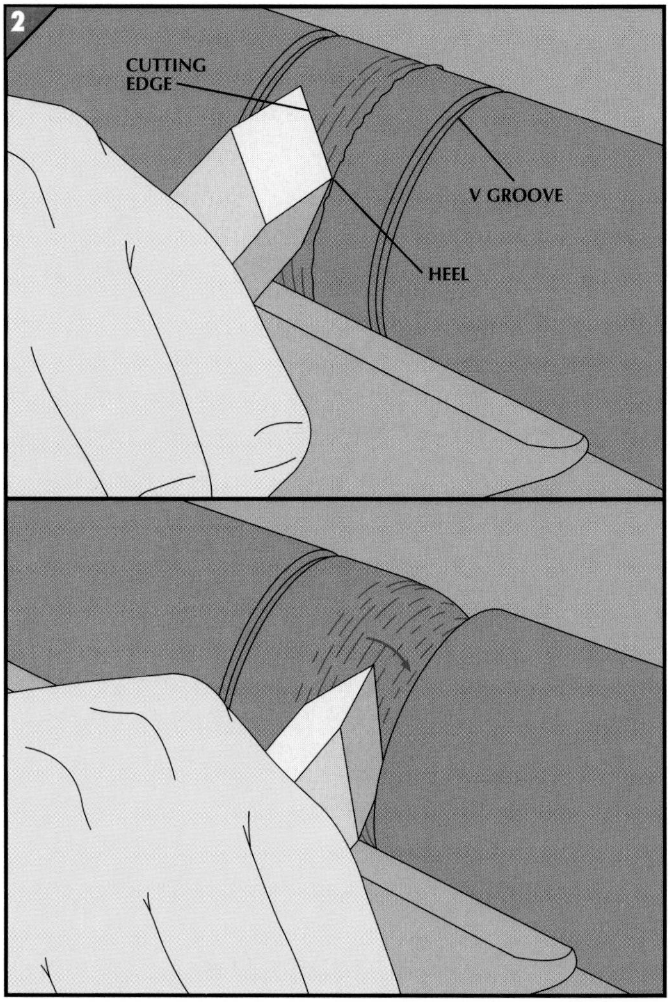

HOLLOWING OUT A COVE

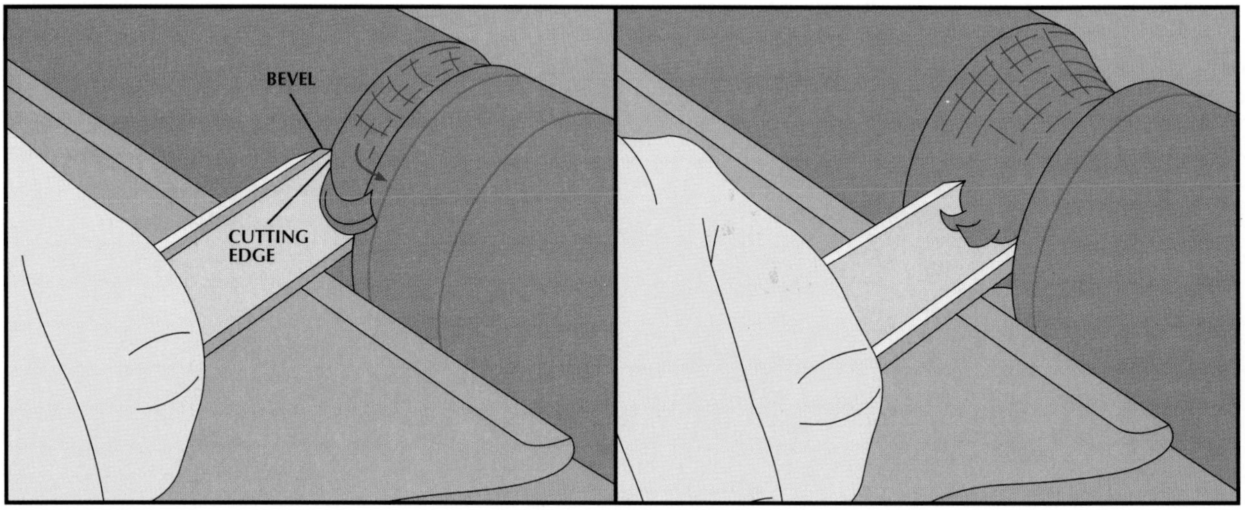

Making the concave cuts.

◆ Turn the blank into a cylinder *(page 94)*.

◆ Mark a cove with a pencil as you would a bead *(page 95, Step 1)*, then position a spindle gouge almost on edge on the tool rest, its bevel rubbing just inside an outside V-groove.

◆ Raise the handle so the cutting edge engages the wood. In one continuous motion, pivot the tool and cut toward the bottom of the cove *(above, left)*, and ending the cut with the blade lying horizontally *(above, right)*.

◆ Cut the other part of the cove, starting from the opposite side.

◆ Deepen the cove with similar cuts, starting each pass inside the marks to avoid making the cut too wide.

CREATING A TAPER

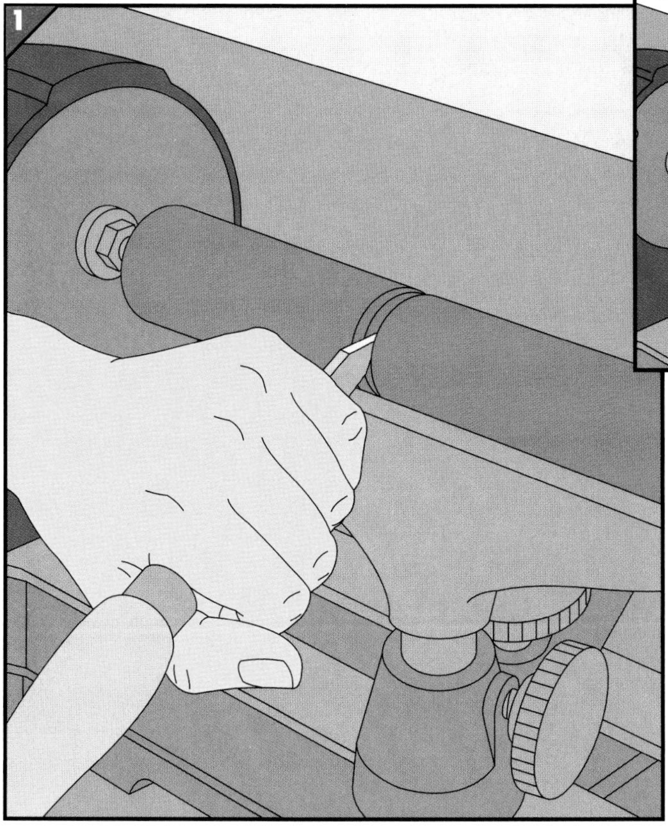

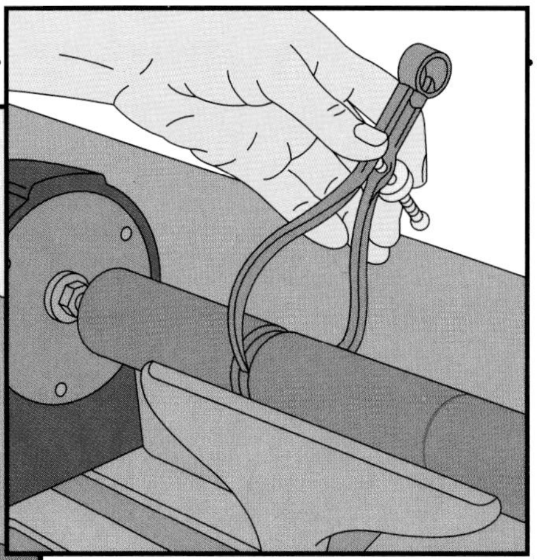

1. Sizing the taper ends.

◆ Turn the blank into a cylinder *(page 94)* about $\frac{1}{8}$ inch larger in diameter than the wide end of the planned taper.
◆ Mark the ends of the taper with a pencil; if the taper will be longer than 8 inches, mark its center as well.
◆ At one end of the taper, place a parting tool on edge on the tool rest, and allow the lower end of the bevel on the cutting edge to rub against the wood; then, raise the handle to drive the cutting edge into the stock. Ease the tip forward into the wood, cutting a groove *(left)*.
◆ Check the depth of the cut frequently with calipers set to the desired diameter *(inset)*. Make each depth cut with this same technique.

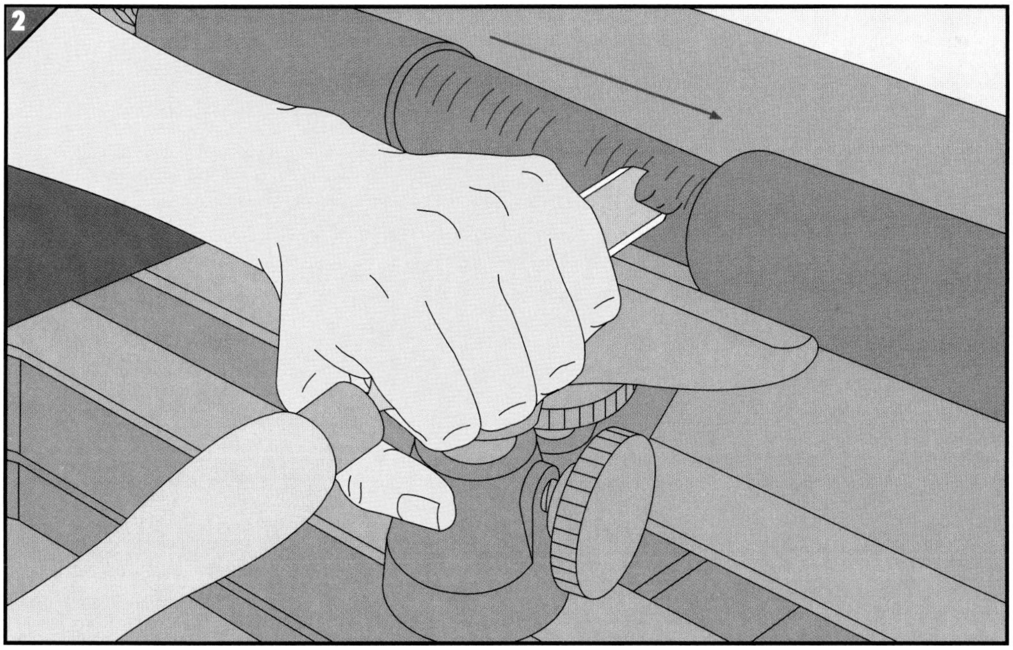

2. Cutting the taper.

◆ Starting at the groove at the wide end of the taper, cut along the entire length of the taper using the same technique as for rough-cutting a cylinder *(page 94, Step 1)*, but gradually apply greater forward pressure with the roughing gouge so as to remove more wood as you approach the narrow end. Repeat this cutting motion until both ends of the taper have the desired diameter.
◆ Plane the surface of the taper with a skew chisel *(page 94, Step 2)*.

TURNING A POMMEL

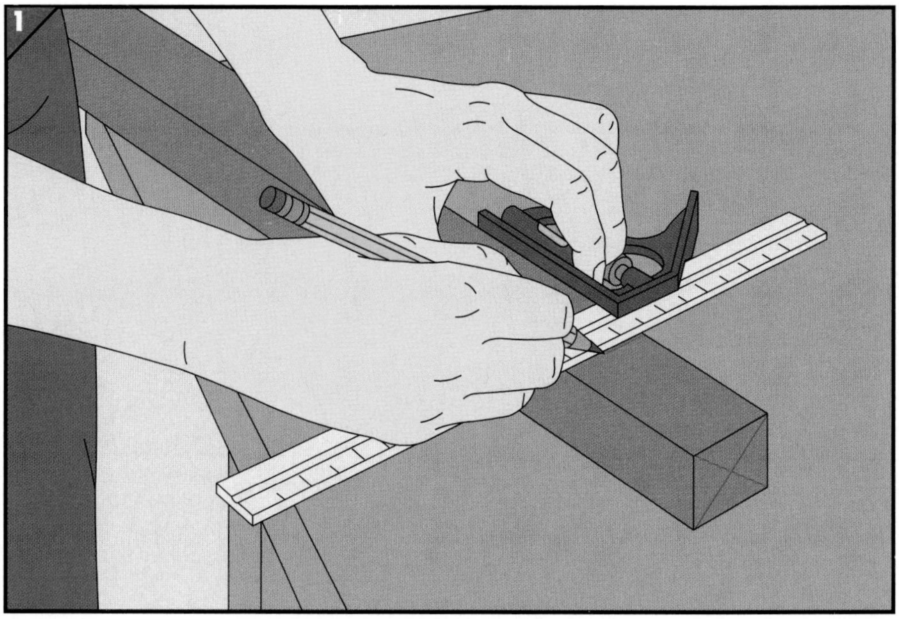

1. Marking the square section.

◆ Cut a length of stock into a square with a table saw, then plane or sand the surfaces smooth.

◆ With a combination square, mark the ends of the section that will remain square after the turning is finished *(right)*.

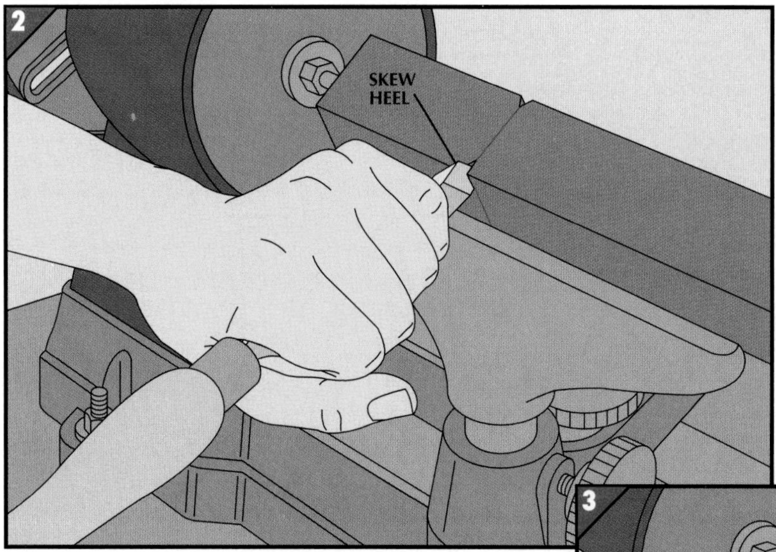

2. Cutting a groove.

◆ Set the tool rest at the center of the blank $\frac{1}{4}$ inch from the corner of the wood.

◆ Turn on the lathe and set a skew chisel, point down, on the tool rest, with the handle angled slightly downward.

◆ Slowly push the point of the blade straight into the wood at the mark. Then roll the tool handle alternately to the left and the right, opening up the cut to form a V groove at each corner about $\frac{1}{2}$ inch wide *(left)*.

◆ Make the same cut at any other marks.

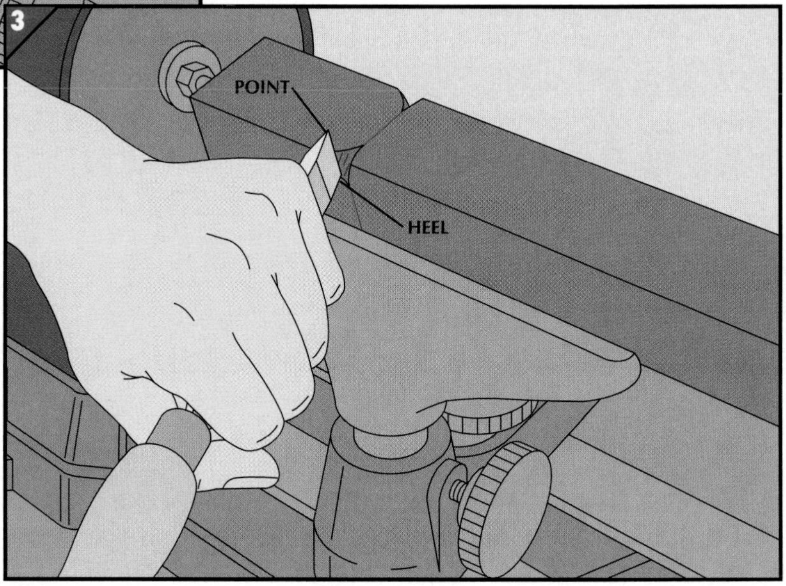

3. Rounding the shoulders.

◆ With the wood still spinning, reposition the chisel on the tool rest in line with the V groove, with the point of the blade on top and angled toward the section that will remain square. The cutting edge should be almost horizontal, the point well above the spinning corners.

◆ Rub the bevel against the wood; then, with a motion similar to that used to shape a bead *(page 96, Step 2)*, raise the tool handle so the cutting edge contacts the wood. Roll the heel of the cutting edge down into the V groove, ending the motion with the cutting edge in a vertical position *(right)*.

◆ Repeat the cut until the shoulder is fully rounded.

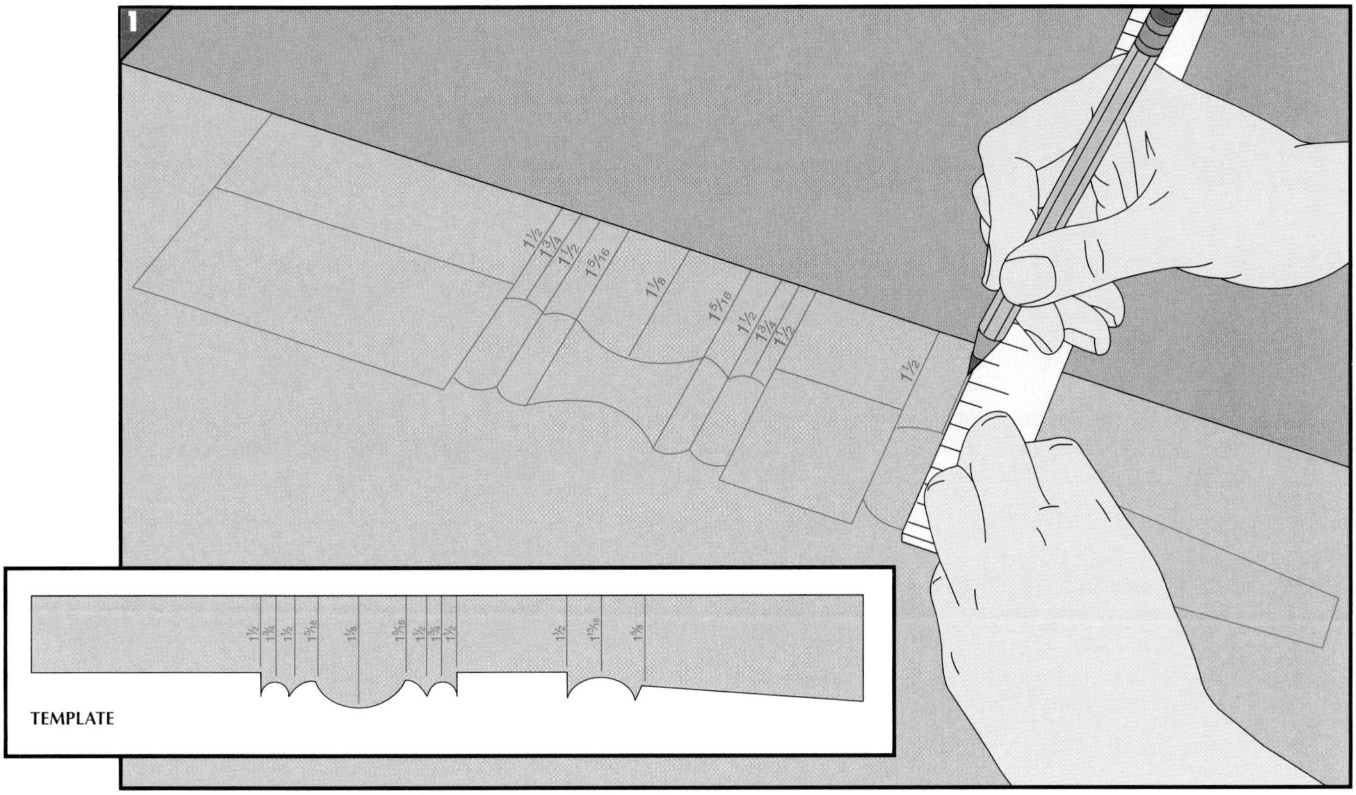

1. Making the template.

◆ Outline the design on a sheet of heavy paper, leaving about 2 inches between the sketch and one edge of the sheet.
◆ Measure the diameters of transition points in the design, then draw a line from each point to the edge of the paper *(above)*, marking the measured diameters on the lines as you go. For a taper longer than 8 inches, also measure and mark the diameter at its midpoint.
◆ Glue the pattern to a piece of $\frac{1}{8}$-inch hardboard, lining up the edges of the paper and the hardboard.
◆ With a band saw, cut out the pattern along the edge nearest the edge of the hardboard to achieve the shape shown in the inset. Smooth the edges of the template with a file.

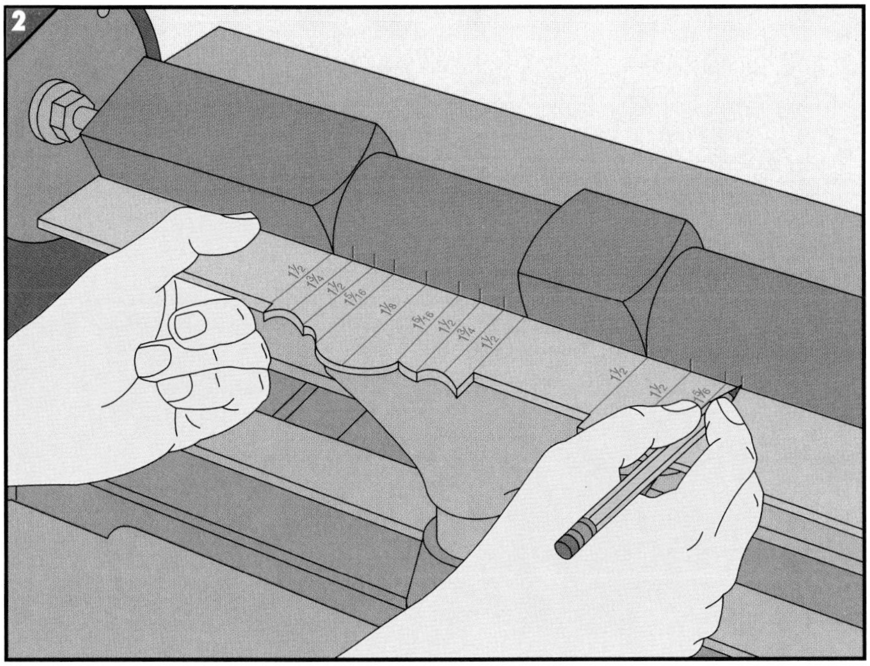

2. Marking guidelines on a blank.

◆ Turn a blank into a cylinder *(page 94)*, leaving any pommel sections square *(page 98)*.
◆ Holding the straight edge of the template against the blank with the ends of the two pieces aligned, extend the marked lines of the template onto the blank *(left)*.
◆ At each mark, place the pencil on the tool rest with its point against the blank and rotate the spindle by hand to extend the guideline around the cylinder.

TRICKS OF THE TRADE

A Layout Tool for Multiple Turnings

The jig shown at right can make quick work of scribing accurate layout lines on several blanks to be turned into the same shape. Sketch the design on a plywood scrap and drive a finishing nail into one edge at each transition point. Snip off the nailheads with wire cutters and file each end to a point. Once a blank has been shaped into a cylinder, set the jig on the tool rest and lightly press it into the spinning wood; the nails will score all the layout lines on the blank at once.

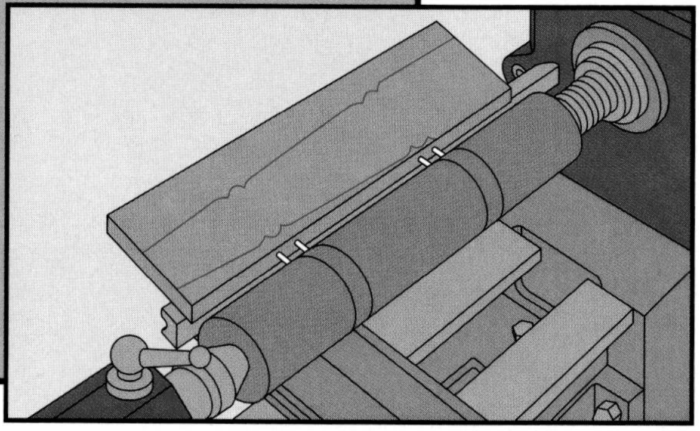

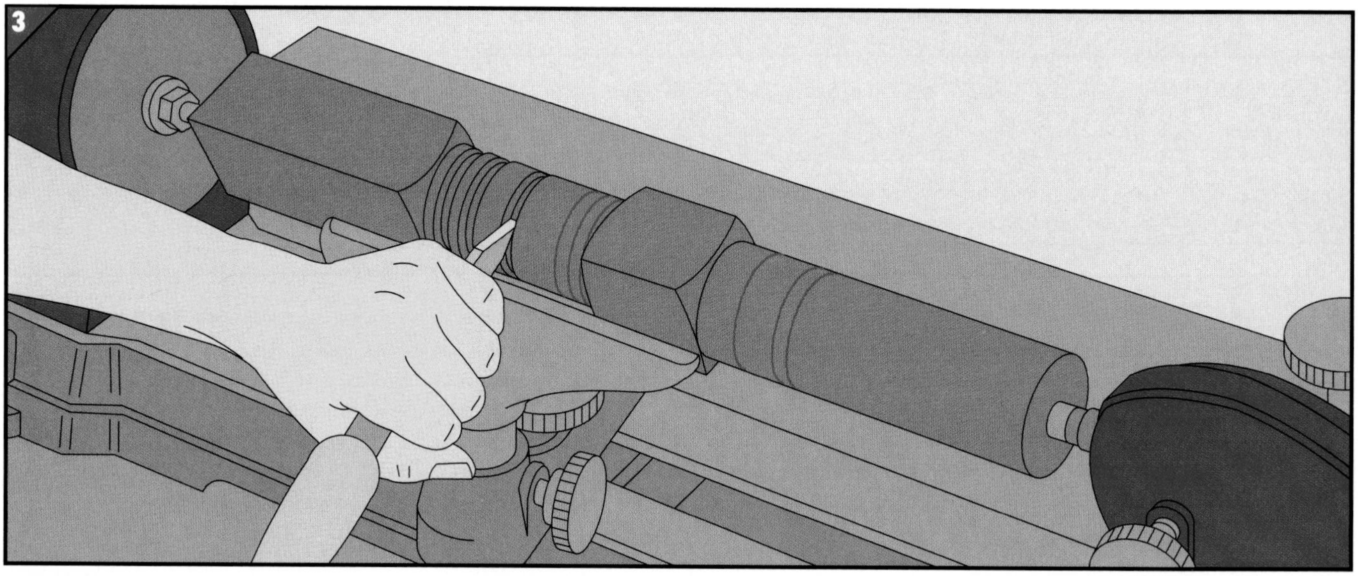

3. Making the parting cuts.

◆ With a parting tool *(page 97, Step 1)*, cut a groove at every guideline that indicates the high or low point of a cove or taper, or the high point of a bead *(above)*. Do not use the parting tool at the low point of a bead or at the shoulder of a rectangular section. Stopping occasionally to check with calipers, make the diameter of each groove equal to the marked measurement on the template.

◆ When all the grooves have been cut to the correct depth, turn the individual elements *(pages 95-99)*.

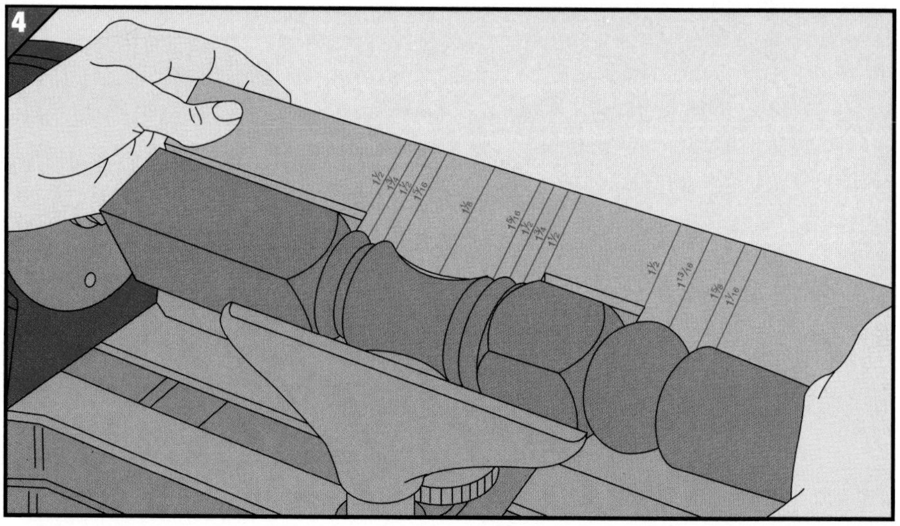

4. Checking your work with the template.

As you shape the blank, stop the lathe periodically and hold the cut edge of the template against your work *(above)*. The template should fit perfectly against the blank—any gaps between the template and the wood indicate that some sections need additional cutting.

FINISHING TURNED WOOD

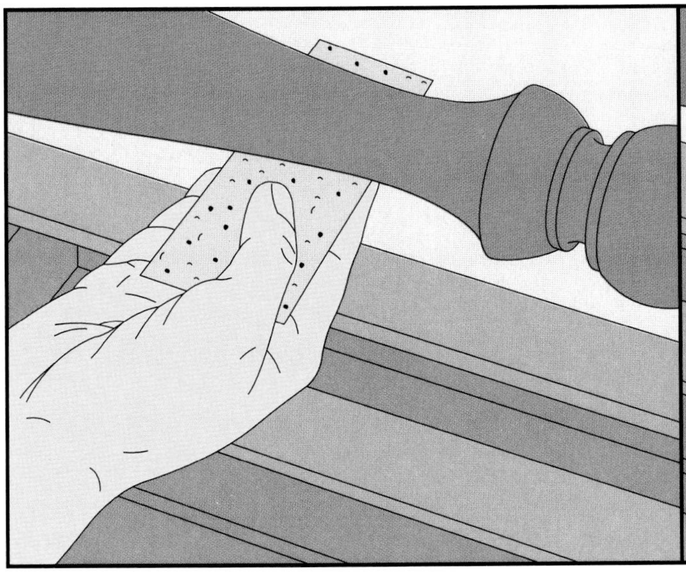

Sanding a spindle turning.
The amount of sanding needed will vary with the quality of the turning job. Crisp, clean turnings may not need any sanding at all. If the wood needs only a light smoothing, leave the lathe turned off and sand the wood with the grain using 220-grit sandpaper.

If the wood is a bit rough, it can be sanded with the lathe spinning and the tool rest removed:
◆ For broad surfaces such as a vase or taper, fold a piece of 120- to 180-grit sandpaper in thirds to a width of about 2 inches. Hold the paper under the spinning stock, pressing lightly and moving steadily back and forth along the surface *(above, left)*. Repeat the procedure with 220- to 280-grit paper.
◆ For tighter areas such as a small cove, wrap the sandpaper around a form such as a dowel or wedge that fits the shape. Hold the form and sandpaper below the stock as it spins, pressing lightly to avoid rubbing away the definition of the shape *(above, right)*. Progress to a finer grade of paper and repeat the sanding procedure.

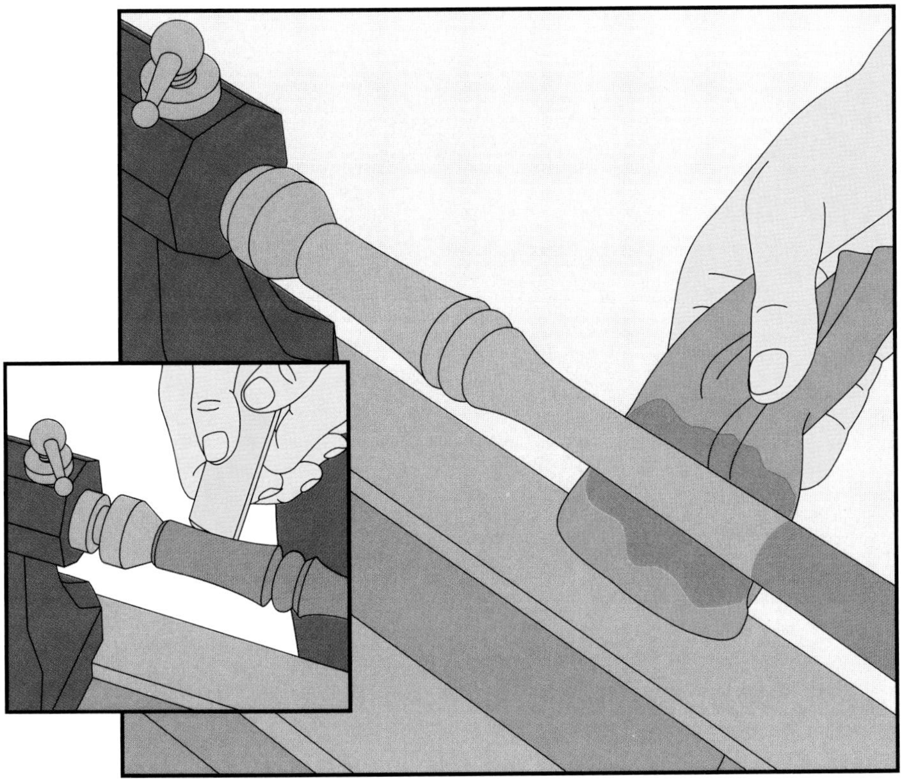

Oiling and waxing a turning.
◆ Set the lathe to its slowest speed.
◆ Dampen a soft cotton cloth with tung oil or linseed oil and rub it into the spinning wood from underneath, making sure the cloth is not wrapped around your fingers *(left)*. Let the oil dry.
◆ To apply a wax polish, move the lathe to a higher speed. Holding a turner's wax stick against the spinning workpiece, move the stick quickly along the wood to prevent wax buildup *(inset)*.
◆ Hold a soft cotton cloth against the wood to buff the finish, rubbing until the wax is melted and the desired gloss is achieved.

Turning Wood on a Faceplate

Turning wood secured to a faceplate allows you to create bowls, doorknobs, newel-post caps, and other shapes that cannot be held between the spindle centers. Although some lathes are equipped for "outboard" turning, which allows large blanks to be fastened to the outer face of the headstock, on most models, the maximum radius of a faceplate workpiece is limited by the distance between the spindle and the lathe bed—about 8 inches.

Securing Blanks: Faceplates that screw onto the headstock spindle and anchor the wood are available in several sizes *(page 91)*. Choose one about $\frac{1}{2}$ inch smaller in diameter than the base of the piece you are planning to turn. Use No. 8 wood screws to fasten most blanks to the faceplate; screws should be as long as possible—up to 2 inches—without extending into a part of the blank that will be cut away during the turning process. Lightweight pieces can be secured with double-sided tape.

Preparing the Wood: As in spindle work, a blank for faceplate turning is first squared with a table saw. Then, locate the center point of the blank and with a compass, mark a circle from the center point $\frac{1}{8}$ inch larger than the largest diameter of the finished piece. Trim away excess wood outside the circle with a band saw.

Round the sides and face of the wood with a bowl gouge—a hefty version of a spindle gouge. Shape and smooth the work with scraping tools, which work better than gouges on wider surfaces—such as the sides of a bowl—and on end grain.

TOOLS

- Faceplate
- Electric drill
- Roughing gouge
- Skew chisel
- Bowl gouge
- Roundnose scraper
- Squarenose scraper

SAFETY TIPS

Protect your eyes with goggles when operating a lathe.

FASHIONING A NEWEL-POST CAP

1. Fastening the stock to the faceplate.

◆ Position the faceplate on one end of the blank, aligning its threaded center hole with the marked center point on the wood. Mark the faceplate screw-hole locations on the blank *(right)*.

◆ Drill a pilot hole at each mark and fasten the faceplate to the stock with No. 8 wood screws, then screw the faceplate to the headstock spindle on the lathe.

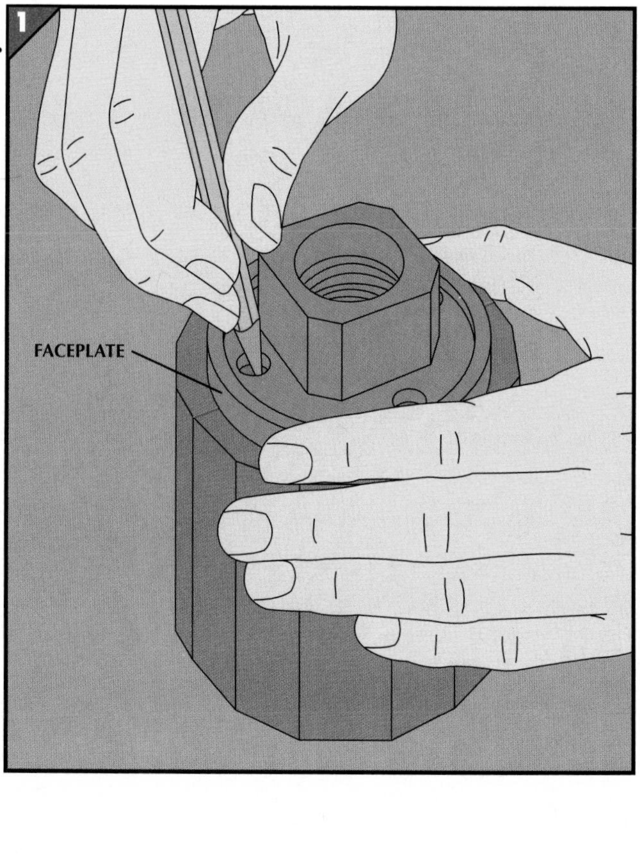

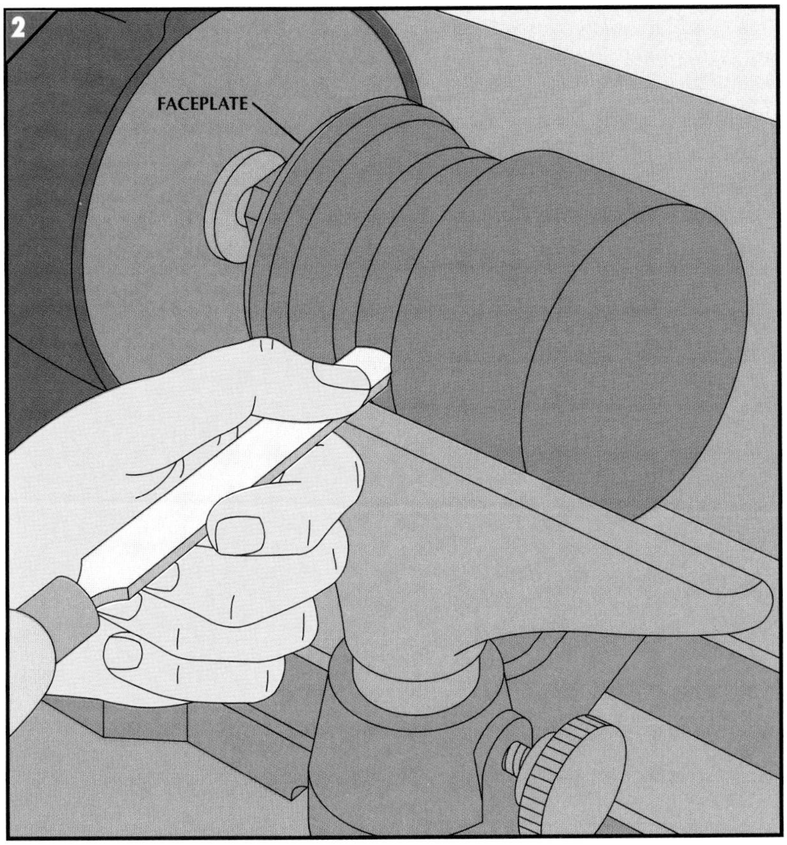

2. Shaping the blank's sides.
◆ Smooth the wood to a cylinder *(page 94)*, then shape any other elements that are part of the design *(pages 95-98)*. Round and shape the front of the piece with a bowl gouge.
◆ To shape a cove around the sides of the blank, set a roundnose scraper on the tool rest at the planned center of the newel-post cap, and hold the tool bevel edge down *(page 92)*. Press the cutting edge straight into the spinning wood to open a groove *(left)*. Widen the groove to the desired cove shape by repeating the same scraping procedure on both sides of the groove, increasing the forward pressure as you go.

3. Rounding the end cap.
◆ To smooth the dome shape on the end of the blank, set the tool rest at about a 45-degree angle to the centerline of the stock and $\frac{1}{4}$ inch from the wood.
◆ Rest a squarenose scraper, bevel down, on the tool rest and push the left corner of the cutting edge into the spinning wood to scrape a shallow groove.
◆ Gradually slide the blade along the tool rest, pivoting the cutting edge in a gentle arc toward the center of the stock without moving the tool past the center *(right)*.
◆ Repeat the scraping motion until the wood is the desired shape, stopping periodically to reposition the tool rest closer to the wood.

Power Sanders

You can speed the process of smoothing the various pieces of a woodworking project with a power sander. A combination belt-and-disk sander *(below)* will take much of the tedium and effort out of sanding.

Choosing a Sander: The belt sander of a combination tool can smooth board faces and edges as well as end grain. With minor adjustments, it can also be used to sand curved surfaces *(page 106)*. For stock wider than the belt, use a hand-held belt sander. To free your hands for better control of the stock, you can build a simple shop-made jig to transform the handheld sander into a stationary tool *(page 107)*. The disk sander of the combination tool is best suited to sanding end grain.

TOOLS

Try square
T-bevel
Circular saw
Screwdriver
Clamps

MATERIALS

Plywood ($\frac{3}{4}$")
Wood screws
($1\frac{1}{4}$" No. 6)

SAFETY TIPS

Wear goggles and a dust mask when power sanding.

Power-Sander Safety

In addition to the safety rules for power tools listed on page 14, observe these precautions:

- ✔ When using the belt sander, feed the stock against the rotation of the belt, to prevent the work from being pulled off the machine.
- ✔ When using the disk sander, hold the workpiece against the downward rotation of the disk, to keep the work from being lifted off the disk.
- ✔ Clean all wood dust from the machine before sanding anything metal; the sparks produced by sanding metal could ignite wood dust.
- ✔ Replace frayed belts and disks, or a disk with loose adhesive; they can fly off the sander.

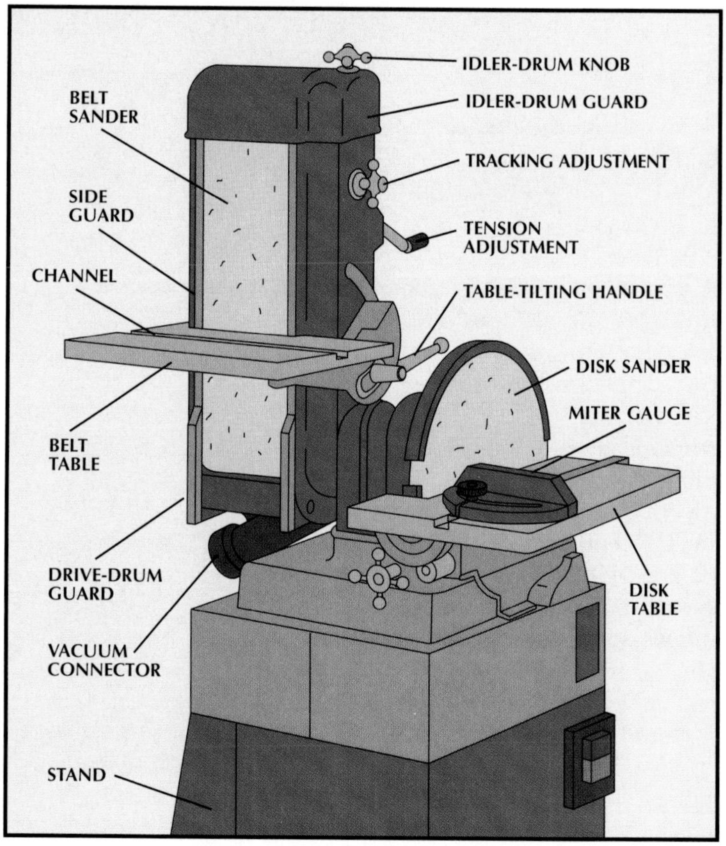

A combination sander.
This shop tool is two sanders powered by a single motor. The belt sander, which tilts from vertical to horizontal, has a continuous strip of abrasive-coated fabric that rides over two drums—the drive drum, turned by the motor, and the idler drum, which turns freely. Handles and knobs on the sides change the position of the idler drum to adjust the tracking and tension of the belt. Guards around the belt can be removed for special sanding jobs. The disk sander, attached to the motor shaft, is a metal plate to which an abrasive disk is glued. Worktables for both sanders—usually having channels for miter gauges—can be tilted and locked at any angle up to 45 degrees for smoothing bevels and miters.

SANDING FLAT SURFACES

Sanding with the grain.

◆ Remove the idler-drum guard and lock the belt unit in a horizontal position.

◆ With the motor on, grip the board with your left hand and feed it onto the belt with your right hand against the rotation of the belt. Keep the grain parallel to the belt and move the board along the length of the belt in a continuous motion, maintaining light, even pressure *(right)*. Make repeated passes over the belt until the surface is smooth.

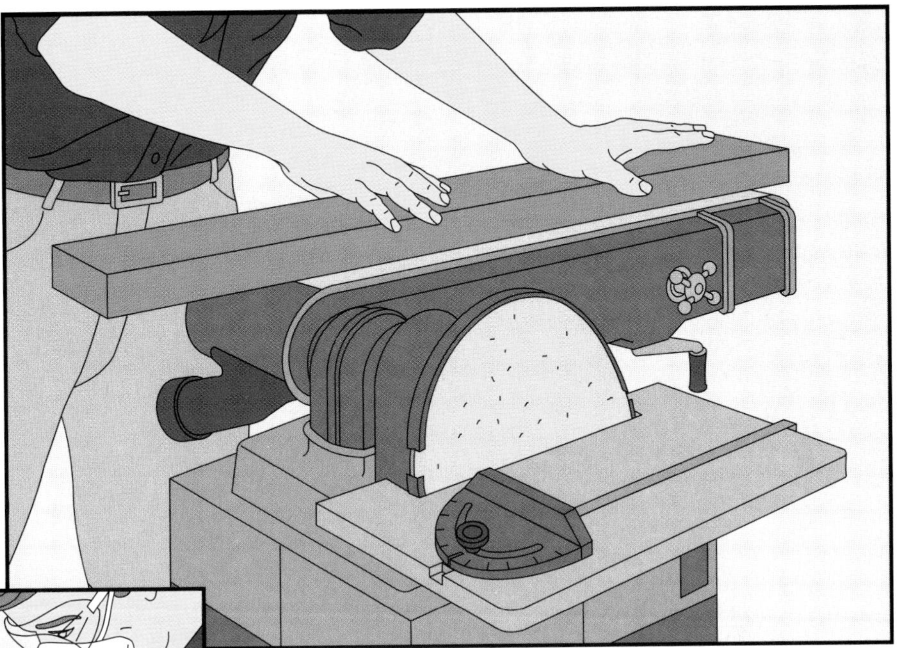

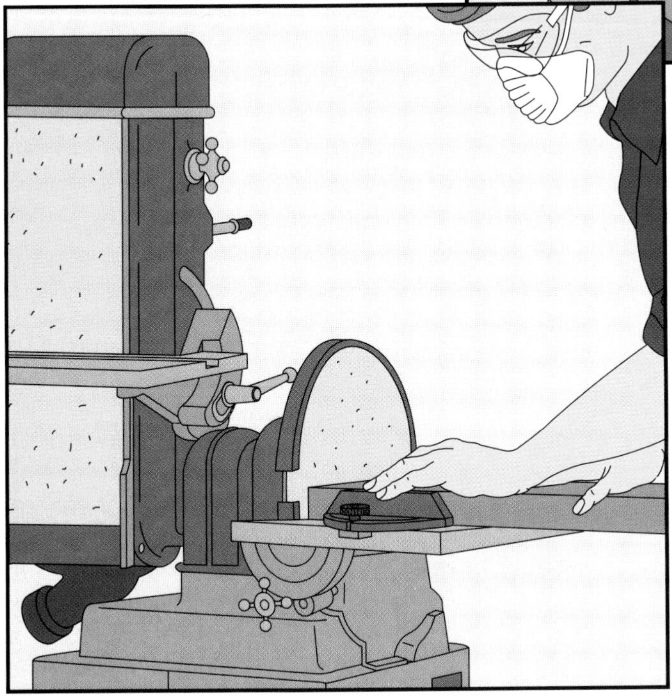

Sanding end grain.

◆ For a square end, position the disk table horizontally, using a try square to make sure it is perpendicular to the sanding disk.

◆ Place the miter gauge—set at a right angle—in its channel, and hold the board against the miter gauge.

◆ With the motor on, press the end of the board against the left side of the disk, on the downward side of its rotation, and move it back and forth between the left edge and the center of the disk, maintaining light, continuous pressure *(above)*. You can use a miter gauge, if necessary, to keep the wood square to the disk.

For a mitered end, adjust the miter gauge to the desired angle and sand as for a square end. To sand a beveled end, set the disk table at the desired angle with a T-bevel.

TRICKS OF THE TRADE

Cleaning Sanding Belts

A fast and easy way to remove sawdust and loose abrasive grit from sanding belts is with a block of neoprene rubber. Set the sander on its side, lock the motor on, and hold the rubber block against the rotating belt for a few seconds. The dust and grit will rub off onto the rubber.

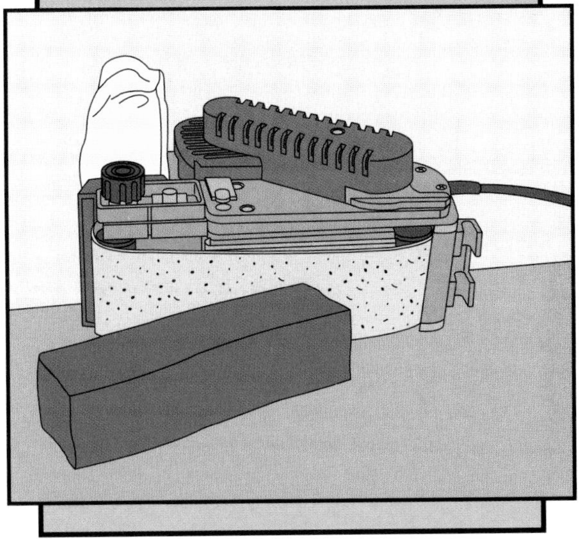

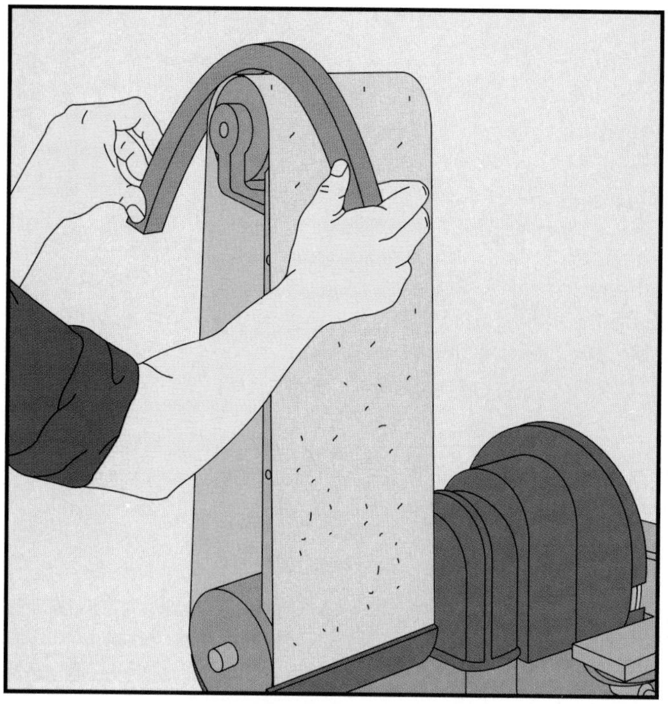

Sanding an inside curve.

◆ Remove the idler-drum guard, loosen the belt-unit locking nut, and lock the unit in its vertical position.

◆ Turn on the motor and gently pass the inside of the curved piece over the belt at the idler drum, against the rotation of the belt; maintain a light, even pressure and feed the piece continuously *(above)*. After each pass, return to your starting point; repeat the procedure until the surface is smooth.

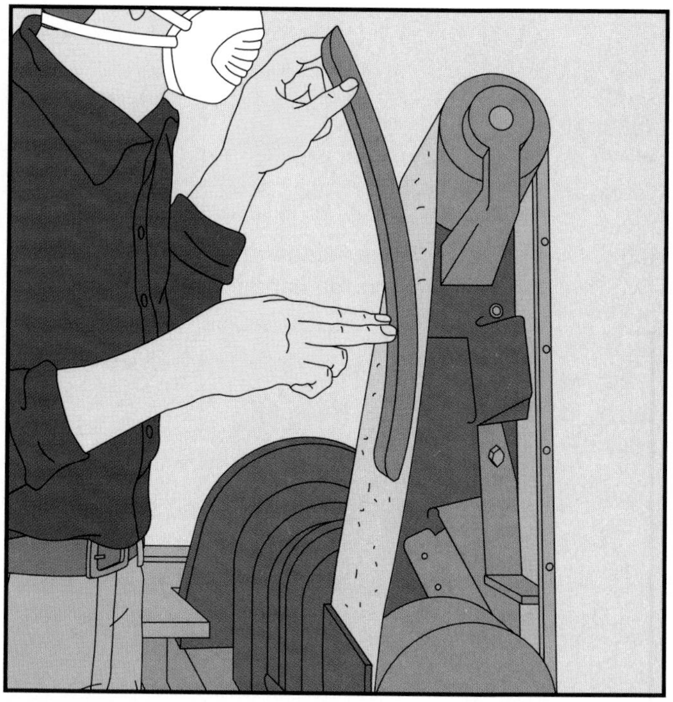

Sanding an outside curve.

◆ With the belt unit locked in its vertical position, remove the idler-drum guard, the side guard, and the back plate. Reduce belt tension so the belt yields slightly when pressed.

◆ Turn on the motor and move the curved piece against the back of the belt, pressing against it slightly so the belt follows the curve of the piece *(above)*. Pay close attention to the tracking of the belt over the drums, and adjust the tracking knob as necessary.

TRICKS OF THE TRADE

A Template for Sanding Curves

A sanding template can help you smooth several pieces to the same curved shape. Cut a piece of softwood on a band saw to the desired shape, smooth it with the belt sander, and attach a piece of scrap wood to its side with $1\frac{1}{4}$-inch No. 6 wood screws *(inset)*. To prepare the sander, remove the idler-drum guard and the side guard, and tilt the belt sander to its horizontal position. Loosen the belt enough to fit the template between the belt and the base plate, then adjust the tension—you may need to buy a longer belt. To use the jig, turn on the sander, adjust the tracking, and hold the workpiece against the belt above the template *(right)*.

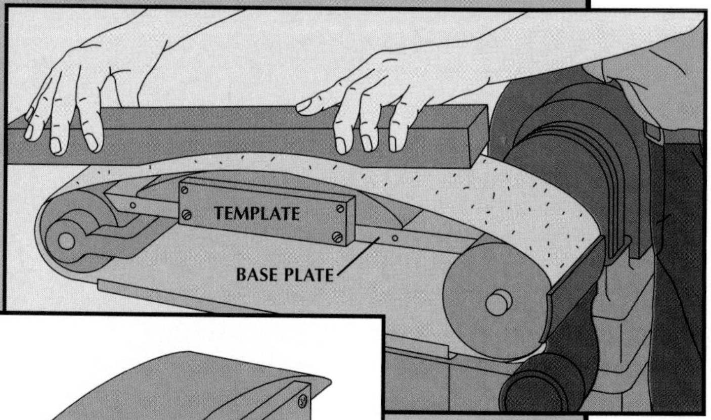

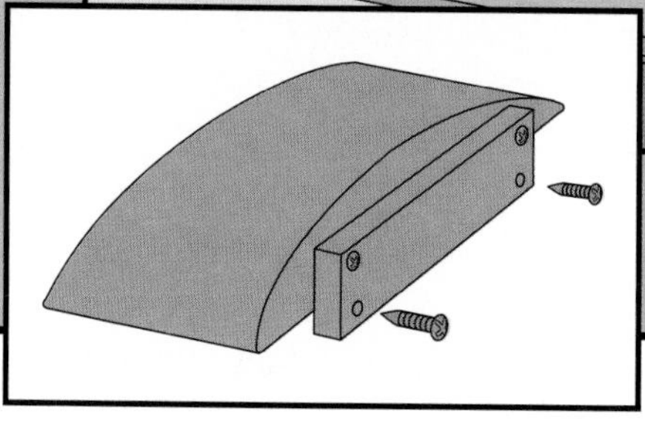

A PORTABLE BELT-SANDER STAND

Smoothing mitered ends.

To give you more control when using a handheld belt sander to smooth ends and edges, mount the tool in a sanding table.

◆ To make the table *(inset)*, first cut the base about 2 feet square from $\frac{3}{4}$-inch plywood and cut another piece 9 inches wide and 2 feet long for the raised table. Set the sander on its side on the base, then cut two support posts to fit in the handles. Fasten the posts to the base with $1\frac{1}{4}$-inch No. 6 wood screws driven from the underside, placed to hold the sander at the desired position. Fasten the raised table to the base so there will be a slight gap between its edge and the belt.

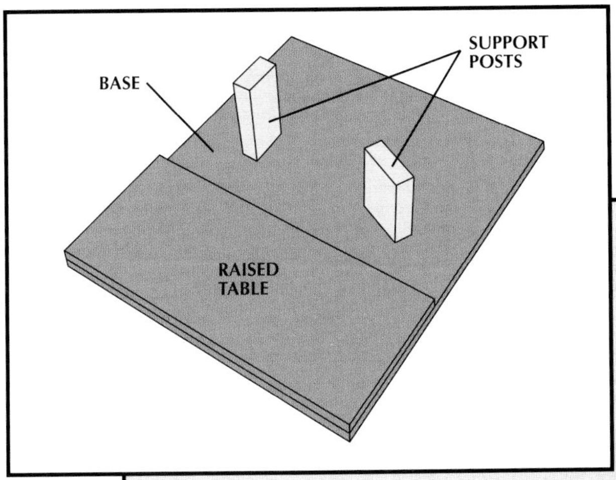

◆ To use the stand, cut a stop block, trimming one end to the desired angle for the piece to be sanded, then attach it to the table with the trimmed end flush with the raised table's edge.

◆ Clamp the stand to a work surface and slip the portable belt sander handles over the support posts.

◆ Turn on the sander and place the workpiece flat on the raised table. With one edge flush against the stop block, gently feed the end to be smoothed into the belt *(below)*.

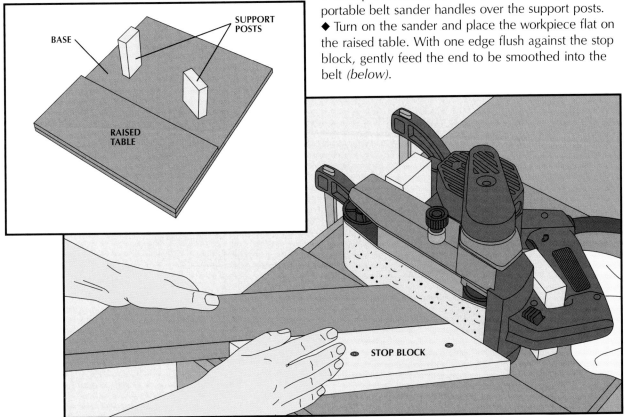

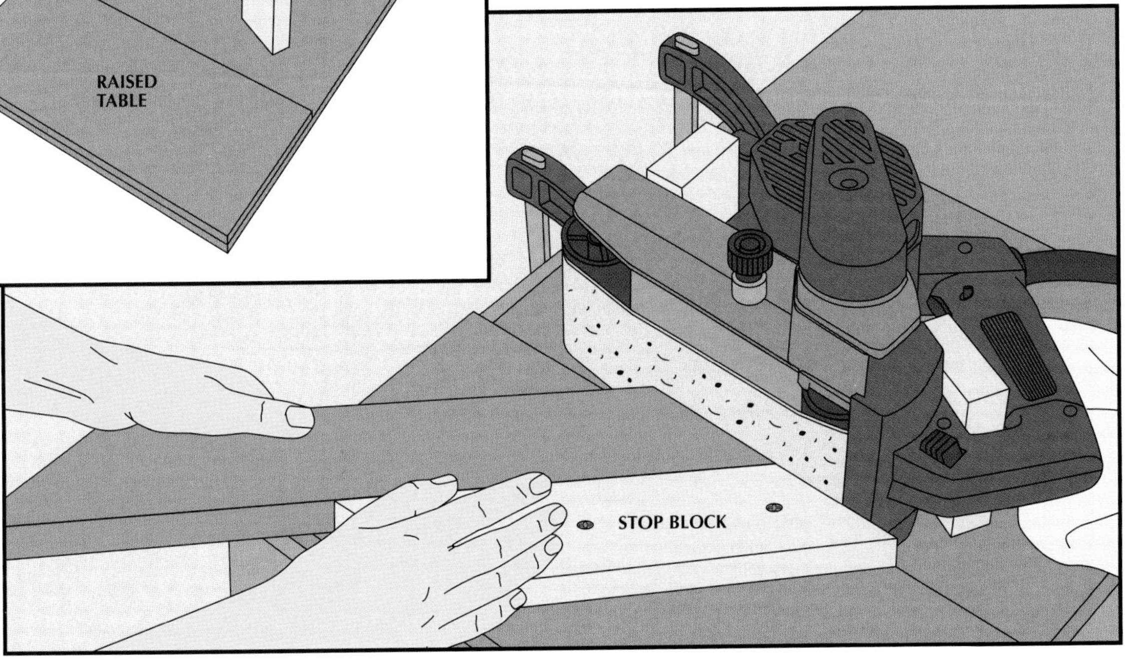

A COMMERCIAL SANDER STAND

Instead of building a stand for your portable belt sander, you can purchase a commercial stand *(right)*. Most manufacturers make stands to fit their sanders. To use a typical model, mount the tool in the stand, then clamp the stand to a work surface. Set the table to the desired angle, turn on the sander and, holding the workpiece flat on the table, advance it into the belt with light pressure.

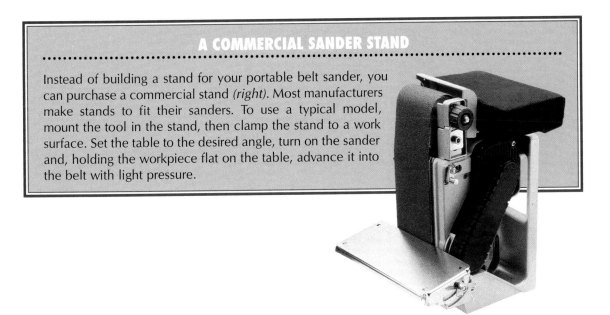

4

Skin-Deep Beauty with Veneers

Many exotic and attractive wood species are available only as veneers. Though almost as fragile as an eggshell, veneer can make plain boards stronger and more resistant to warping. More important, it frees the craftsman to display the grain in ways that are economically or structurally impossible with solid wood.

Trimming excess veneer →

Covering a Wood Base with Veneer

Veneers are sliced from logs, burls, stumps, and crotches in sheets as thin as $\frac{1}{40}$ inch. Their edges are generally left untrimmed, and they are sold by the square foot. Another form of veneer is sliced only $\frac{1}{64}$ inch thick, glued to a paper backing, and is sold in 8-foot rolls.

Planning the Job: Make the base to be veneered from a stable wood such as pine or plywood. Sand off splinters and fill holes with wood putty. With stock that is less than $\frac{1}{2}$ inch thick, veneer both surfaces—otherwise, the piece will warp. Unlike veneer in rolls, sheets of richly patterned woods, which tend to be brittle, first need to be flattened. Dampen each sheet with a sponge, then press it between two pieces of plywood. As the veneer flattens, increase the pressure gradually with clamps. Apply the veneer while it is still slightly damp to the touch.

Veneering Techniques: Veneer usually covers flat surfaces *(pages 112-113)*, although curves can also be veneered *(page 114)*. On a solid-wood base, apply veneer so its grain runs parallel to that of the base.

Glue veneer to plywood so the grains are perpendicular to each other. The base can be covered with a single sheet or several arranged in a pattern *(below)*. Splice multiple sections carefully so the seam between them is invisible. To complete the job, decorative bands can be added and edging applied to hide the end grain *(pages 119-120)*.

Avoid finishing veneers with water-base stains, which may cause the wood to buckle. Any other type of finish is acceptable.

An integral part of the art of veneering is repair, including replacing damaged areas with an invisible patch *(page 115-116)* and flattening an air pocket *(page 117)*.

TOOLS

- Straightedge
- Clamps
- Utility knife
- Veneer saw
- Paint roller
- Awl
- Hand roller
- Handsaw
- Veneer hammer
- Craft knife
- Wood chisel
- Glue injector
- Bar clamps
- Block plane

MATERIALS

- Veneer
- Wood glue
- Veneer pins
- Veneer tape
- Plywood
- Wax paper
- Leather scrap
- 2 x 4s
- Sandpaper (very fine-grade)
- Contact cement
- Edge banding
- Scrap board

PAIR-BONDED VENEERS

Combining veneers for effect.
Consecutive sheets of veneer cut from a flitch—a squared-off log—are nearly identical in pattern, but can be arranged to create different designs *(right)*. Two sheets that present a mirror image of each other, as if they were consecutive pages of a book, are called book-matched veneer; you can extend book-matching over a large surface by turning every second sheet end for end. Veneer sheets—ideally long, narrow ones—laid in a repeating pattern just as they come from the stack are called slip-matched. Four sheets of straight-grained veneer can be arranged in a diamond pattern or as a reverse diamond, in which the grain radiates from a central point.

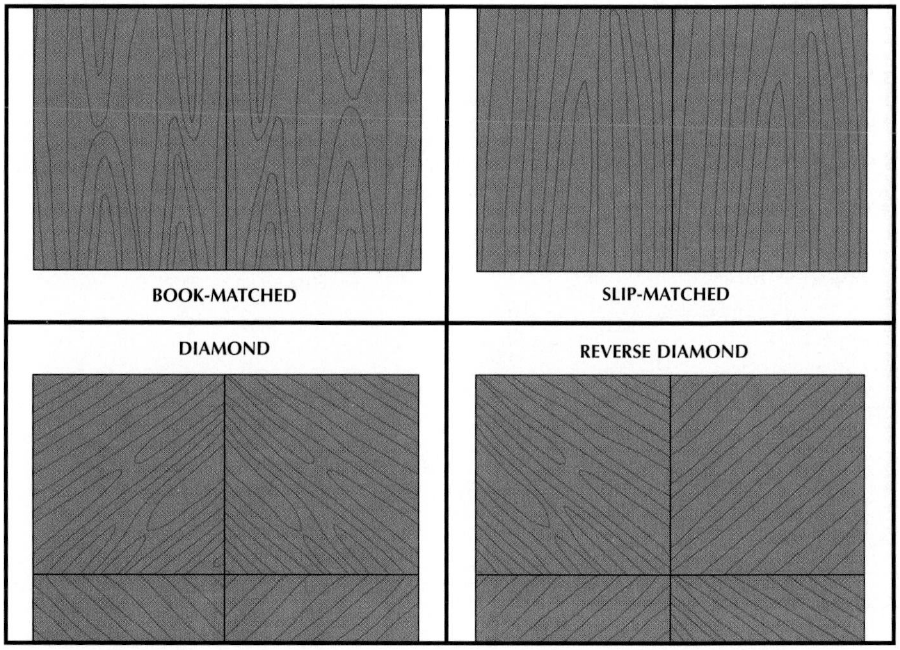

Tools of the trade.

Veneering employs a raft of specialized implements for cutting and gluing. Cutting tools include a veneer saw, whose curved blade and fine teeth ensure a clean edge, and a router plane. The plane can be used instead of a power router to excavate shallow grooves for inlays: You first need to outline the groove with a craft knife and a straightedge, then guide the plane's blade freehand along the scored lines to clear out the waste. A veneer punch, which excises damaged veneer and makes a patch to fit, and a craft knife are handy for repairs—as is a needle-tip glue injector, used to introduce glue under veneer that has separated from the underlying base. For durable glue joints between veneer and base, the veneer is pressed to a flat surface with a hand roller and to a curved surface with a veneer hammer. This hammer has a semicircular edge at one end to prevent scratching the veneer, and an angled face at the other end for working in tight places, and is never used to strike anything.

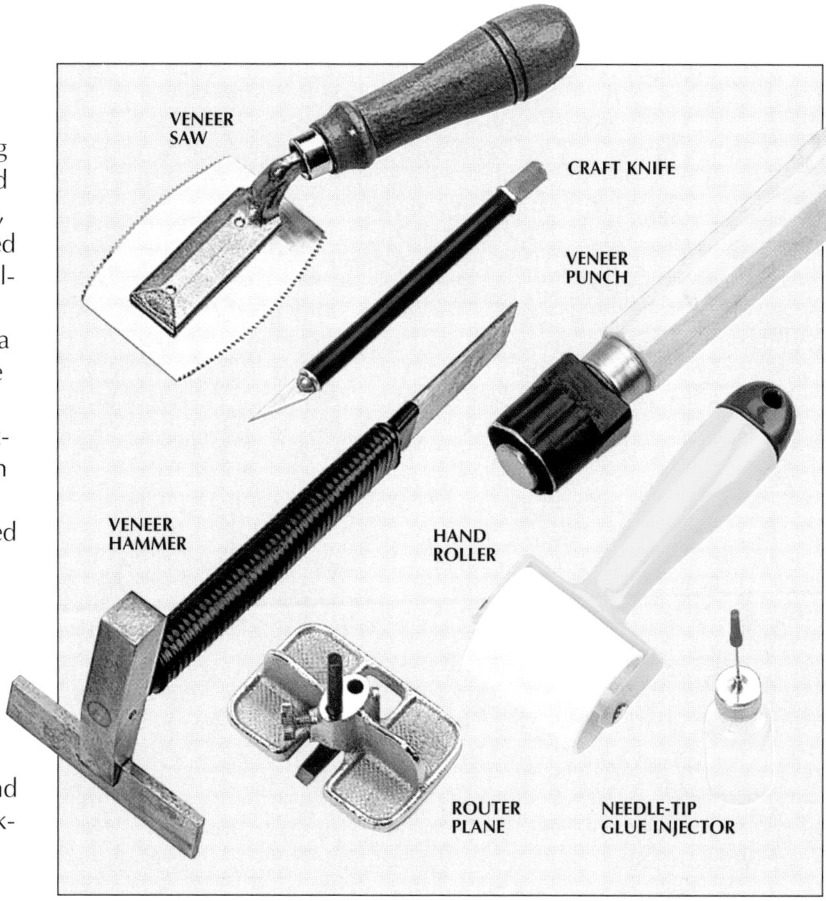

Selecting a Veneering Glue

✓ Polyvinyl acetate (white glue) is an inexpensive, water-soluble adhesive that starts to dry in three to five minutes, thus requiring swift clamping. Apply it with a paint roller, a brush, or a comb-type glue spreader. With highly figured veneers, which warp when exposed to water, spread glue only on the base. Clean all application tools in warm water.

✓ Aliphatic-resin glue, commonly called carpenter's or yellow glue, starts to dry in about five minutes—clamp the pieces being bonded quickly. Yellow glue is the best type to use for hammer veneering *(page 114)*. Spread the glue on both the base and the back of the veneer with a paint roller. Wait until the glue is tacky—five minutes—before pressing the veneer to the base. Tools should be cleaned immediately with water.

✓ Contact cement bonds instantly, needing no clamping. This feature makes it ideal for veneering edges, but it does not allow for repositioning once the veneer is applied. Work in a well-ventilated room, using a paintbrush to spread the cement on both the veneer and the base. Let it dry until it is no longer sticky. Then carefully press the veneer in place with your fingers and a roller. Clean your tools with lacquer thinner.

✓ Hide glue, which is made from the hide and hooves of animals, has been the classic veneering glue for centuries. Sold as a powder and mixed with water, it starts to dry about 10 minutes after it is applied. Hide glue dries at room temperature to form a durable bond and softens when heated, making it easy to effect minor adjustments and repairs. But because it must be heated during use to about 150°F, it is seldom used by nonprofessionals.

✓ Iron-on glue sheets consist of paper that is coated on both sides with hot-melt glue. The sheets are placed between the base and the veneer, then pressed with a household iron set at low heat. They can be cut to shape with scissors. Quick and convenient to use to cover small areas, the sheets produce a less durable bond than the more conventional glues.

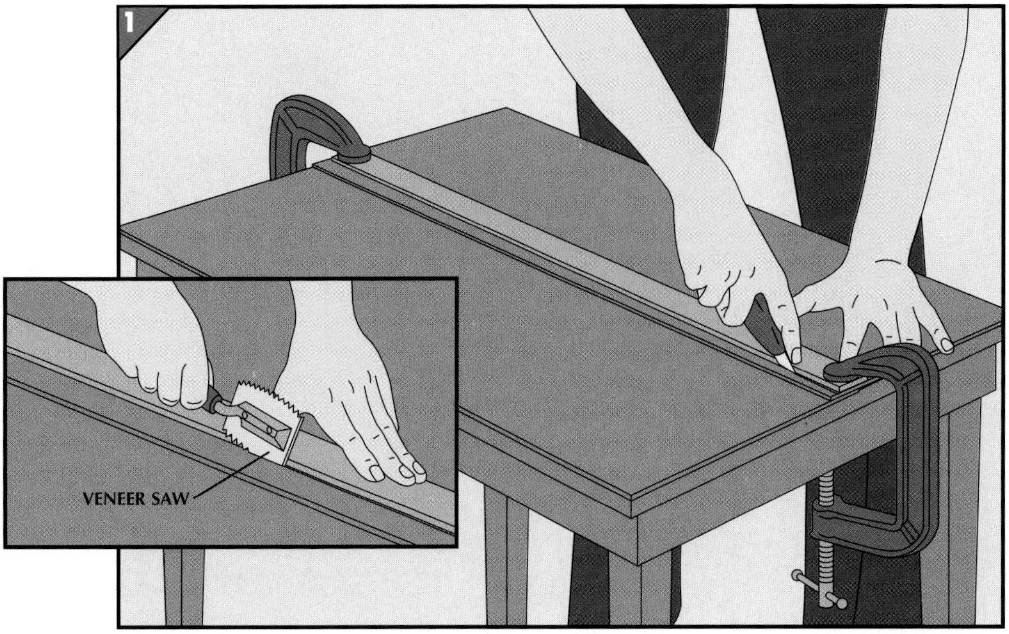

1. Splicing adjoining sheets.
Before beginning, prepare for clamping the veneer: Cut a piece of $\frac{3}{4}$-inch plywood slightly larger than the surface to be veneered, as well as three or four 2-by-4s to match the width of the plywood.
◆ Arrange two sheets of veneer on the base surface in the desired pattern so their adjoining edges overlap by $\frac{1}{2}$ inch and their outside edges extend over the sides of the base by at least $\frac{1}{4}$ inch.
◆ Clamp a straightedge along the overlap and run a utility knife along the guide to cut through both sheets at once *(above)*; use short strokes to prevent the blade from wandering and following the grain.

To cut a seam with a veneer saw, place the tapered edge of the blade against the straightedge, and pull the blade along the overlap, cutting with short, smooth strokes in one direction *(inset)*.

2. Spreading the glue.
◆ Lay the veneer good face down on a work surface covered with newspaper. Spread the appropriate glue *(page 111)* thickly and evenly on the veneer with a small paint roller *(right)*. To prevent the veneer from shifting and glue from smearing its face, hold the sheets steady with an awl.
◆ Apply glue to the base, wiping any drips with a rag.
◆ Position the veneer on the base, matching the grain patterns along seams and maintaining an even overlap along the edges of the base. Press and smooth the surface with your hands, shifting the veneer sections slightly to close any gaps in the seam.
◆ Secure the sheets with veneer pins spaced 6 inches apart and about 3 inches from the seam *(photograph)*; the pins' needlelike points leave nearly invisible holes.

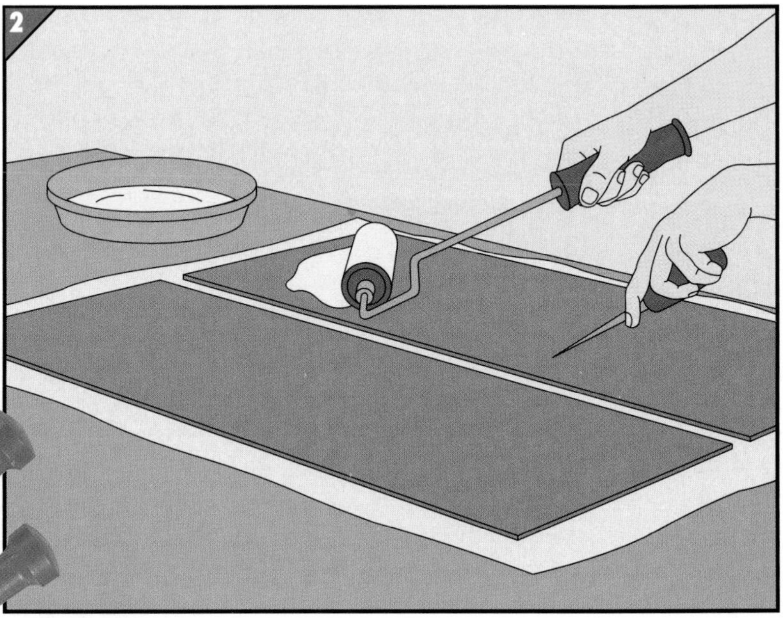

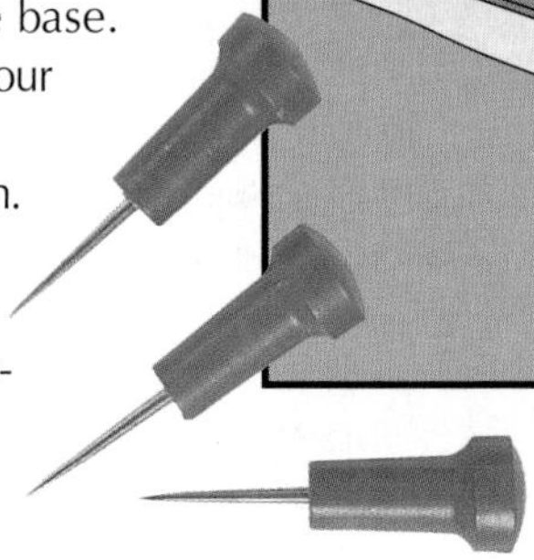

3. Rolling the veneer.

◆ Press out air pockets and excess glue by pushing a hand roller from the center of the base toward the edges, wiping off the extruded glue as you go *(right)*.
◆ Roll along the seam to press it flat.
◆ Cut a piece of veneer tape—special gummed paper tape that won't lift slivers when removed—the length of the seam. Dampen the tape with a sponge, then smooth it in place along the seam. At 12-inch intervals, fasten 4-inch strips of tape across the seam.
◆ Remove the veneer pins.

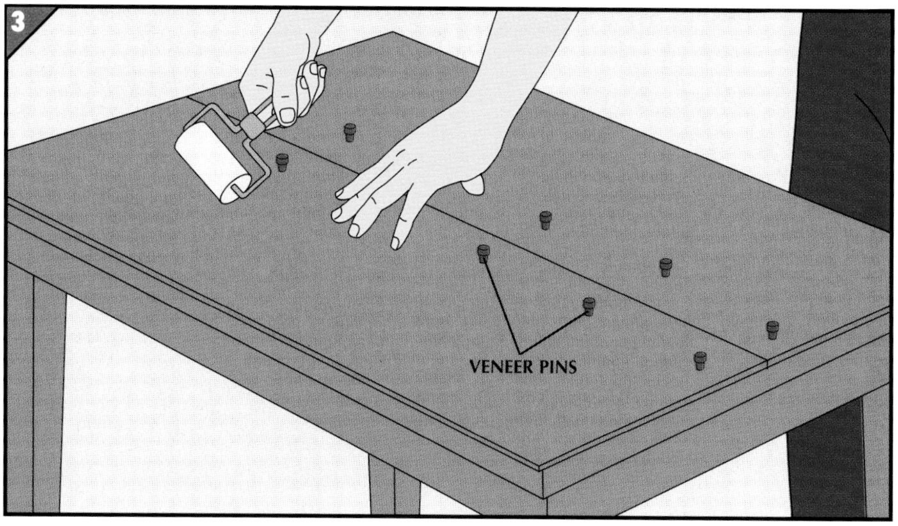

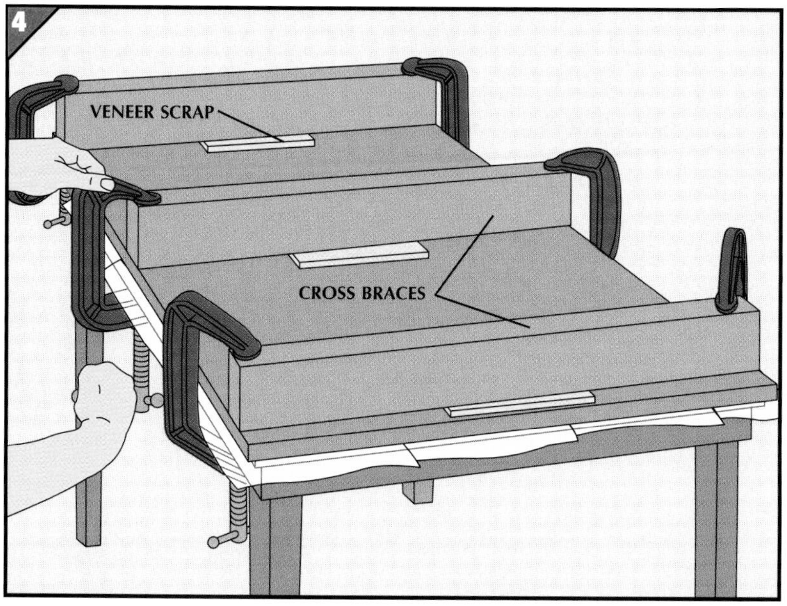

4. Clamping the veneer.

◆ Cover the veneer with wax paper and set the plywood from Step 1 on the veneer.
◆ Set the 2-by-4s on edge across the plywood at 16-inch intervals, slipping a veneer scrap beneath each one. Hold the cross braces in place with clamps, then start tightening the clamps that secure the center cross brace, so that glue will be forced from the center of the plywood toward its edges *(left)*. Wipe off any extruded glue and continue tightening the clamps until glue no longer squeezes out, then tighten the clamps that secure the remaining cross braces.
◆ Let the glue dry 12 hours, then remove the clamps and 2-by-4s.

5. Trimming the edges.

◆ Protecting your worktable with the plywood, set the veneered surface upside down.
◆ Trim the excess veneer from the edges with a veneer saw, starting at a corner *(right)* and cutting nearly to the next corner. Then cut in the opposite direction, to keep from tearing fragile veneer corners.
◆ When you have trimmed all of the edges, set the veneered surface right side up; dampen the paper tape with a sponge and remove it. Lightly sand away any residual glue or tape with very fine-grade sandpaper.

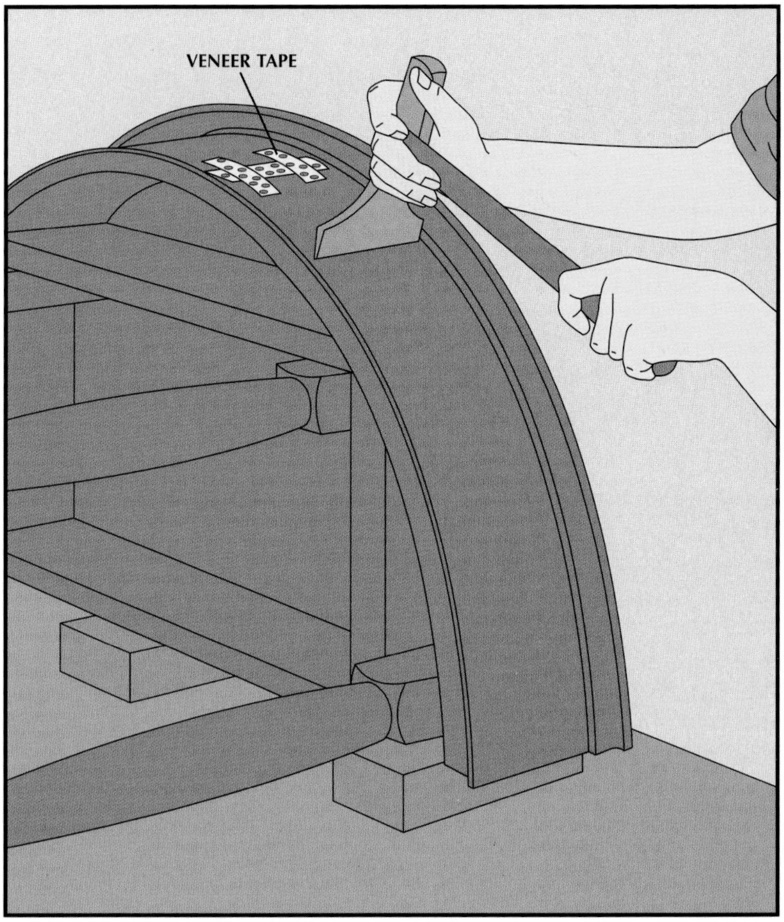

Using a veneer hammer.

◆ If the base is lightweight, clamp it to the worktable.

◆ To splice veneers, fasten the pieces together with veneer tape before gluing them to the base.

◆ Apply glue and lay the veneer on the base, then smooth it with a veneer hammer, forcing out excess glue and flattening any air pockets. Then bear down more forcefully, pressing against the head of the hammer, and stroke repeatedly along the veneer in the direction of the grain, working over the taped veneers as if they were a single continuous sheet *(right)*.

◆ Let the glue dry overnight, then remove the veneer tape.

TRICKS OF THE TRADE

Shop-Made Veneer Hammer

A homemade veneer hammer can be as effective as a store-bought model. For the handle, cut a $\frac{3}{4}$-inch dowel 11 inches long. Make the head from $\frac{3}{4}$-inch hardwood, cutting it $3\frac{1}{2}$ inches long by $2\frac{1}{2}$ inches wide. Drill a hole in the center of the head for the handle and glue the two parts together. Make the blade of $\frac{1}{4}$-inch-thick brass or aluminum plate, set to extend $\frac{1}{4}$ inch beyond the bottom edge of the head. Do not use iron or steel for the plate—either could react with the tannic acid present in most woods and leave stains on the veneer surface. File the blade's working edge smooth and round the corners to keep them from scratching the veneer. Drill matching holes through the plate and the head, and use stove bolts and wing nuts to fasten them together so you can remove the blade for cleaning.

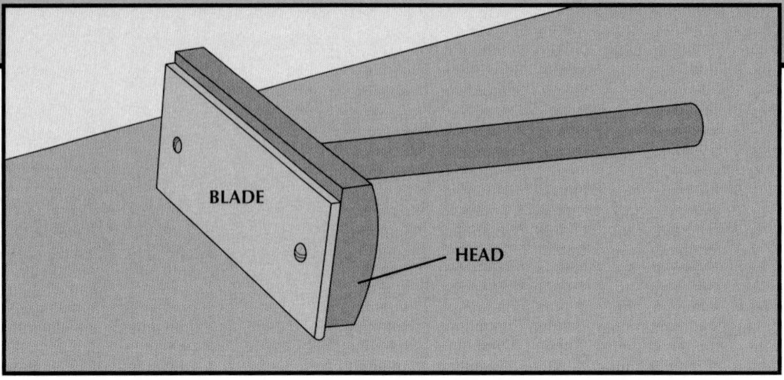

REPLACING DAMAGED VENEER WITH A DIAMOND PATCH

1. Outlining the patch.
A veneer punch *(page 111)* is a nearly foolproof way to repair veneer. Simply place the punch over the damage and strike the tool sharply with a hammer. Cut a patch in the same way, then chisel out the damaged veneer and glue the patch in the recess as shown on page 116. Alternatively, you can proceed with a craft knife as follows:
◆ Cut a diamond-shaped patch slightly larger than the damaged area from veneer that matches the surface being repaired. To ensure a tight fit, slightly undercut the sides of the patch.
◆ Position the patch over the damaged surface so the grain of the two pieces runs in the same direction, and outline it with a sharp pencil *(right)*.

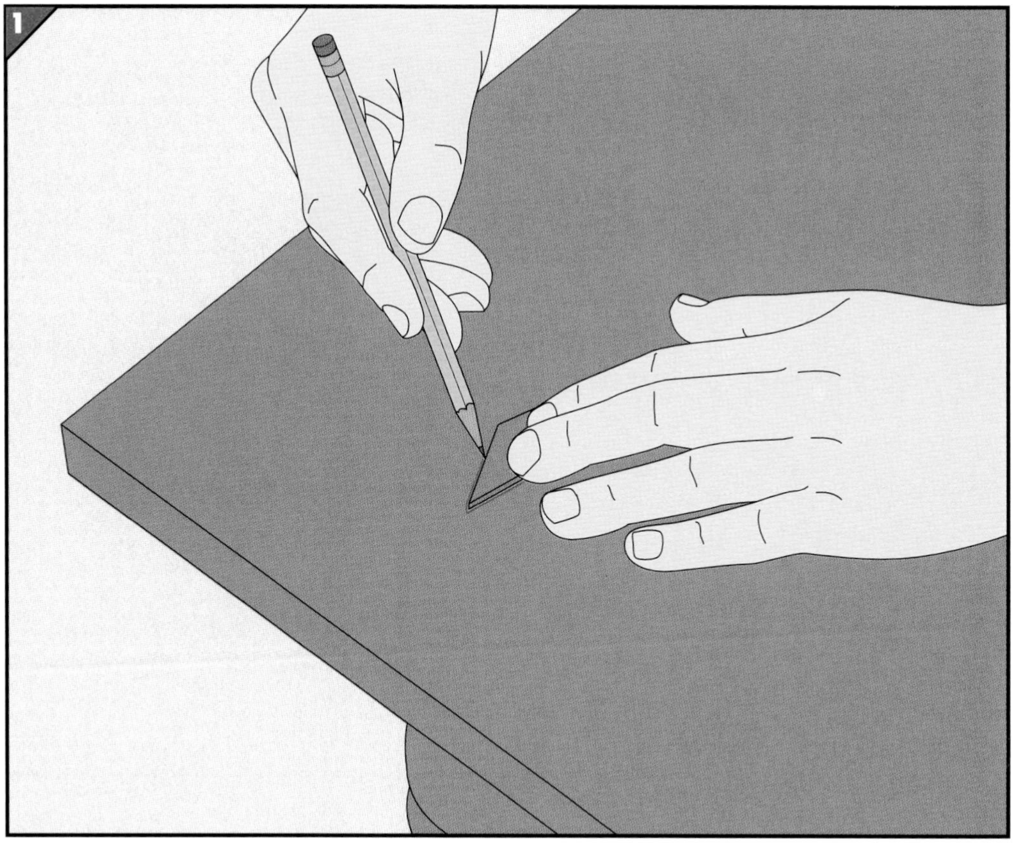

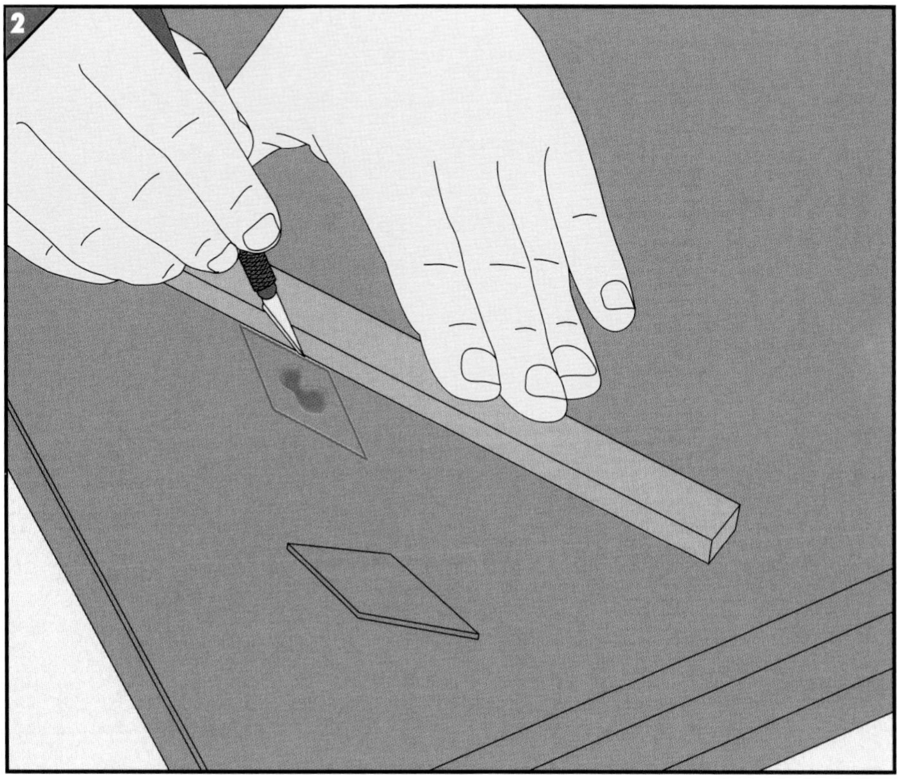

2. Cutting the recess.
Using a hardwood board or a straightedge as a guide, cut just to the waste side of the marked lines with the craft knife, slicing through the veneer *(left)*.

3. Clearing the recess.
Starting at the center of the damaged area and working outward, remove the old veneer within the cut outline with a wood chisel held bevel side down *(right)*. Or, use a dogleg chisel—its offset blade is designed for cleaning out flat recesses *(photograph)*.

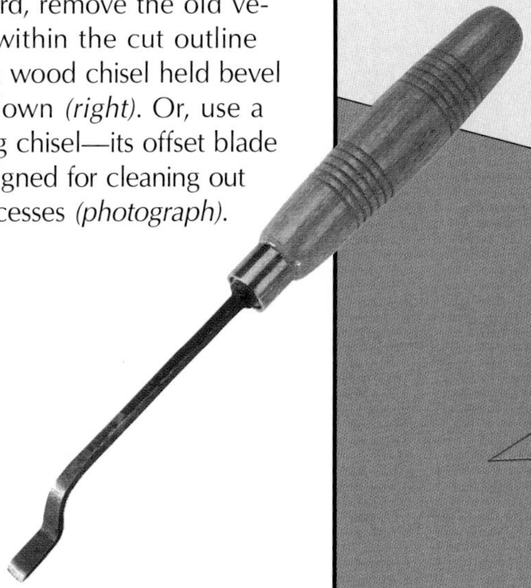

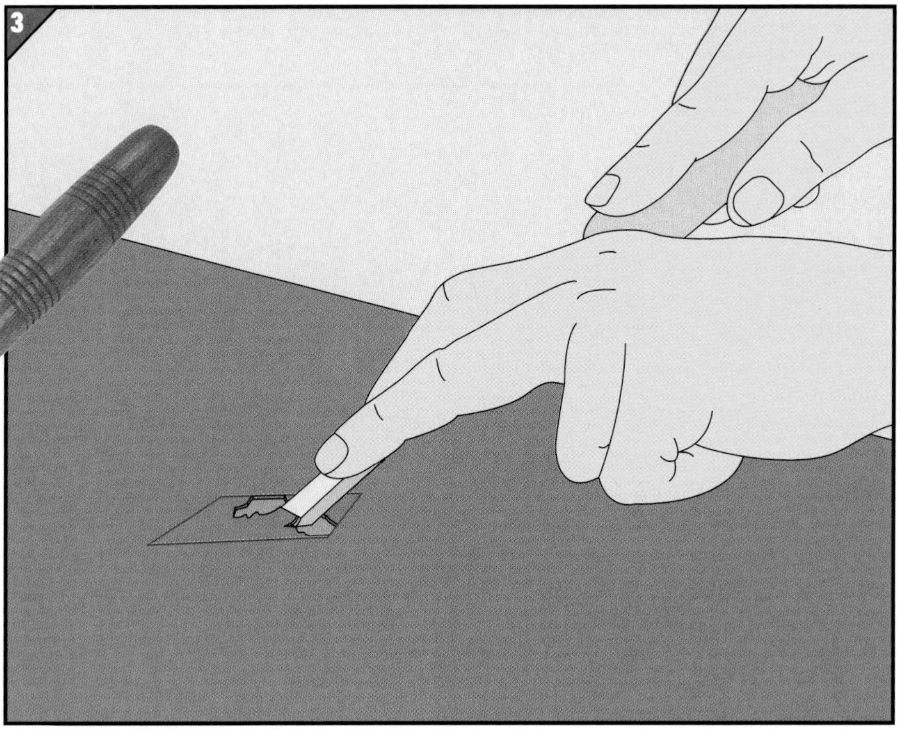

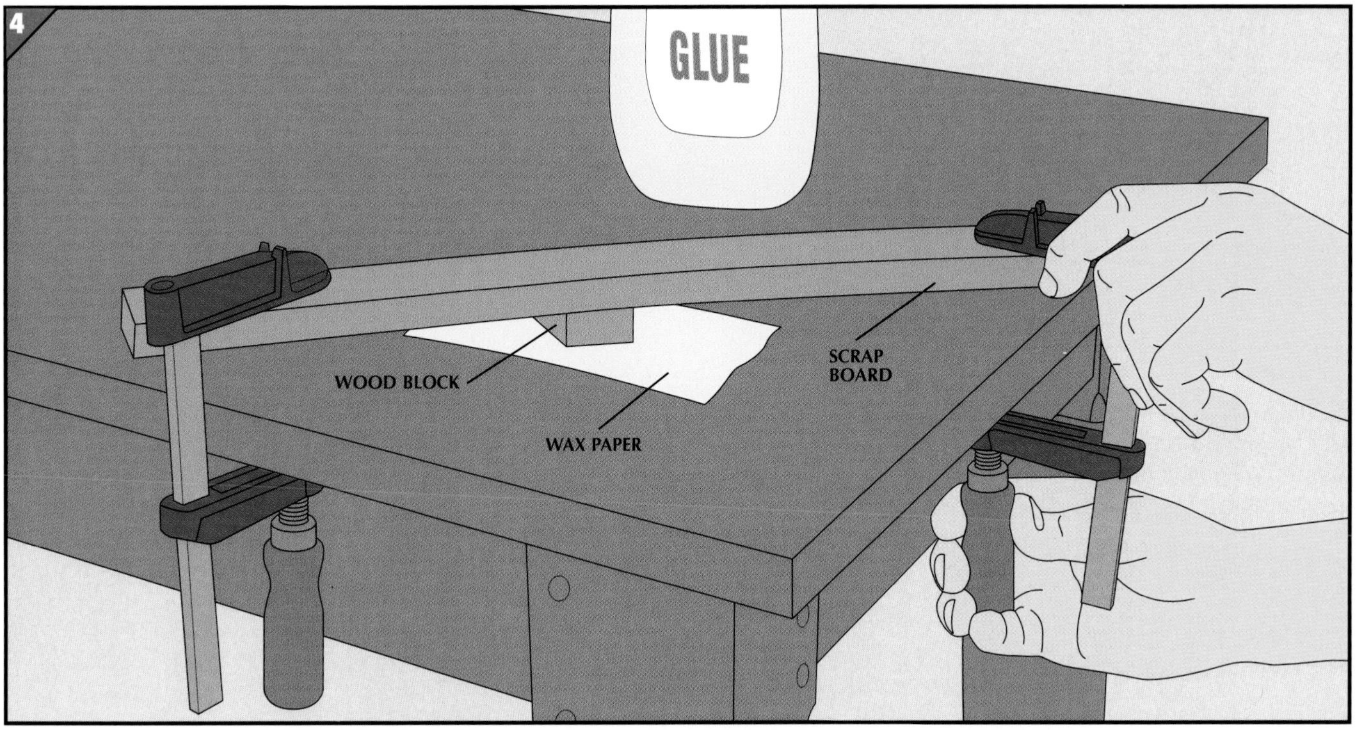

4. Gluing the patch.
◆ Cut a diamond-shaped wood block slightly smaller than the patch.
◆ Spread white or yellow glue in the recess and set the patch in place. Lay a piece of wax paper over the patch, then center the wood block over the patch.
◆ Clamp down the wood block; if it is too far from the edge of the table, set a scrap board across the block and clamp it to the edges *(above)*.

FIXING BLISTERS

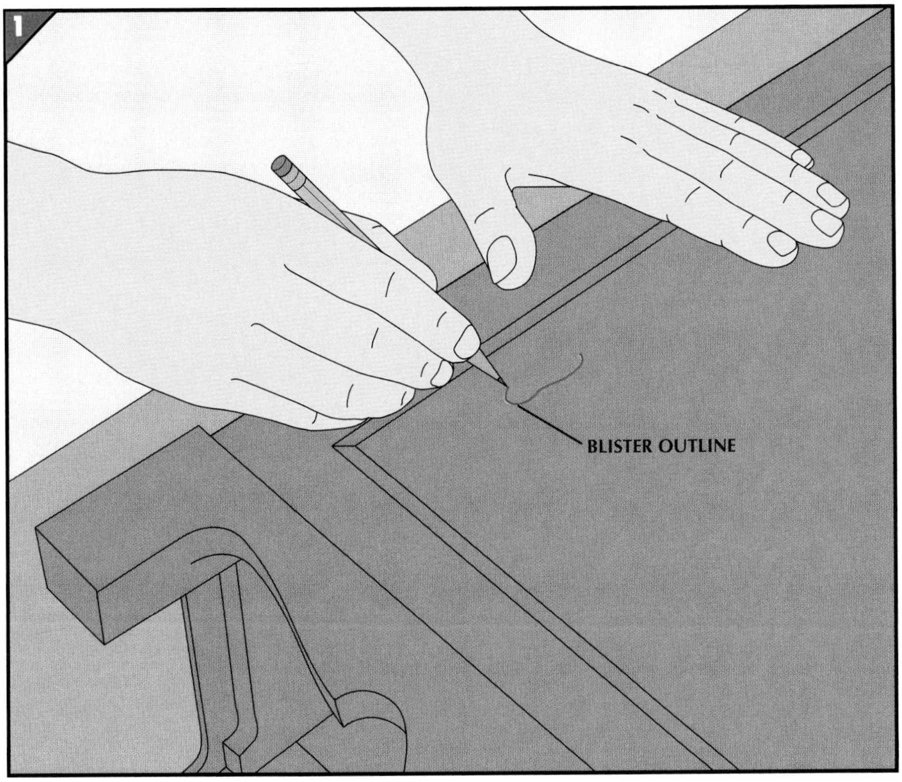

1. Outlining the blister.
Determine the extent of the air pocket by tapping around the area with a fingernail; the blistered section will produce a hollow sound. With a pencil, lightly outline the blister on the surface *(left)*.

2. Slicing the blister open.
◆ With a craft knife, slit the blister open along its center, following the wood grain and keeping within the penciled outline *(right)*.
◆ Pressing down on one side of the slit, use the knife blade to scrape out the old glue and debris from under the blister. Clean under the other side of the blister in the same way.

3. Injecting glue under the blister.

◆ Gently pry open one of the flaps with the craft knife and apply some adhesive with a needle-tip glue or syringe-style injector *(right)*; glue the other flap in the same way. If you don't have a glue injector, you can apply the adhesive with the tip of a finishing nail.

◆ Wipe away excess glue with a damp cloth.

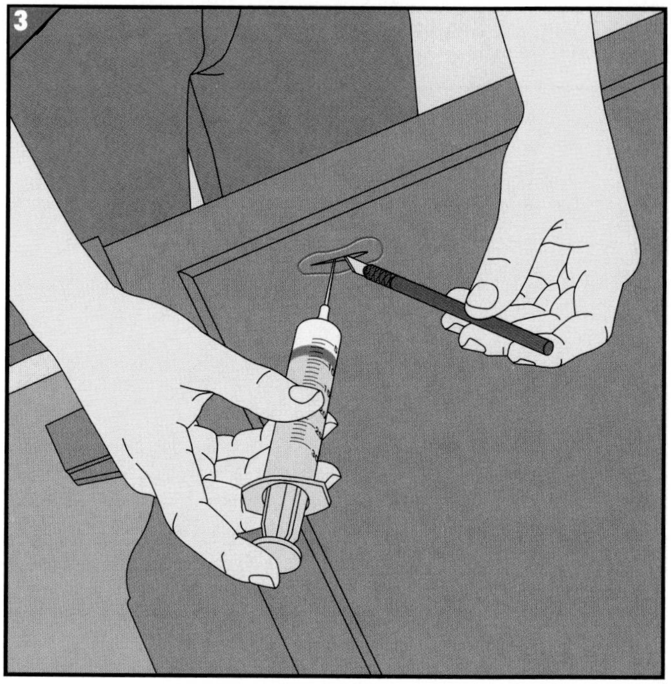

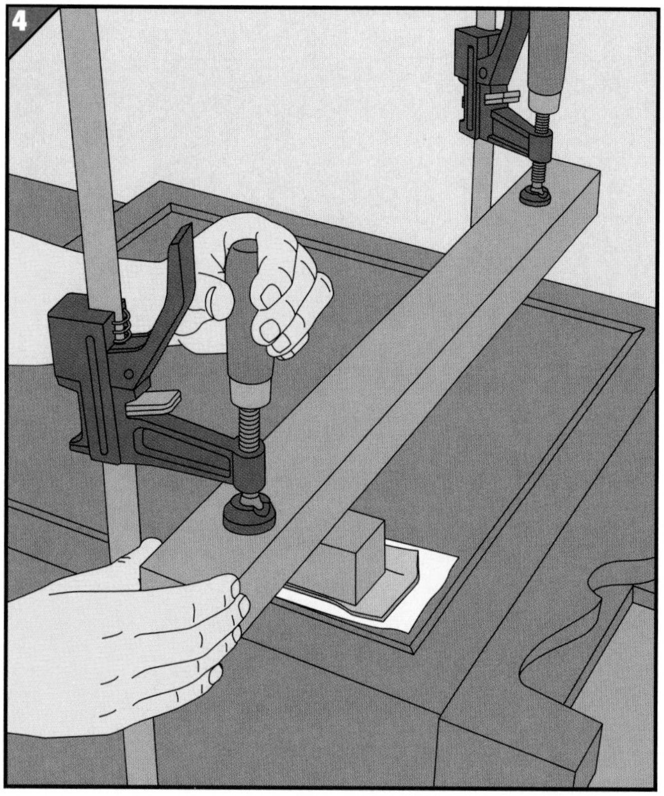

4. Securing the veneer.

◆ Cover the repair with wax paper and a piece of scrap leather to protect the surface. Place a wood block on the leather.

◆ Clamp the block against the surface. If the clamps can't reach the area, secure a board across the block; bar clamps may be necessary to span a large surface *(left)*.

TRICKS OF THE TRADE

Refastening a Hide-Glue Bond

The veneer on most antiques is bonded with hide glue. One advantage of this adhesive is that it can be reactivated with heat. To flatten a blister in hide-glued veneer, place a slightly dampened cloth on the affected area, set a household iron to moderate heat, and press it against the cloth. Lift the iron within a few minutes *(right)*—the glue should have softened and the pressure applied by the iron will have smoothed out the blister; once the blister is flat, clamp the veneer *(Step 4, above)*. If this method doesn't work, slice open the veneer and repair it as shown beginning on page 117.

SPLICING A DECORATIVE BAND

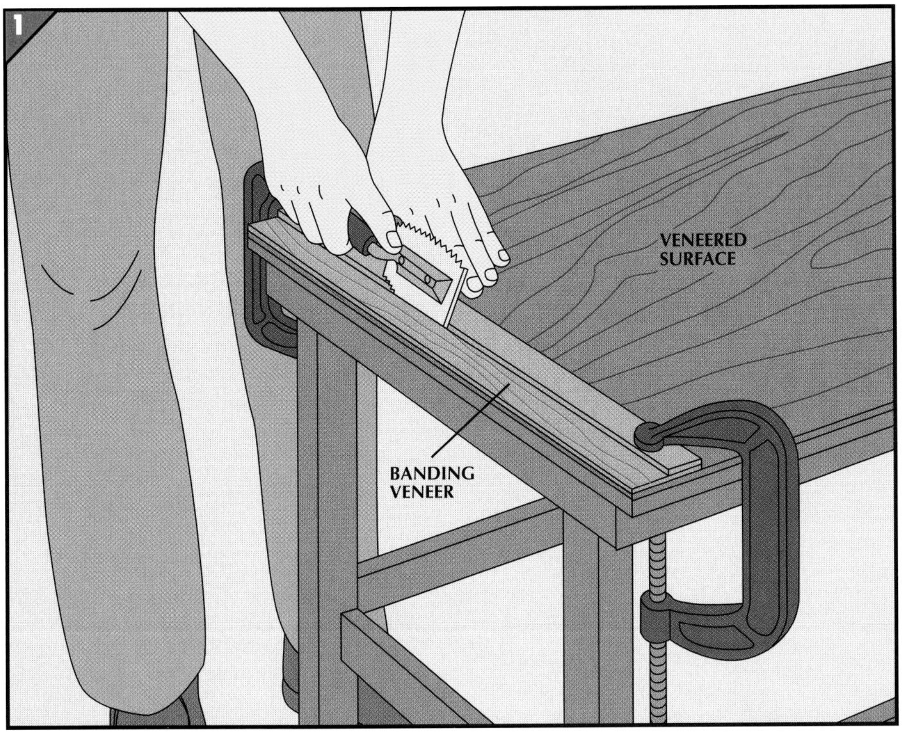

1. Cutting the seams.

◆ From veneer of a contrasting color or from the same source as the surface, cut banding strips for the ends and sides of the surface: Cut the end strips with their grain perpendicular to that of the surface; cut the side strips with their grain parallel to it.

◆ Set the banding veneer along one edge of the veneered surface so it overhangs slightly.

◆ Clamp a straightedge along the planned seam line between the two pieces of veneer, and slice through both layers at once with a veneer saw *(left)*.

◆ Repeat the procedure along the other edges of the veneered surface, numbering each banding piece to record its position and marking its seam line.

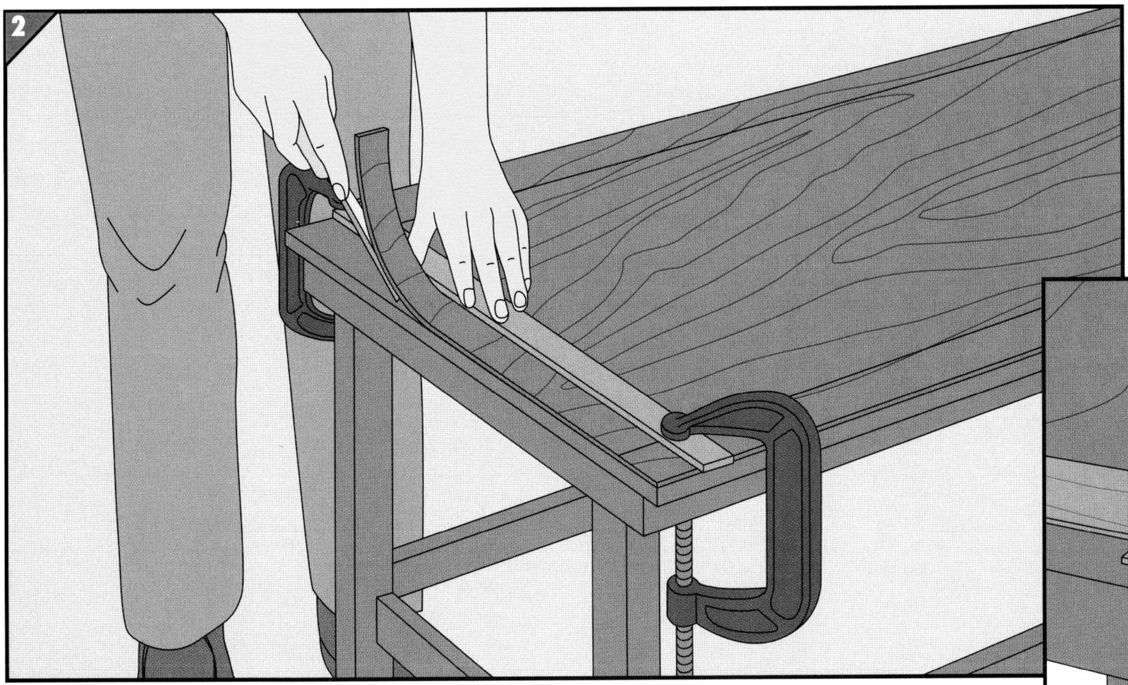

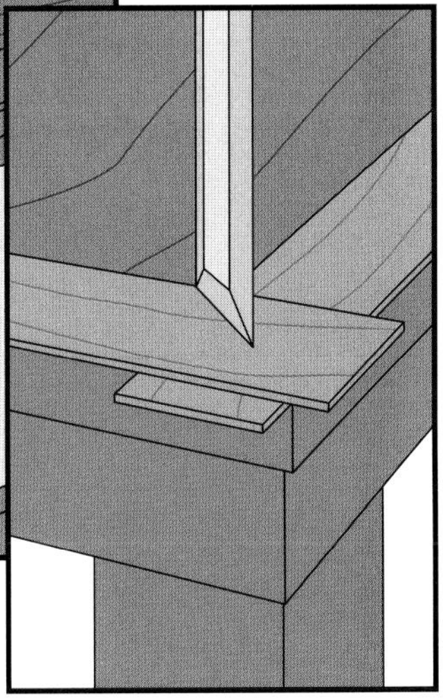

2. Lifting the existing veneer.

◆ Clamp the straightedge along the seam line of the veneered surface.

◆ Holding a wood chisel bevel down, pry off the edges of the veneer, pressing down on the straightedge as you work to avoid damaging the veneer inside the seam line *(above)*. Remove the veneer from the other edges in the same way.

◆ Scrape dried glue from cleared areas.

◆ Fasten the pieces of banding in place with veneer tape, matching the seam lines and overlapping the ends of the banding at each corner.

◆ Miter the overlapping ends with a chisel *(inset)* or a craft knife and straightedge. When all the corners have been mitered, dampen the veneer tape and remove it.

◆ Spread contact cement on the back of the pieces of banding and on the cleared edges of the surface. When the contact cement loses its stickiness, lay overlapping strips of wax paper, about 6 inches wide, over the cement-covered edge.

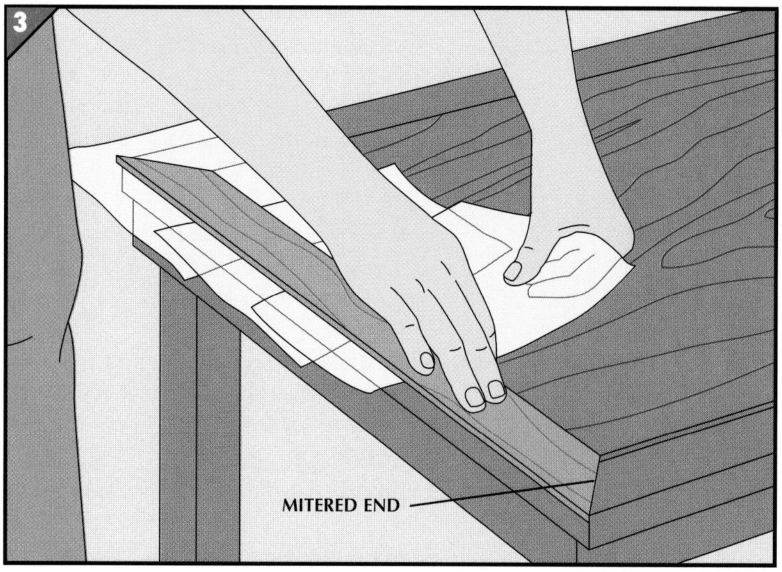

3. Applying the banding.
◆ Lay the banding over the wax paper and, starting at a corner, slowly pull away the strips of paper, one at a time, while pressing the veneer against the surface *(left)*.
◆ Flatten the banding with a roller.
◆ Install the other banding sections in the same way, being especially careful to fit the mitered ends together precisely.

4. Trimming the banding.
◆ Adjust a block plane for a very shallow cut.
◆ Holding the plane with its sole flat on the edge, shave away the overhanging edges of banding *(right)*.

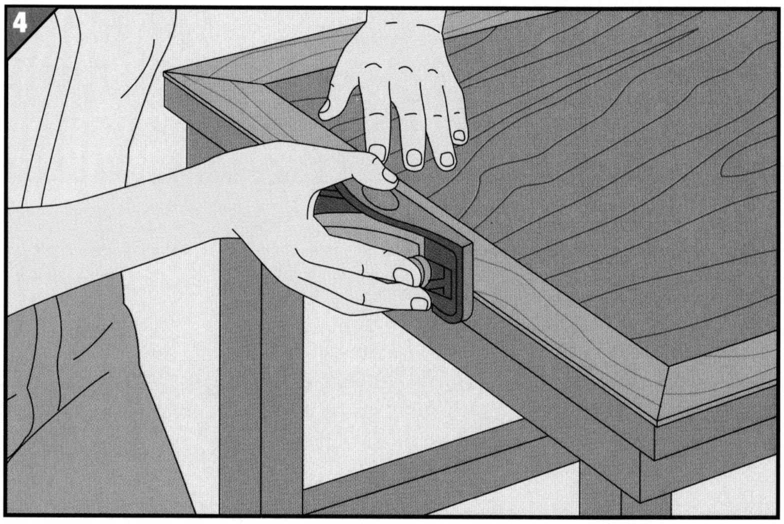

APPLYING EDGING

Rolling on the veneer.
◆ From a veneer sheet, cut pieces of banding as wide as and slightly longer than the edges being covered.
◆ Apply a thin coat of contact cement along the edges and on the banding.
◆ When the cement is no longer sticky, start at one corner and position the edging with one hand as you press it smooth with a hand roller *(right)*.
◆ With a chisel, trim the excess, then glue on the other pieces the same way.

Self-adhesive banding, sold in rolls of various widths, is applied with a household iron set at moderately high heat, which softens the glue.

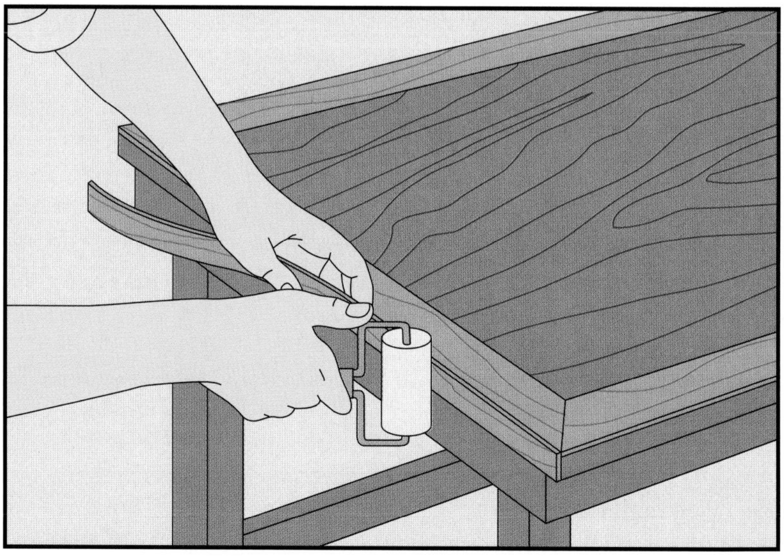

Highlighting Wood Surfaces with Inlays

Although veneer is typically applied over an entire surface, you can also set it into recesses cut into the surface—a technique called inlaying. Natural or colored wood veneers are the most common types, but leather, ivory, and mother-of-pearl are also used.

Types of Inlay: The simplest inlays are border strips and medallions *(below and pages 122-125)*. A more elaborate form is marquetry—small irregularly shaped wood chips assembled like a mosaic to form a symbol or picture. Another type—parquetry—uses straight-edged chips to form geometric patterns. You can make inlays yourself, using the technique for cutting and fitting adjoining pieces *(pages 119-120)*, but ready-made inserts are available from woodworking suppliers.

The inlays often come set in a piece of scrap veneer, with brown paper glued to the outside face. Most range from $\frac{1}{28}$ inch to $\frac{1}{14}$ inch thick. Border strips come in 3-foot lengths and in widths ranging from about $\frac{1}{16}$ inch to $1\frac{1}{2}$ inches. Order extra strips to ensure an exact match in case you ever need to patch the inlay.

There are several ways to vary the effect by coloring or shading the inlays. Colorfast fabric dyes or inks are good for tinting light-colored absorbent woods such as poplar or holly. Or, dip the edge of a piece into a tray of fine sand heated over a burner to scorch the wood. When dyeing or scorching the inlays, make the color a little darker than the final color—finish sanding will remove the surface layer.

Cutting the Recess: A router is best for cutting a recess in solid wood. For a veneered surface, use the techniques for removing a damaged area for a patch *(pages 115-116)*.

TOOLS

- Router
- Straight bit
- Clamps
- Wood chisel
- Mallet
- Craft knife
- Straightedge
- Hammer
- Awl
- Skew chisel
- Carving gouge
- Dogleg chisel
- Band saw

MATERIALS

- Straightedge board
- Border inlay strips
- Veneer tape
- Wood glue
- Wax paper
- Plywood
- Bricks
- Medallion inlay
- Sandpaper (fine-grade)
- Wood block
- 2 x 4

SAFETY TIPS

Protect your eyes with goggles when using a router or band saw.

A BORDER STRIP IN SOLID WOOD

1. Routing a straight groove.

◆ Outline the inlay recess on the surface and fit a router with a straight bit whose diameter matches the groove width. Measure the distance between the bit and the edge of the router base, and clamp a straight board a corresponding distance from one inside edge of the outline.

◆ Set the bit to a cutting depth slightly less than the thickness of the inlay. Then, with the router base against the straightedge, turn on the tool, lower it to the surface *(right)*, and cut the groove from left to right, without routing beyond the ends of the outline. At the end of the cut, turn off the router and let the bit stop spinning before lifting the tool from the surface.

◆ Cut the other recess grooves in the same way.

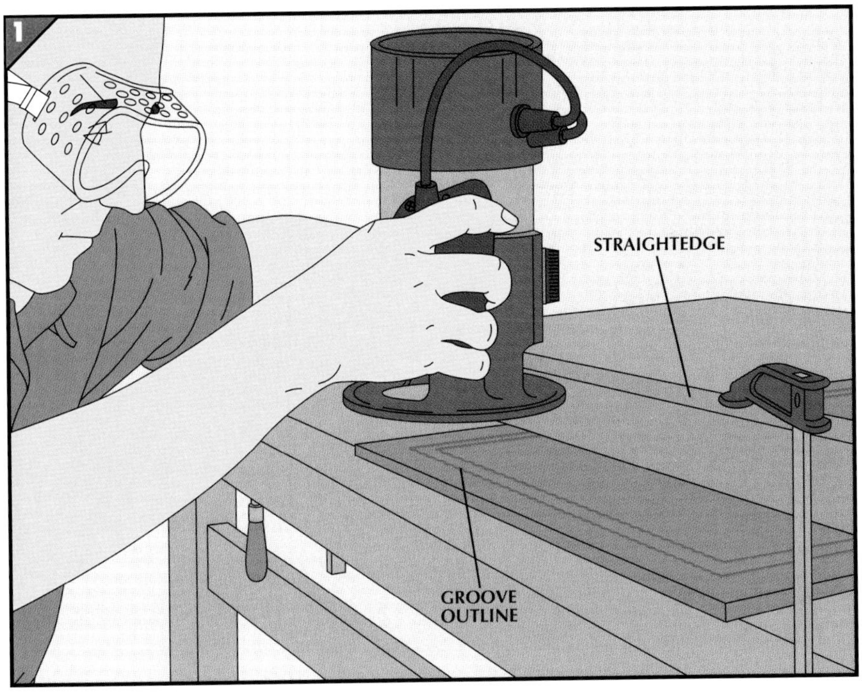

2. Squaring the corners.

◆ Holding a chisel at one outer corner of the recess with the flat side of the blade against the edge of the groove, tap the handle lightly with a mallet *(right)*.

◆ Make an identical cut on the other side of the corner.

◆ Lever out the waste with the chisel.

◆ Clear any splinters from the recess with a craft knife.

This job can be done with a corner chisel *(photograph)*—designed to make a 90-degree cut with one blow. Its two perpendicular cutting edges form a corner-shaped blade.

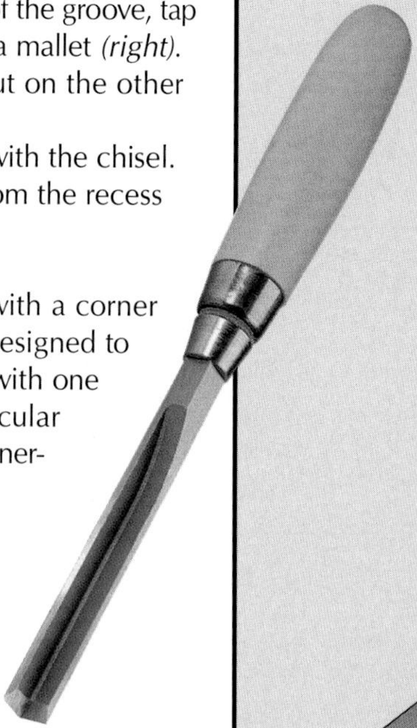

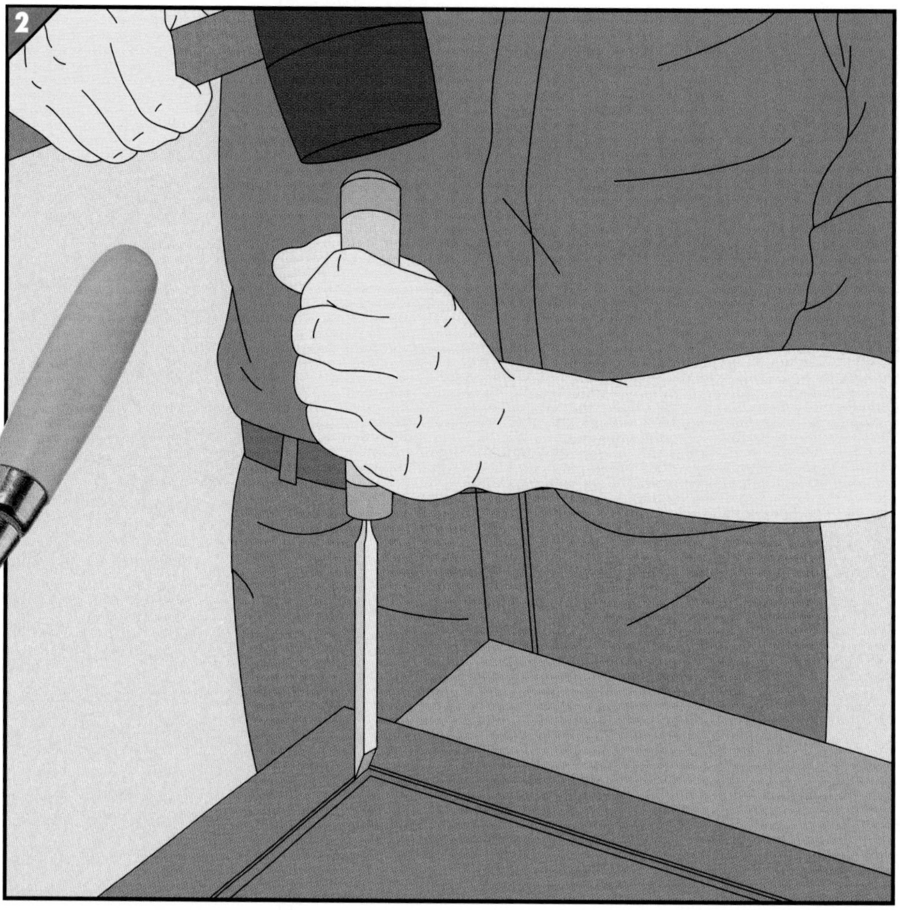

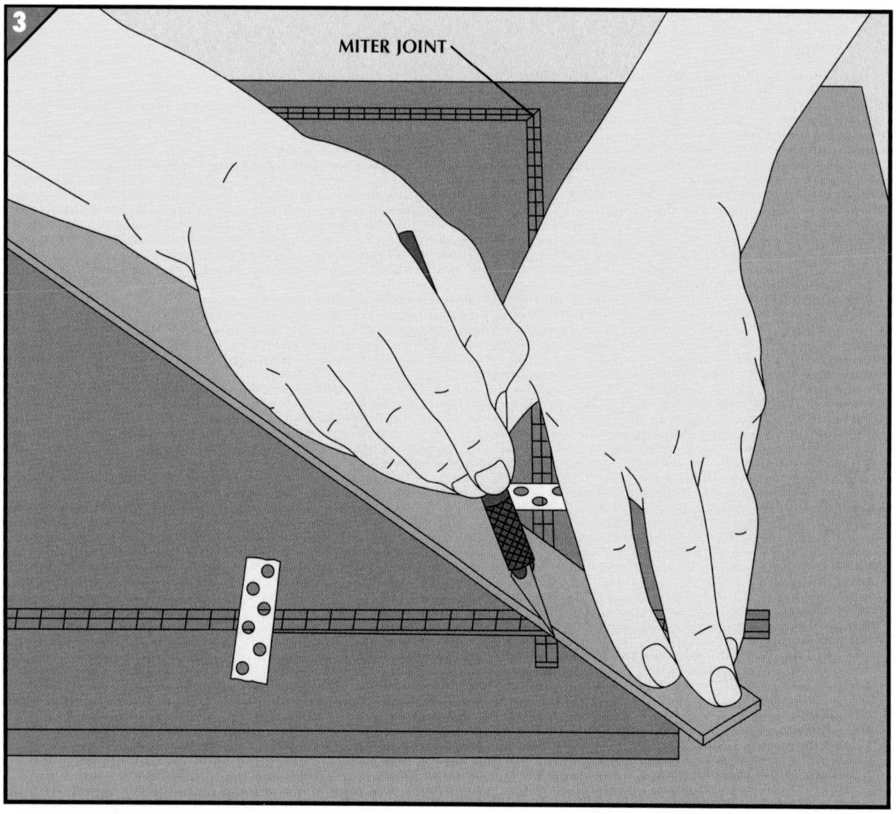

3. Fitting the inlay.

◆ Lay the inlay strips in the grooves, letting their ends overlap so the patterns match at the corners.

◆ Secure each strip to the surface with veneer tape.

◆ Holding a straightedge across one corner and a craft knife aligned with the outside of the corner, cut through both pieces of inlay at a 45-degree angle to create a miter joint.

◆ Cut the remaining corners in the same way *(left)*.

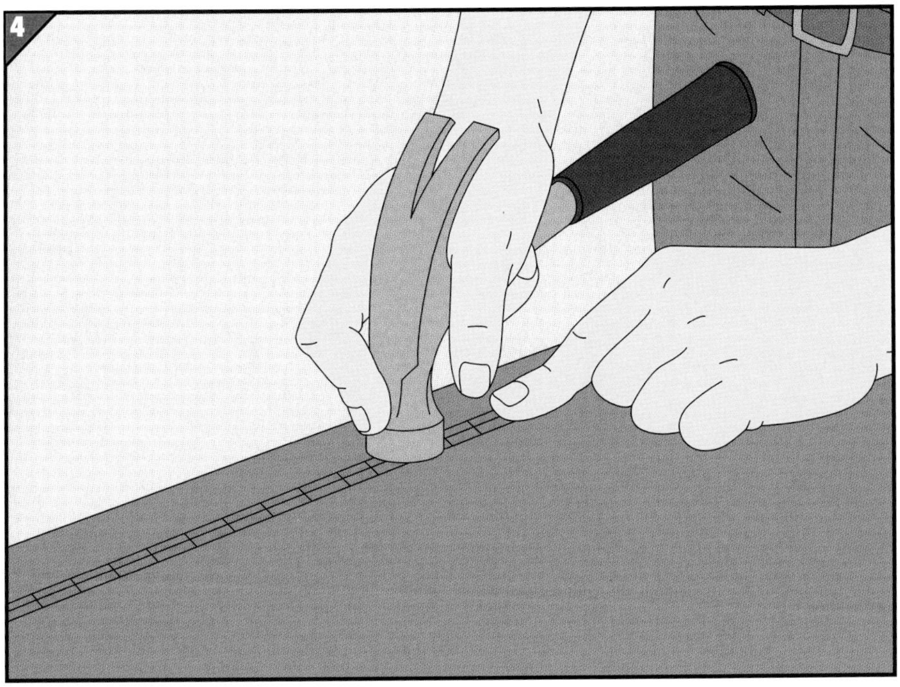

4. Gluing down the border.

◆ Remove the inlay strips from their grooves, spread a thin coat of wood glue on the back of each one, and replace the pieces in the grooves.

◆ With the smooth face of a hammer, press the strips firmly into the grooves, making sure each one is properly aligned before pressing it into place *(left)*.

◆ Wipe away extruded glue with a damp cloth and cover the strips with wax paper. Then, lay a piece of plywood or particleboard over the surface, and weigh it down with bricks until the glue cures.

◆ Sand the inlay flush with the surrounding surface using fine-grade sandpaper.

RECESSING A MEDALLION

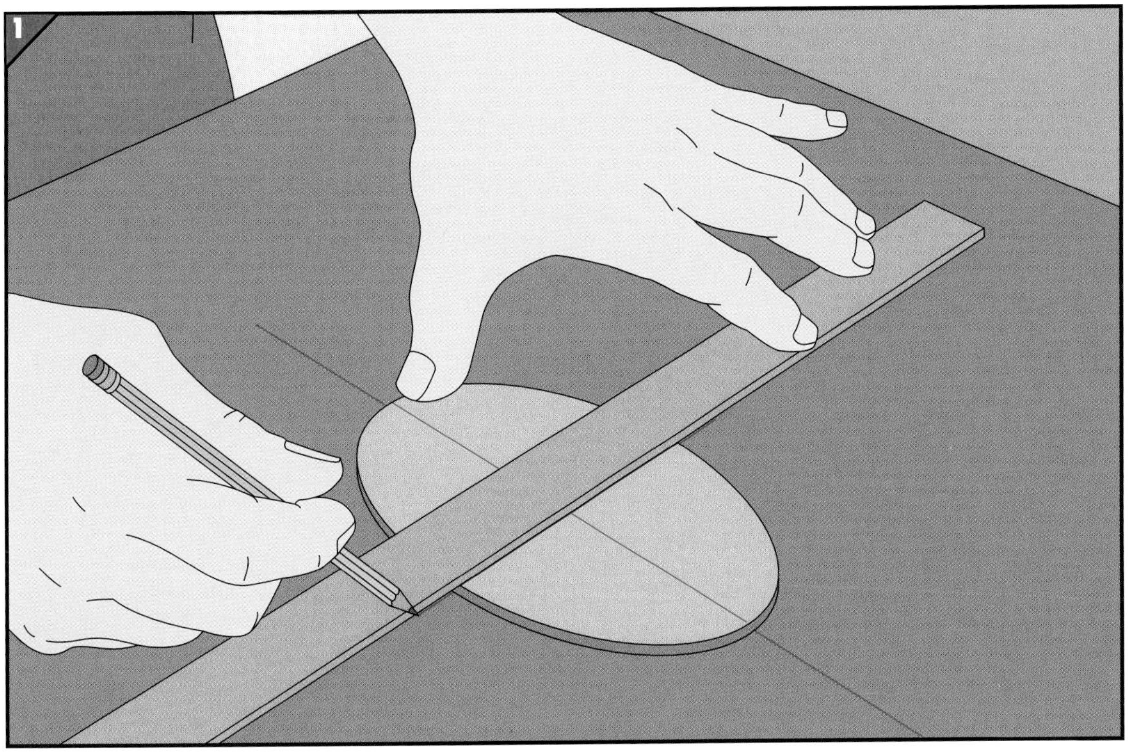

1. Outlining the shape.

◆ Position the inlay on the surface with the brown paper facing up. Then, with a straightedge and a pencil, mark two lines—perpendicular to each other and centered over the inlay—across the inlay and onto the surface *(above)*.

◆ Keeping the marks aligned, score the outline of the inlay onto the surface with an awl.

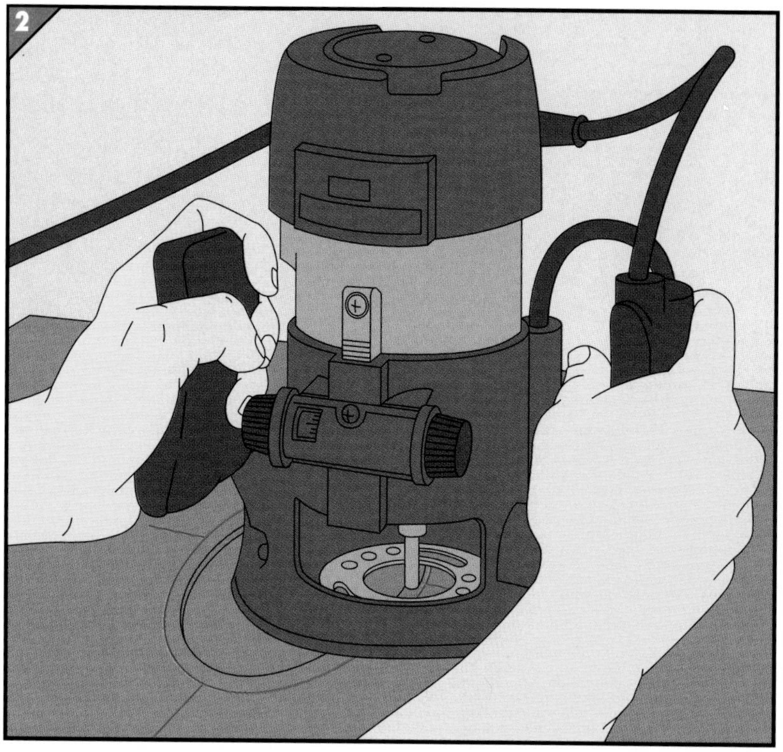

2. Routing the recess freehand.

◆ Install a straight bit in the router, then set the cutting depth to slightly less than the thickness of the inlay.

◆ Start the router and lower the bit onto the surface near the middle of the recess outline.

◆ Move the router clockwise within the outline, cutting out the waste to within $\frac{1}{16}$ inch of the marked shape *(left)*.

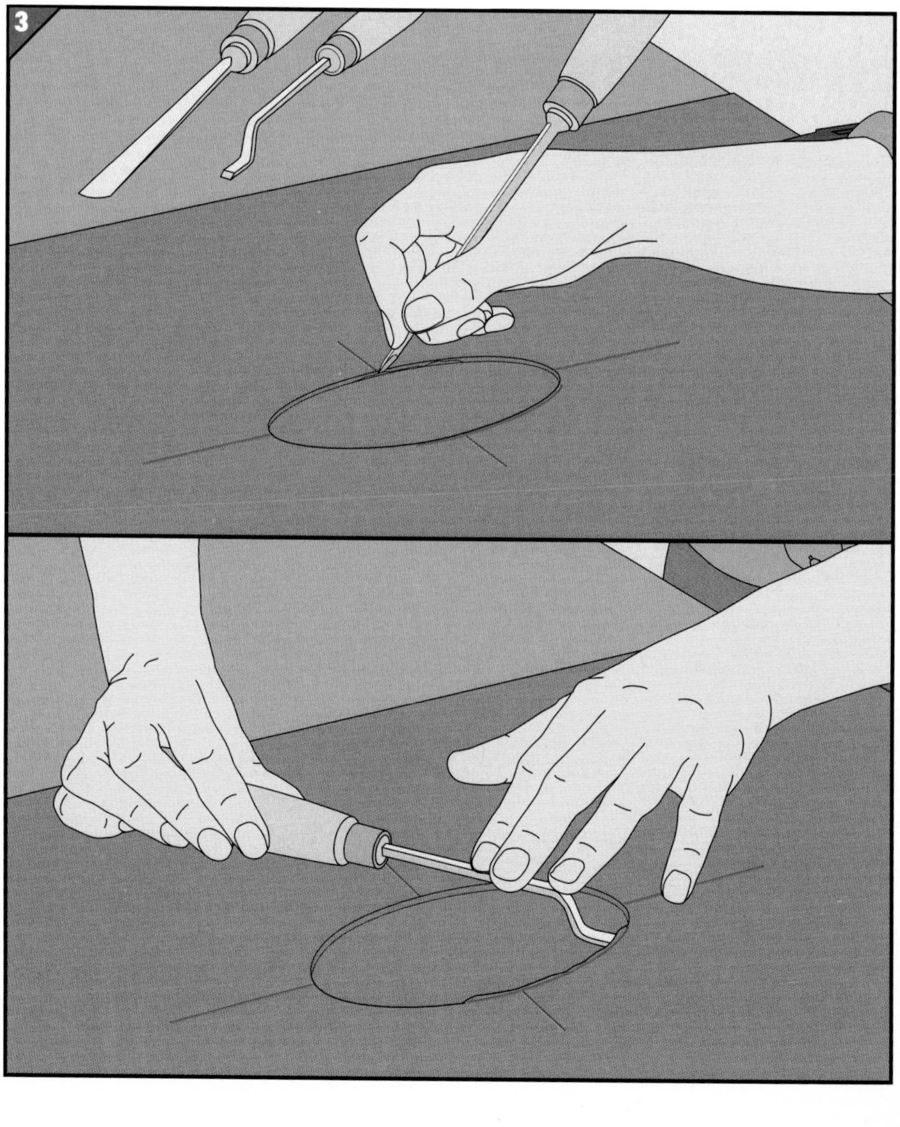

3. Finishing the recess.

◆ Cut waste wood from the straightest sections of the rim of the recess by slicing straight down just inside the outline with a skew chisel *(right, top)*.

◆ Trim curved sections using a carving gouge with the same profile as the curve.

◆ Remove waste from the bottom of the recess with a dogleg chisel *(right, bottom)*.

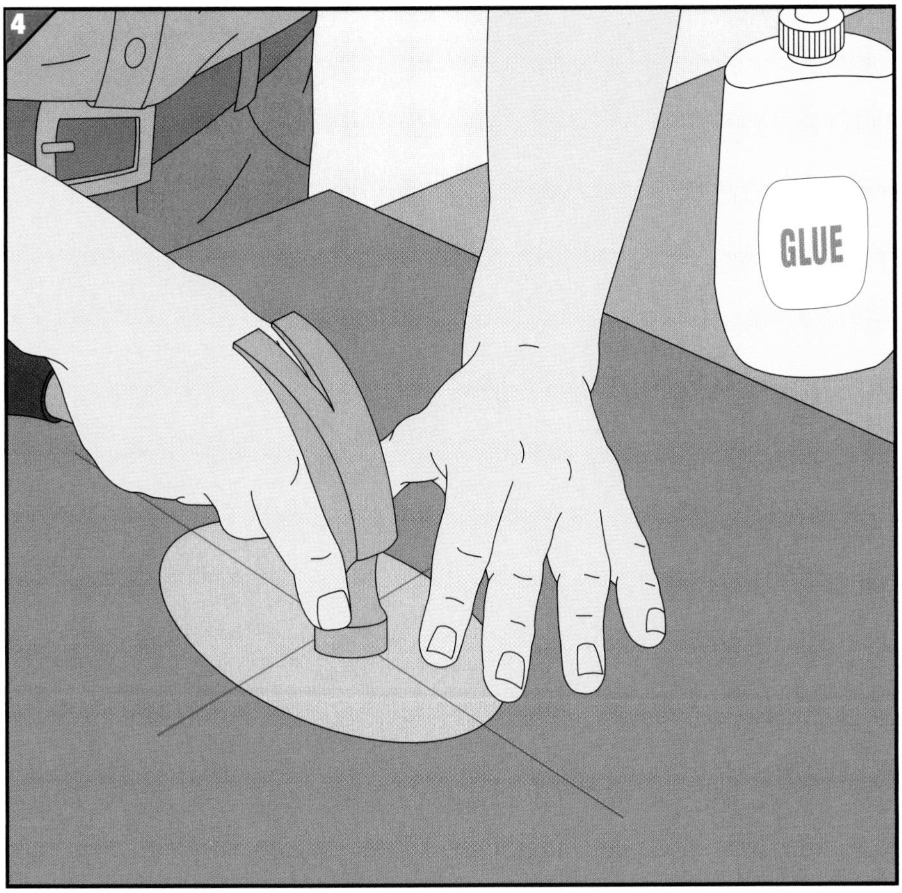

4. Inserting the inlay.

◆ Test the fit of the inlay in the recess, placing it with the brown paper facing up, and the perpendicular marks aligned. If necessary, sand the edges of the inlay with fine-grade sandpaper to fit snugly.

◆ Spread a thin coat of wood glue in the recess and set the inlay in place.

◆ Rub the face of a hammer over the inlay, working from the center outward in a circular motion *(left)*.

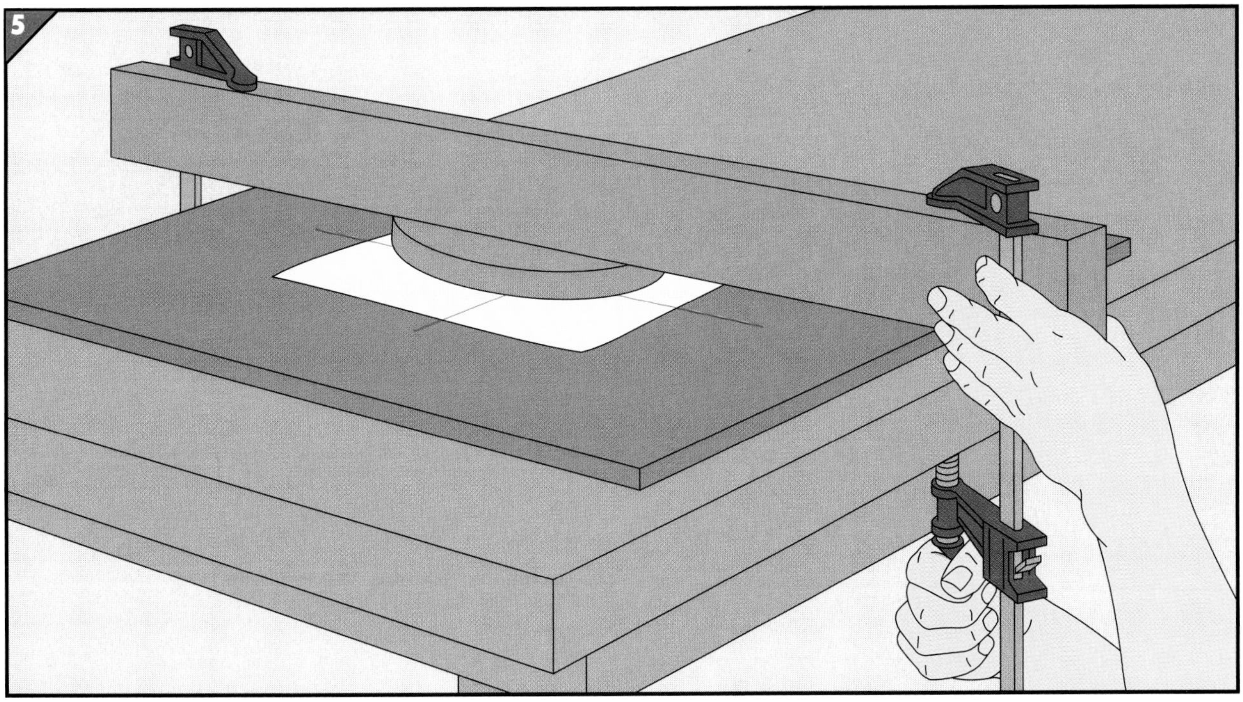

5. Clamping the insert.

◆ Cut a wood block slightly smaller than the inlay; give the block the same shape as the inlay so it will exert pressure only on the medallion.

◆ Cover the inlay with a sheet of wax paper, and place the block over the inlay.

◆ Center a 2-by-4 on edge across the block and clamp the ends of the board to the work surface until the glue cures *(above)*.

◆ Gently sand away the brown paper and the inlay to bring it flush with the surrounding surface.

INDEX

TIME®
LIFE
BOOKS

Time-Life Books is a division of Time Life Inc.

TIME LIFE INC.
PRESIDENT and CEO: George Artandi

TIME-LIFE BOOKS
PRESIDENT: Stephen R. Frary
PUBLISHER/MANAGING EDITOR: Neil Kagan

HOME REPAIR AND IMPROVEMENT: Advanced Woodworking
EDITOR: Lee Hassig
MARKETING DIRECTOR: James Gillespie
Design Director: Barbara M. Sheppard
Art Director: Kate McConnell
Associate Editor/Research and Writing: Karen Sweet
Marketing Manager: Wells Spence

Director of Finance: Christopher Hearing
Director of Book Production: Marjann Caldwell
Director of Operations: Betsi McGrath
Director of Photography and Research: John Conrad Weiser
Director of Editorial Administration: Barbara Levitt
Production Manager: Marlene Zack
Quality Assurance Manager: James King
Library: Louise D. Forstall

ST. REMY MULTIMEDIA INC.
President and Chief Executive Officer: Fernand Lecoq
President and Chief Operating Officer: Pierre Léveillé
Vice President, Finance: Natalie Watanabe
Managing Editor: Carolyn Jackson
Managing Art Director: Diane Denoncourt
Production Manager: Michelle Turbide

Staff for *Advanced Woodworking*

Series Editors: Marc Cassini, Heather Mills
Art Director: Michel Giguère
Assistant Editor: John Dowling
Designers: Jean-Guy Doiron, Robert Labelle
Editorial Assistant: James Piecowye
Coordinator: Dominique Gagné
Copy Editor: Judy Yelon
Indexer: Linda Cardella Cournoyer
Systems Coordinator: Éric Beaulieu
Technical Support: Jean Sirois
Other Staff: Linda Castle, Lorraine Doré, Geneviève Dubé, Liane Keightley, Anne-Marie Lemay, Robert Paquet, Rebecca Smollett

PICTURE CREDITS
Cover: Photograph, Robert Chartier. Art, Maryo Proulx.

Illustrators: Jack Arthur, Terry Atkinson from Arts & Words, Gilles Beauchemin, Frederic F. Bigio from B-C Graphics, François Daxhelet, Roger Essley, Charles Forsythe, Gerry Gallagher, William J. Hennessy Jr., Elsie J. Hennig, Walter Hilmers Jr. from HJ Commercial Art, John Jones, Dick Lee, John Martinez, John Massey, Joan McGurren, Eduino J. Pereira from Art & Words, Jacques Perrault, Snowden Associates

Photographers: **End papers:** Glenn Moores and Chantal Lamarre. **13:** Electrophysics. **21:** Woodcraft Supply Corp. **26, 37, 38 (both), 52, 55, 66:** Glenn Moores and Chantal Lamarre. **67:** Ryobi America Corp. **68, 86, 88, 89, 91:** Glenn Moores and Chantal Lamarre. **107:** DeWalt Industrial Tool Company Inc. **111, 112, 116, 122:** Glenn Moores and Chantal Lamarre.

ACKNOWLEDGMENTS
The editors wish to thank the following individuals and institutions: Delta International Machinery Corp., Guelph, Ontario; DeWalt Industrial Tool Co. Inc., Richmond Hill, Ontario; Electrophysics, London, Ontario; Louis V. Genuario, Genuario Construction Co., Inc., Alexandria, VA; Chuck Hicks, Whiteside Machine Co., Claremont, NC; Record Tools Inc., Pickering, Ontario; Ryobi America Corp., Anderson, SC; Michael Watkins, Adjustable Clamp Co., Chicago, IL; Woodcraft Supply Corp., Parkersburg, WV; The Woodworkers' Store, Medina, MN

First printing. Printed in U.S.A.
Published simultaneously in Canada.
School and library distribution by Time-Life Education, P.O. Box 85026, Richmond, Virginia 23285-5026.

Library of Congress Cataloging-in-Publication Data
Advanced Woodworking / by the editors of Time-Life Books.
p. cm. — (Home repair and improvement)
Includes index.
ISBN 0-7835-3912-6
1. Woodwork.
I. Time-Life Books. II. Series.
TT180.A2 1997
684'.08—dc21 97-26696